# IT Strategy
# for Business

*Edited by*

## Joe Peppard
Cranfield School of Management

PITMAN
PUBLISHING

Pitman Publishing
128 Long Acre, London WC2E 9AN

A Division of Pearson Professional Limited

© Longman Group UK Limited 1993

First published in Great Britain 1993

**British Library Cataloguing in Publication Data**
A catalogue record for this book is available from the British Library.

ISBN 0 273 60024 9

10  9  8

Printed and bound in Great Britain by
Biddles Ltd, Guildford and King's Lynn

# IT Strategy for Business

# Contents

# PART III    IT and Strategic Issues

# PART IV    Successful Implementation

# Preface

Being competitive in the 1990s will depend on the effective application of information systems and technology (IS/IT). However, implementing IS/IT no longer means automating a manual task to make it more efficient but rather taking a strategic perspective to ensure that investment in IS/IT is contributing to an organisation's business strategy. ( Increasingly, IT is being used by innovative organisations to facilitate the re-engineering of their business processes and in some instances to radically change the way in which they conduct business. IS/IT is no longer a technical problem but a business issue. )

In many organisations, more and more managers are being asked to subscribe to the IS/IT planning process. However, it is surprising the number of managers at senior levels and line positions in organisations who do not have at least an awareness of developments in information systems and technology. And I don't mean here a knowledge of personal computers and spreadsheets! At a strategic level, senior managers need a clear vision of the competitive impact of IS/IT. Line managers must be able to identify opportunities for applying IS/IT to business problems.

It is these very issues which were the driving force behind a course which I ran on the 1990/91 MBA program at the Business School at Trinity College Dublin, entitled *Information Systems: Strategy and Management*. This seminar-based elective saw many of the contributors to this book present papers. Their brief was to keep their presentation and discussion at a 'high level', not to get bogged down in detail, to raise management issues and, most importantly, to take a strategic perspective. This has not changed.

The objective of this book is to increase the awareness which managers at all levels (and potential managers) have of IS/IT and the role it can play in increasing competitiveness. After reading this book the reader should be equipped with a greater appreciation and understanding of IS/IT and how it impacts on their organisation, and be in a position to assess the competitive impact of IS/IT, identify opportunities for applying IS/IT and how to link IS/IT strategy with business strategy. Implementing an IS/IT strategy and managing the associated change is also considered.

I am only too aware of the problems with contributed volumes where very often there is repetition of material, blatant contradictions, or material that bears no relation to the book's objectives. My task as editor was to ensure that all contributions fitted together within the overall context of the book. The authors are all leading authorities in the area to which they subscribed. Individual chapters should be capable of being read on their own but equally as an integral part of the book. Each author undoubtedly has his/her own style, which perhaps will make reading interesting, but I have tried to ensure some consistency in presentation and layout. To avoid overlap of material, which was inevitable when the manuscripts were first submitted, I placed the material where I felt it was best located. I hope that I have managed to produce a readable volume. This is for you the reader to judge.

There is only a limited amount which can be contained in each chapter; all of the chapter topics warrant a book in themselves. The focus is clearly on presenting a *high-level* view of relevant issues. I have incorporated some *value-added* within each chapter by including additional readings, grouped under suitable subheadings, where further information can be found. I have also tried to reference case study sources so that they can be followed up if necessary. This should appeal not only to the student reader but also to practising managers who may need to gather further information. A glossary of some of the more technical terms is also included.

I must thank the contributors for preparing their manuscripts on time and putting up with my persistent hassle. I must also express my appreciation to my colleagues in the information systems group at the Cranfield School of Management. They have helped shape my thinking on IS/IT: I'm sure they will recognise their influence.

Finally, a special word of thanks to John Cushion of Pitman who provided superb back up and support throughout this project.

Joe Peppard
Kempston, November 1992

# Contributors

**Frank Bannister**
Frank is a Managing Consultant with Price Waterhouse. He started his career in Operation Research in the Irish Civil Service, joining PW in 1978. He is a leading authority on Open Systems and is well known in Ireland as a writer on Open Systems, computer modelling and related topics. He is an external lecturer at Trinity College, Dublin and the Irish Management Institute. He is also much in demand as a public lecturer and has lectured extensively both in Ireland and abroad on Open Systems, Decision Support Systems, and end-user computing.


**Leo Blennerhasset**
Leo is an Associate Partner with Andersen Consulting. Since graduating from Trinity College, Dublin in 1981, with an honours Business Studies degree, he has accumulated significant experience in the integration of strategy, operations, people and systems for medium and large organisations in a number of countries.


**Donal Daly**
Donal is Group Managing Director of Expert Edge Computer Systems, a leading European computer software company specialising in the development, distribution and design of expert system software. He is a graduate of the Electrical Engineering faculty of University College, Cork, but has spent all his professional career in the computer industry. Donal is author of *Expert Systems Introduced*, has written several articles on expert systems and has lectured widely on the subject.

**Eamonn P. Galvin**

Eamonn is a Senior Consultant with the Dublin office of Andersen Consulting. He has been involved with a wide range of clients, including assignments in the insurance, transport and retail industries. His work has included strategic studies and organisational reviews as well as mainline IT systems installation work. He is an honours graduate of University College Dublin where he also completed a postgraduate degree. Prior to joining Andersens he worked as a research assistant at the School of Business Studies, Trinity College, Dublin. He has lectured extensively in marketing.

**Garrett Hickey**

Garrett is a Partner in Price Waterhouse. Since graduating from Trinity College, Dublin in 1977, he has been a full time information systems professional - both as a systems development head for a major international bank as well as a consultant. Throughout his career he has chiefly focused on the planning, design, installation, and support of applications systems - and on the management and control of these activities - for banks, financial institutions and medium to large scale organisations. Since 1989, he has been a partner in Price Waterhouse, based in Dublin, with responsibility for the information systems consulting practice in Ireland for banks and financial institutions.

**Rob Lambert**

Rob is a Lecturer in Management Information Systems at the Cranfield School of Management. He worked within industry for over ten years with organisations such as Rank Xerox, FW Woolworths and Plessey. He latterly held the position of Systems Consultant. He taught at Brooklands School of Management prior to joining Cranfield in 1985. Rob has developed and taught on a range of management programs aimed at improving managerial and organisational performance. He is particularly interested in the role of information systems in achieving corporate objectives and improving managerial performance and is currently working with major organisations in the oil, pharmaceutical and insurance industries.

**Brian McLoughlin**

Brian is Director, Information Technology Services with Deloitte and Touche, one of the world's leading accounting and management consultancy firms. He has over 20 years experience in the IT industry, advising a wide variety of businesses and organisations on the strategic application of information technologies and their implementation. He has lectured and published articles on a range of topics, including database systems, object-oriented languages, EDI and client/server systems.

**Robin Menzies**

Robin is a partner in the Dublin office of Coopers & Lybrand. A qualified accountant, he has specialised in computer audit and security since 1980. He is responsible for the security consultancy services in the Irish firm. He has also been involved in the establishment and operation of the European Security Forum, and in this context has conducted a number of pan-European research projects into computer security matters, covering topics such as Balancing Investment and Risk, Risk Analysis and legislation dealing with IT security.


**Ian Oram**

Ian is a Principal in Tagg Oram Partnership. He has seventeen years consultancy and management experience of telecommunications and computing in the public and private sectors. He holds degrees in physics and computing science from Imperial College, London, is a Chartered Engineer and a graduate of the Cranfield MBA programme. He has worked throughout the European Community and the Nordic area as well as in the USA. A specialist in the area of system integration and networks with an emphasis on telecommunications, databases and human computer interaction, his work has included the development of an information technology strategy for a UK police force and the definition and establishment of support function and communications networks in Europe for a major US software company. His publications include *Can an Expert be a Leader*.


**Joe Peppard**

Joe is currently based at the Cranfield School of Management. An honours Business Studies graduate of Trinity College, Dublin, he previously spent five years lecturing at his *alma mater*. He has considerable expertise in the areas of information systems strategy, business re-engineering, electronic data interchange and executive information systems and has consulted with a number of organisations in these areas. Joe has published articles in both academic and general business journals. He is a current Irish international marathon runner.


**Ciaran Redmond**

Ciaran is President of Fouyssac Investments Ltd., a securities trading company. He has over 18 years experience in information systems and has held positions in a diverse and broad range of systems areas. His work has covered the areas of commercial systems, planning, military electronics, communications and advanced artificial intelligence research and development. In his former role as Vice President - Information Systems with GPA Group plc., the aircraft leasing company, he was well known for his development and advocacy of artificial intelligence based corporate systems. His company specialises in futures and options trading using advanced trading stations built on an artificial intelligence base. He also provides consultancy to international clients in adaptive networks, artificial intelligence, intelligent document management and advanced communications.


**Katy Steward**

Katy is in her final year of a PhD program at The Management School, Imperial College London. She is working under Professor Sandra Dawson in the area of *Technological Communication and Organisation Learning*, conducting fieldwork in the exploration and production business of an oil company. Prior to starting her PhD she did her MBA at the Management School, specialising in innovation, and has a BA in Social Anthropology from Cambridge. Katy worked, for a number of years, for Cambridge Education Consultants, a consultancy specialising in education and training in developing countries.

**Richard L. Vail**

Richard is Senior Lecturer in Business Studies at Trinity College, Dublin. He has worked as an officer in the US Army and an engineer for Westinghouse. Dr. Vail has also conducted research and taught at the University of Colorado, Boulder, Templeton College, Oxford, and the Irish Management Institute. In addition to teaching graduate and undergraduate courses he has supervised research students, taught on company training courses and provided consulting. He specialises in manufacturing systems management, service systems management, and business research methodology.

# 1

# Information, Technology, and Strategy

This book deals with the strategic dimension of information systems and information technology (IS/IT). The audience is anyone involved in evaluating the role IS/IT plays in organisations, determining potential areas where IS/IT might be used to achieve competitive advantage, developing an IS/IT strategy, or simply requiring an understanding of the business issues which current technological developments raise.

The objective of the book is to increase the awareness that managers have of IS/IT and the role it can play in increasing competitiveness. After reading this book the reader should be in a position to assess the competitive impact of IS/IT on their organisation and how to link IS/IT strategy with corporate strategy. This book will also equip the reader with a greater appreciation and understanding of the various information technologies and the issues which they raise. It will also consider how directions in IT innovations will influence IS/IT strategies.

IS/IT offers new management and business opportunities and can be applied strategically in at least four different ways:

- to gain a competitive advantage
- to improve productivity and performance
- to facilitate new ways of managing and organising
- to develop new businesses.[1]

However, the strategic application of IS/IT raises a number of key business concerns. These concerns, which directly influence the effectiveness of IS/IT in an organisation, can be categorised under the headings of *planning, technology,* and *people.*

*Planning*        Just as organisations coordinate and plan their business direction they must also plan their investment in technology. No business strategy is now complete without an IS/IT strategy. IS/IT must not only support business strategy but may also provide a strategic opportunity in its own right.

*Technology*      In many organisations a gulf exists between management and the 'technology people' (the IT professionals). To identify potential competitive advantage opportunities and to align the IS/IT strategy with the business strategy, management must be able to bridge this gap. An in-depth knowledge of technical details is not necessary but rather an understanding of the technologies' capabilities, the opportunities they present, and the strategic issues they raise. Every IS/IT strategic planning process makes assumptions about the nature and the role of technological developments.

*People*          The IS/IT plan is only a blueprint, which must be put into action. Implementation involves developing the various applications which result from the IS/IT strategy and managing this process. Implementation of an IS/IT plan also involves change, and this change must be managed effectively. People are generally frightened of change so they need the support of a well managed change process. Ineffective implementation is the prime reason why IT investments fail to result in business gains.

There must, of course, be an underlying understanding of the strategic significance of IS/IT and its role in the management of the information resource. The overall driving force of the IS/IT planning process is the underlying business strategy: the IS/IT strategy is derived from the business strategy.

This book is structured to reflect these concerns and address the issues they raise. If it has one theme, it is that IS/IT is a strategic resource that can create or support business strategy. Each of the four sections deals with topics which we consider important in developing strategies for IS/IT. Figure 1.1 illustrates schematically the structure of the book and outlines the themes to be addressed in each of these sections.

In part 1 we set the strategic agenda for the remainder of the book. The objective is to create awareness of the role of IS/IT in today's organisation and the implications this has for competition. We look at how IS/IT has become more strategic in nature and identify some of the issues this raises. We also examine the business environment which organisations face in the 1990s and look at how they are likely to respond to these challenges. Particular emphasis is placed on how IS/IT can be used for competitive advantage in the marketplace.

Part 2 looks at developing an IS/IT strategy. It presents one approach (and there are a number) to IS/IT strategy formulation. Building on concepts and techniques from strategic management a planning framework is presented.

**Figure 1.1** The structure of the book.

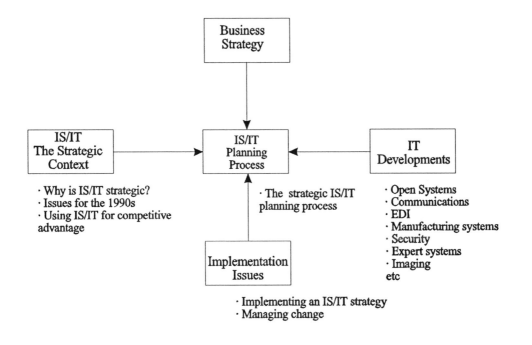

Part 3 examines some of the technologies that are likely to have a major impact on both the business strategy and the IS/IT strategy.

Finally, in part 4 we look at the implementation of an IS/IT plan and address some of the change issues that need to be managed.

## 1.1  The book in context

Within many organisations IT tends not to be viewed as a strategic resource, but rather as an administrative expense.[2]  As such, IS/IT decisions tend to be delegated by senior management to the IT professionals (i.e. the technical personnel) in the organisations.  We believe that IS/IT is too important to be left solely to the technology people.  However, a recent IS/IT survey[3] indicated that  a cultural gap still exists between IT professionals and the rest of the organisation.   It also suggested that top management do not appreciate information technology's potential for improving business performance.

Today, more and more managers at all levels are being asked to subscribe to the IS/IT planning process.  However, their background in the management functions of sales, finance, marketing, etc. means that many of them are unable to articulate potential IS/IT opportunities.

Managers don't need an in-depth knowledge of computers or telecommunications to identify opportunities where IS/IT might be used strategically or to manage IS/IT investments effectively.   What they do need to understand is how IS/IT can contribute effectively to achieve business objectives in their organisations.

## 1.2  What is IS/IT?

For many of us, when we hear the phrase IS/IT we immediately think about computers and communication: the emphasis is clearly on the technical aspect.  We must admit that many technological innovations are very impressive; however, one should not loose sight of the *raison d'etre* of these systems.  Just as a high quality fountain pen is rarely sufficient to write a bestseller, technology itself is usually not sufficient for superior performance.  Technology is only a means to an end and for any organisation this end is the effective management of the information resource.

In many books and articles the terms information system and information technology are used interchangeably.  This can be confusing, especially when one considers that information systems existed long before the computer was invented.  At the outset, we would therefore like to make a clearer distinction between these two terms.

Information system (IS) refers to

*the flow of information in an organisation and between organisations, encompassing the information the business creates, uses and stores.*

The concern is with the efficient utilisation of resources for providing the required level of information support for the management of business operations. It represents the applications perspective. However, as we shall see throughout this book many IS applications depend on technology in order to be viable options.

Information technology (IT) represents the technical perspective and includes telecommunications, computers and automation technologies. More formally, it is

*the enabling mechanism which facilitates the processing and flow of this information, as well as the technologies used in the physical processing to produce a product or provide a service.*

So the familiar bank ATM (automated teller machine) is composed of an IS element, which is the application providing the service, in this case 24 hour cash dispensing, account balance inquiry, etc. and the IT elements of telecommunications, computers, and software which are the mechanism through which this service is delivered.

## 1.3  Information in and around organisations

The information age is well and truly upon us.[4]  The most universally obvious effect is shown in the changing distribution of work across the whole economy. If profiles of working populations in the developed world are examined, they show that the largest proportion of workers are now engaged in some form of information handling work. Today's business organisation is an information-based organisation.[5]

A major driving force is information technology itself, computers and communications if you will, which are vastly increasing the amount of information in and around organisations. IT is also leading to greater shrinkage of time and distance effects and greater interrelatedness within an industry and organisation. Increasing competition nationally and globally and economic conditions are also responsible for this information-based organisation requiring business organisations to be more responsive, flexible and innovative if they are to compete successfully.

Information is the lifeblood of any organisation and everything an organisation does involves using information in some way. It is intricately bound up with the control of other resources. *Information both supports and is involved in the total business process.*

Consider the activities of a typical manufacturing firm. From an initial product idea to customer delivery represents a flow of information (see figure 1.2). Not only does progression from one step to the next require the transfer of information but each step itself requires that information be processed and perhaps stored.

Design information is sent to production planning where manufacturing operations are planned to ensure maximum utilisation of available resources within the available capacity to satisfy requirements. Raw material releases are scheduled; workers are assigned to tasks and activities; jobs are assigned to machines. Throughout the whole production process the status of jobs is continually monitored to ensure work is progressing as planned. Quality is also checked to maintain quality standards.

**Figure 1.2** Information flow in a manufacturing organisation.

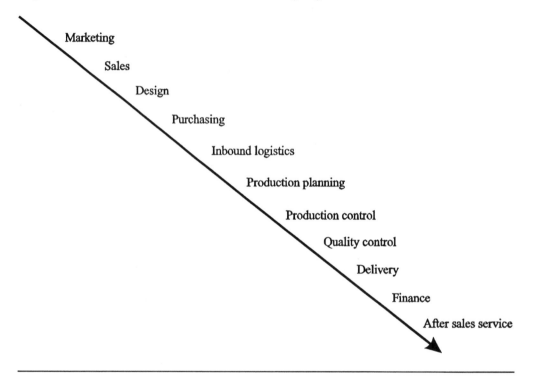

Information is not just something which is internal to an organisation. Organisations also exchange information with their environments as illustrated in figure 1.3. Purchase orders are sent to suppliers; sales orders are received from customers; financial information is delivered to shareholders. Market and intelligence information is required to determine what markets to enter, products to sell, and what strategic posture to adopt. Information is also used in the regulation of business activities; for example, government legislation placing restrictions on trading practices or stock exchange rules regarding disclosures. Thus within an organisation there is a wide variety of information produced, consumed and stored.

**Figure 1.3** Information exchange with the environment.

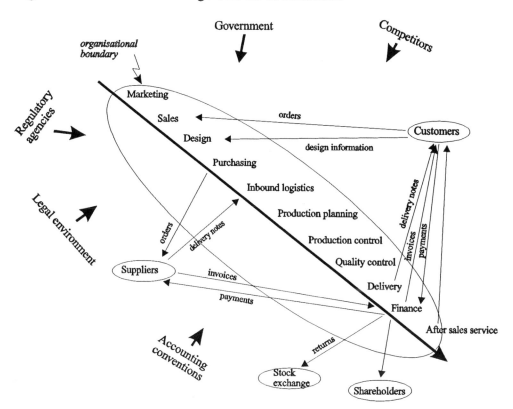

Although technology has been applied for physical processing (i.e. converting raw materials into finished products) since the industrial revolution, this activity is becoming very much more information intensive. Changing customer needs and the desire for customisation require not only flexible production technologies but also an information delivery mechanism to respond to these changing demands. Consider the car industry. There was a time when you could have any colour Ford car as long as it was black! Todays customer is more discerning, often requiring a car tailored to their own specifications. Not only must the production line be flexible to facilitate numerous variations, but information about customer requirements must ensure that the car which is ordered is the one which is eventually produced and delivered. Toyota is reputedly able to deliver an automobile with colour and accessories to customer specifications within five days of the order being placed. Clothing manufacturers are turning to computer-aided design (CAD) techniques to increase the speed with which they can modify products to conform to style changes or retailers' specific orders.

Many automated processes increasingly yield information as a byproduct, thus increasing organisational knowledge. *Informate*[6] is the term which has been coined to describe this phenomenon. Many production processes now display information from multiple sensors and require operators to make decisions which previously they didn't have to. This requires production workers to acquire new skills and work with new information tools. They must also be "empowered" to make decisions without the need for functional separation and control activities.

## Information in products

Davis and Davidson[7] have argued that in the future products are likely to be more information based and that organisations need to "informationalise" their products if they are to increase the value to customers. Indeed, some products are intangible and have no physical components at all. For a fee, Dun and Bradstreet customers can access their database of company financial information. Reuters provide an online information service of share prices and international news. As a result of electronic checkout scanners supermarkets are now able to sell information relating to customer buying patterns to suppliers who can then analyse this information and adjust their marketing campaigns to reflect buying trends.

## Is competition through information or IT?

A distinction can be made between competing through IT and competing through information. For example, to improve customer service, some companies have put terminals at customer locations which are linked directly to their stock and ordering system. This allows the customer to easily check stock availability and to place orders directly. This information has always been available, although not directly to customers. However, IT does make it directly available to customers. This is clearly an example of competing through *IT*.

On the other hand, suppose a firm has identified criteria for evaluating potential acquisitions. If it uses a commercial database to identify acquisition prospects that meet these criteria, this is an example of competing through *information*.

## Information management

Given the crucial role that information plays in and around organisations it is imperative that this information be managed effectively. *Information management* is primarily concerned with the delivery of information (both internal and external) to organisational members from the shop floor workers to the CEO. We are not talking about technology, nor even necessarily about the application of technology. Rather, we are talking about remaining competitive in a complex and changing marketplace and about new ways of managing the information resource although increasingly this will involve the use of IT. Information is a strategic resource and it has been argued that the way organisations use information shapes policy, intentionally or not.[8]

## 1.4  Strategy and strategic planning

Strategy has become a key term in every major organisation. The essence of business strategy lies in creating future competitive advantages faster than competitors. It is seen as involving a complete reappraisal of the organisation in relation to its environment and is a blueprint for which alternative entrepreneurial, competitive and functional area approaches will be pursued in positioning the organisation.

Almost every strategic management prescription and nearly every corporate planning system is premised on a strategic hierarchy in which corporate strategy guides business unit strategy and business unit strategies guide functional tactics. The rationale here is that, left to its own devices, each functional department will inevitably pursue approaches dictated by its professional orientation and the interests of those in charge. In this hierarchy, senior management makes strategy and lower levels execute it. The dichotomy between formulation and implementation is familiar and widely accepted.

Traditionally, organisations are seen to conduct strategic planning by establishing objectives and a course of action to meet the objectives. Typically, strategy formulation begins with the assessment of threats and opportunities in the company's external environment. Executives interpret external data and conclude which issues are critical to the firm. When this information is contrasted with the company's own strengths and weaknesses it leads, firstly, to a definition of the company's distinctive 'competences' and, secondly, to the citing of an overall corporate vision.

Numerous formal frameworks have been proposed in the management literature to aid in strategy formulation. These systematic approaches focus on the degree of fit between existing resources and current opportunities. The BCG Matrix with its 'cash cow', 'star', 'dog' or 'problem child' or Ansoff's product portfolio are just two widely used tools.

As a result of the work of Michael Porter, a Harvard University Professor, the 1980s saw a pronounced emphasis on industry and competitor analysis and the search for competitive advantage. So influential has Porter's work been that we apply many of his ideas in developing an IS/IT strategy.

Figure 1.4 illustrates the strategic planning process, for which these tools  may be used in the analysis.   However, it is beyond the scope of this book to consider strategic management in any detail.   For those readers unfamiliar with strategy techniques there is a vast body of literature which they may wish to refer to.  Some references can be found at the end of this chapter.

## Strategic information management

When we consider the term **strategic information management** three important notions emerge.   The first relates to the *development and support of the strategic management process*.   Although information for such purposes has always been collected, recently we have seen IT being applied to strategic management in three ways:

- aiding in the collection of strategic information (competitor information, market intelligence, industry reports etc.)[9]
- aiding in the strategic planning process (via strategic databases or formal planning models)[10]
- developing a strategic plan (using artificial intelligence techniques).[11]

The second notion refers to developing systems to provide *information in support of business operations*.   This view seeks to align IS/IT strategy with business strategy and using IS/IT for competitive advantage.

The third notion relates to *competing through information* and the technology which facilitates its generation.

For the purpose of this book, we shall refer to strategic information management as

**IS/IT strategies which significantly improve information use and context in order to enhance performance and coordinate activities across functional and business unit lines, as well as the interactions with external entities, in pursuit of competitive advantage.**

Box 1.1 illustrates the key role of information management in the parcel delivery industry.

**Figure 1.4**  An outline of the strategic planning process.

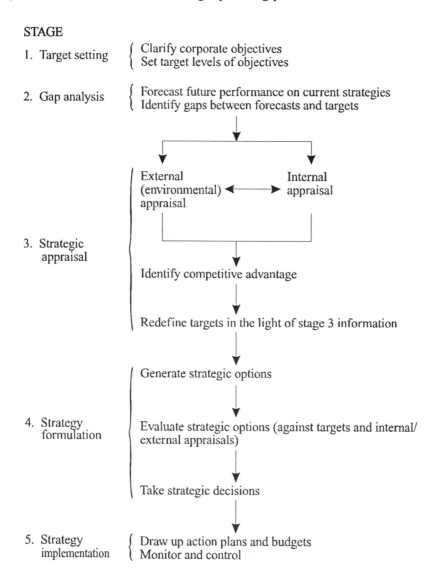

STAGE

1. Target setting { Clarify corporate objectives
                    Set target levels of objectives

2. Gap analysis { Forecast future performance on current strategies
                   Identify gaps between forecasts and targets

3. Strategic
   appraisal

   External
   (environmental) ◄─────► Internal
   appraisal                appraisal

   Identify competitive advantage

   Redefine targets in the light of stage 3 information

4. Strategy
   formulation

   Generate strategic options

   Evaluate strategic options (against targets and internal/
   external appraisals)

   Take strategic decisions

5. Strategy      { Draw up action plans and budgets
   implementation  Monitor and control

Adapted from J. Argenti, *Practical Corporate Planning*, Allen & Unwin, London, 1980.

The courier and express parcel delivery industry has changed from one based on transport to one which is critically dependent on information technology. Systems are used to schedule vehicle fleets and to help plan the most efficient routes to delivery destinations. However companies are facing increasing demands from customers to provide them with consignment tracking and fast reporting of management information.

To meet these demands courier and express companies, such as Federal Express, DHL, United Parcel Service, and TNT have invested millions of pounds in information technology. Information technology is being used in two key ways. Firstly, the global majors operate in many countries and the operational efficiencies of operating in many different countries are dependent on increasingly sophisticated computer networks to hold them together. Secondly, IT enhances the relationship with customers.

Much of the IT development to date focusses on consignment tracking. However, some advanced systems now track shipments at various points in their door-to-door movement such as the pick-up from consigner, arrival at the delivery service company's local depot, arrival/despatch at the main parcel sorting hub, arrival at the local depot nearest to the premise of the consignee and the final delivery.

Consider the case of UPS. In the early 1980s UPS operated a manual package handling system. Although efficient, it couldn't match Federal Express Corporation in technology. UPS's Chief Executive Kent "Oz" Nelson realized back then that the leader in information management would be the leader in international package distribution. The company embarked in a heavy but focused programme of investment in IT. It spent $50m for a global network; $100m for a data centre in Mahwah, New Jersey; and $350m for a Delivery Information Acquisition Device (DIAD), a handheld computer for drivers, and creating a machine-readable label that holds more data than bar codes.

The DIAD unit acts as a two-way communication system between drivers out on the road and their depot. It is used to receive parcel collection details and to transmit proof of delivery back to the company's central consignment tracking system. This has meant that it is not now necessary to search through paper receipts to find who signed for a package if it goes astray. Customers sign on the handheld computer and once a day drivers transmit the signatures to Mahwah, New Jersey, where they can be viewed.

UPS is also spending $150 million on a cellular data network called UPSNET to keep track of the 1 million plus packages it picks up and delivers every day. The network currently links 1,300 distribution warehouses in 46 countries.Although by the late 1980s profits were affected by automation and overseas expansion, UPS earnings are now rebounding.

Expertise in IT gained in parcel delivery has also allowed Federal Express to launch a specialist logistics division called Federal Express Business Logistics (FEBL).  Since 1990 FEB Logistics has been developing a network of international distribution centres called *partsbank*.  While partsbanks may look like ordinary distribution warehouses their role is to provide multiple users with international logistics operations which transcend national boundaries.

A typical partsbank user might be an electronics company based in the US, sourcing products and components from several countries in the Pacific Rim, and needing to service its customers in Europe.  FEBL would manage the total global logistics for such a company, including customs procedures.

**Box 1.1**  What has IT got to do with parcel delivery?
Sources: The new realism in office systems, *Business Week*, June 15th, 1992, pp. 48-53;  Tracking: customers call the tune, *Financial Times*, July 24th, 1991;  The fruitful, tangled trees of knowledge, *The Economist*, June 20th, 1992, pp. 129-132;  Logistics for a shrinking world, *Electronic Trader*, February 1992, pp. 14-15

## 1.5  Strategic information systems

In order to manage information strategically, organisations develop what are known as *strategic information systems, strategic IS/IT* or *competitive information systems*. Technically, such systems may be no different from traditional IS/IT systems, however they can be distinguished by their focus on treating information as a strategic resource.  Their objective is not just to automate existing information flows and operations to increase efficiency but to give the business competitive advantage.

By using IS/IT strategically, organisations attempt to externally disturb the competitive forces at work in an industry and in so doing change the industry structure.  Consider the impact which IS/IT has had in the financial services industry from 'Big Bang' through to 24 hour electronic trading in equities.  The once familiar open call system of the stock exchange has been replaced by buyers and sellers linking together electronically to buy and sell shares.  A physical presence in the exchange is now no longer necessary.

The innovative use of computer-related technology has enabled a wide range of firms in many different industries to create new products, provide superior service, and dramatically reduce costs, thereby gaining a significant and sustainable competitive edge over their competition.  Box 1.2 illustrates a number of examples of applying IS/IT in such a manner.

### American Hospital Supply

American Hospital Supply, as its name suggests, has selected the health care industry as its niche in the wholesale business. To gain an important edge over its rivals, AHS pioneered an order entry distribution system that links most of the firm's customers to its computers. In addition to ordering merchandise the system also allows customers to control their inventories by having direct access to AHS's stock records, increasing the likelihood of their coming to rely upon AHS as a key supplier. The fact that the company's initial move to electronic ordering was spearheaded by a regional manager seeking to meets the needs of a single customer suggests that starting small may be the key to success.

### Thompson Holidays

Thompson Holidays is a tour operator selling holidays to the general public through travel agents. Until 1982, enquiries and bookings were made by telephone, often resulting in chaos during peak periods. When its online reservation system TOP was introduced, agents could make on-screen bookings of holidays.

Technology has become the basis of Thompson's business; the firm's market leadership is actually founded on technological supremacy. It was the first tour operator to offer on-screen bookings to high street agents.

During a single day at the start of the 1986 holiday sales campaign 105,000 holidays were booked through TOP resulting in Thompson carrying over one million passengers that year. It is this ability to handle mass bookings that has enabled Thompson to pursue its fiercely aggressive marketing strategy, and to stimulate huge demand.

### Otis Elevators

Otis Elevators, the US manufacturer of elevators, identified 'customer service' as being a key element of its customer strategy. It decided that one of the things that would give its customers most satisfaction was a prompt lift repair service. So it built an automated system, called Otisline, to dispatch repairmen. When something starts going wrong with Otis's newer lifts, they (the lifts!) automatically call in their complaints to the computer - without human intervention. Otis's rivals suddenly had to compete on quality of service as well as the price and quality of lifts themselves.

**Box 1.2** Some examples of using IS/IT for competitive advantage.

Competitive advantage through IS/IT is not only to make an old process more efficient or quicker but to transform it and radically change the way business is conducted. For example, firms traditionally pay bills on receipt of invoices and pay by cheque. This process could be redesigned so that payment is made on receipt of goods rather than an invoice (what is known as *self-billing*). After all, the invoice just reconfirms the delivery. Instead of sending a cheque, an electronic payment instruction is sent to the payor's bank. The payor's account is debited and the payee's account is credited. A traditional way of doing business has been redesigned to take advantage of IT.

We are not arguing that traditional systems are no longer appropriate. On the contrary. Strategic systems supplement existing systems and in many cases derive from them. However some interesting characteristics emerge if we compare their differing emphasis:[12]

| **Strategic IS/IT** | **Traditional IS/IT** |
|---|---|
| 1. External focus on customers, suppliers, competition, and other outside bodies. | Focus on internal processes. |
| 2. Adding value - differentiation through better products or services. | Cost reduction. |
| 3. Sharing the benefits - within the organisation and with customers or suppliers; even with competitors through appropriate strategic alliances. | Localised benefits. |
| 4. Understanding customers needs and delivering value and solutions to problems. | Solving internal problems. |
| 5. Business-driven innovation without emphasis on the latest technology. | Technology-led development. |
| 6. Incremental development - stepped approach, often by 'trial and error', or prototyping. | Total system defined and developed. |

7.  Exploiting the information to          No exploitation beyond initial
    develop the business - for example,    system.
    by market segmentation.

In thinking about the role IS/IT should play in an organisation, managers must understand the nature of the competitive position of the company or business unit and how it competes. This position and competition situation significantly influence the degree to which IS/IT is strategically important to a unit, the way investment in IS technologies should be considered and the way planning should be executed.

In chapter 3 we look more closely at using IS/IT to gain competitive advantage. One of the problems with IT is that managers very often focus on the technology and not enough consideration is given to gaining sustainable advantage from IT. However, despite the many cases of IS/IT being used for competitive advantage (many more are presented in chapter 3) there is little evidence to suggest that this occurs as a result of the strategy formulation process.[13]

## 1.6  Strategy and IS/IT

If we examine the strategy literature technology is treated as an implementation issue. This presents two problems: *how does technology enter into the strategy formulation process?* and *how are technological capabilities fostered and recognised so as to create the basis for competitive advantage?* It is imperative to recognise that there is a difference between having an IS/IT strategy and having an IS/IT strategy that is aligned to the business strategy.

For many organisations IS/IT investment has tended to be piecemeal and haphazard. Coordination and integration of systems is very often not a consideration. This has been  exacerbated in many organisations with the advent of cheap micros and local area network (LAN) software.  Aligning IS/IT with existing business strategy requires the development of both an IS strategy (what  is required in relation to information systems), and an IT strategy (how it is going to be delivered). The key is that business strategy drives IS/IT strategy.  See the Wal-Mart example in box 1.3.

However, beyond using IS/IT to support existing business strategy, firms have the opportunity in using IT, proactively, to create new opportunities for the business. Figure 1.5 illustrates this by showing IS/IT as an input to the strategy development process.

In 1979 K-mart was the largest discount retailer in the US. With 1,891 stores and average revenues per store of $7.25 million, K-mart enjoyed size advantages. This allowed economies of scale in purchasing, distribution, and marketing. By contrast, Wal-Mart was a small niche retailer in the South with only 229 stores and average revenues about half of those of K-mart stores.

Today, Wal-Mart is the largest and highest profit retailer in the world. Growing nearly 25% a year, the company achieved the highest sales per square foot, inventory turns, and operating profit of any discount retailer.

The secret of Wal-Mart's success lies in its business strategy and in using IT as a lever in supporting that strategy. The strategy's focus was on satisfying customer needs...to provide customers access to quality goods, to make these goods available when and where customers want them, to develop a cost structure that enables competitive pricing. The key to achieving these goals was to make the way the company replenished inventory the centerpiece of its competitive strategy.

Over the last five years, Wal-Mart has invested $600 million in IT. Senior management understood early that while hot products come and go, a good delivery system is lasting. At its computerized warehouses, many goods enter at one loading dock and leave from another without ever resting on a shelf.

By collecting and analyzing sales data from stores on a daily basis, Wal-Mart can immediately learn what merchandise is moving slowly and thus avoid over stocking and deep discounting. Wal-Mart's 3,800 vendors also get daily sales data directly from stores. And 1,500 have the same decision and analysis software that Wal-Mart's own buyers use to check how a product performs in various markets.

Wal-Mart's success shows how important it is to get strategy right before investing in IT.

**Box 1.3** Aligning IS/IT strategy with business strategy at Wal-Mart.
Adapted from *Business Week*, June 15, 1992; G. Stalk, P. Evans and L.E. Shulman, Competing on capabilities: the new rules of corporate strategy, *Harvard Business Review*, March-April 1992, pp. 57-69.

It is important that we make this distinction between IS strategy and IT strategy. It is at the IS strategy formulation stage where business managers are involved. However, identifying IS/IT opportunities requires an understanding of IT developments.

---

**Figure 1.5** IS/IT strategy in context.

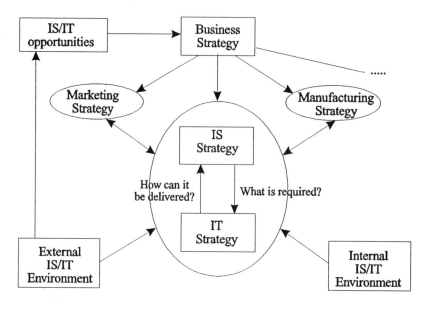

---

*IS strategy*:   is concerned primarily with aligning IS development with business needs and with seeking strategic advantage from IT. It determines requirements to meet business needs, i.e. the applications to be developed.

*IT strategy*:   relates to how these requirements are going to be delivered and is technology focused. Questions it seeks to answer relate to hardware and software. It determines the technology which is going to be used, the enabling mechanism.

So, for example, a wholesaler with a business objective to improve customer service may decide to enhance order management. To accomplish this customers will be permitted to send orders directly to the wholesaler via a telecommunications link. The IS strategy relates to the system to achieve this. The IT strategy is concerned with how this strategy is going to be implemented: the hardware and software to be used, communications standards, etc.

Indeed, for many organisations, the IS strategy is often lacking. Many firms jump straight into IT procurement. This lack of an information systems strategy results in:

- IT investments that do not support business objectives.
- inferior management information.
- competitors, suppliers and customers gaining advantages over the organisation.
- localised justification of investments producing benefits which are counter-productive in the overall business context.
- loss of control of IS/IT leading to individuals often striving to achieve incompatible objectives through IS/IT.
- implementations being late, over budget and unsuccessful.
- continual changes, causing conflict and reducing productivity.

# 1.7  IS/IT strategy formulation

The importance of having an IS/IT strategy that is aligned to business strategy cannot be overemphasised. A study by Ernst and Young [14] found that only 2 out of the 86 organisations they surveyed had IT and business strategies aligned. The business strategy indicates what top management are trying to accomplish; too often IS/IT projects are initiated without being aware of this 'vision'. For example, as part of its business strategy one industrial products company's senior management decided to eliminate administrative tangles by cutting the number of distributors carrying its products. Meanwhile, it delegated hardware and software selections to the IS/IT group in each division. These groups were unaware of what top management was trying to accomplish and top management was unaware of the decision each IS/IT group was making. By the time senior management realised that it would be much easier to consolidate the distributors if all divisions were using the same operating system it was too late. Each division had already bought or built applications that were incompatible. It took the company years to reconfigure the ordering systems so distributors had access to all the products. [15]

The vision of senior management must be communicated to IS/IT professionals. Perhaps if executives were more aware of the role IS/IT played in their ordering system the above problem would never have arisen. Similarly, if IS/IT professionals knew the management view, the situation would also not have occurred.

Kim Clark [16] argues that advantage goes, as it always has, to superior strategy and execution. The IS/IT strategy is derived from the underlying business strategy. The choice of strategy will depend on a number of factors, including the type of industry, its competitive situation, the position of the organisation in the industry and of course the goals and objectives of the organisation.  In chapter 4 we outline an approach to developing an IS/IT strategy.


## 1.8  IS/IT technologies and issues

It is one of the ironies of business strategic planning that those furthest from the customer generally formulate it.  Similarly, people with little understanding of IT usually decide on IT investment decisions.  This is especially true for small-to-medium sized companies who don't normally have the inhouse technological expertise.  While senior managers aren't expected to have an indepth knowledge of technologies, they should, however, be aware of their capabilities and the issues involved.

**Every IS/IT planning process must make assumptions about the nature and role of technological evolution.**  There are two main reasons for this

- implementing an IS/IT strategy takes time
- technology is rapidly changing.

One of the consequences of this is that you plan now to develop a system with a technology which may be obsolete by the time it is actually fully implemented.

"Open systems" is set to be the theme of the 1990s. In 1990, the European Market in open systems was worth $30.5 billion and is growing at 12% a year according to market research company, Data Quest Europe.  The basic premise of the open systems philosophy is that it allows systems from different hardware and software vendors to be connected to each other in a seamless manner.  In chapter 5 we consider this concept and  present some of the issues that it raises, particularly regarding investment in IT.

Chapter 6 reviews the emerging field of telecommunications.  Telecommunications is the technology of information transfer.  Large, geographically dispersed organisations especially need good communication systems to coordinate the activities of many people in diverse locations.  Communications can be used by all organisations to reduce the costs and delays associated with more traditional means of communication, improve sales through better customer service, and establish better means of communicating with suppliers and customers.  The ultimate goal of this evolution in communications is called the integrated services digital network (ISDN) where a wide range of traffic types (voice, data, image, video)  and value added services will be supported by a global telecommunications network.

Over the past few years, mainly as a result of open systems and advances in communications, organisations have begun to link to each other electronically. So, for example, instead of sending orders through the post, which can take several days, they can now be sent electronically in real-time. Chapter 7 considers developments in electronic data interchange (EDI). As a tool, it can be used to slash inventory, improve cash flow, streamline a company's operation, and often forge a competitive advantage.

In chapter 8 we address issues relating to information systems security. Two themes dominate: personal privacy and protection of the information resource. The proliferation of databases containing personal data led to data protection acts being enacted in many countries. These seek to protect personal data contained in many corporate and public databases. The IS/IT investment itself must also be protected, especially if competition is through technology. Many organisations could not now function without their systems. Take for example the results of disruption to a production and sales system. This would typically involve production control, inventory control, sales order entry, invoicing, distribution, demand forecasting, and purchase ordering. The immediate costs of a system failure (in addition to the cost of restoring the system itself) might easily include:

- a complete halt to production;
- a lack of finished products to distribute to customers;
- a build-up of materials and components inventory;
- inability to locate inventory and control distribution properly;
- inability to process sales orders;
- a severe cash flow problem caused by the above.

Just-in-time (JIT), flexible manufacturing systems (FMS), optimised production techniques (OPT) and total quality management (TQM) are just some of the strategies adopted by successful manufacturing firms. Coupling advanced manufacturing technologies and strategic information management will divide world class competitors from the also-rans in virtually every manufacturing industry. The winners will be firms that recognise, at the managerial, functional and technical levels, the strategic value of knowledge and information resources in manufacturing. The losers will be companies that continue to view manufacturing solely in terms of hardware and technology, relegating information management to a secondary role. Chapter 9 looks at developments in manufacturing systems and presents some guidelines for successful strategic applications.

Research in artificial intelligence (AI) seeks to expand the frontiers of information management, and spans a new era: the "intelligence age". Probably the most successful results to date in AI are *expert systems* which seek to encapsulate the knowledge of experts in specific domains. Many successful applications have been constructed over the past ten years in domains such as bank lending, machine breakdown diagnosis, and tax calculations. However, most of these systems are based on principles developed in the 1960s and 70s. In chapter 10 we consider trends in expert systems to date and ponder what the future is likely to hold. Taking a strategic view we consider some of the issues they raise.

Neural networks, intelligent databases, voice recognition, multimedia, virtual reality and document image processing are touted as some of the technologies that are poised to be the major technologies of the late 1990s. Managers should be aware of these innovations and the likely impact they are likely to have on organisations and competition. In chapter 11 we explore some of these emerging technologies and address their strategic significance. One important question that this chapter addresses is whether or not these emerging technologies are solutions looking for a problem.

## 1.9 Implementing an IS/IT strategy

Formulating an IS/IT strategy is one thing, implementing it is another. Organisations are social structures composed of people and IS/IT has a direct effect on their role in the organisation. It is important that actions and changes required to implement an IS/IT strategy are anticipated so as to maximise the benefits. Implementing an IS/IT plan involves change. Employees are given new roles and responsibilities; there is change in the way tasks are performed and how people work with each other. Information itself is a resource that is closely linked with status, enhances authority, and shapes relationships. Changes in the availability of information can result in disruption and organisation conflict. To gain maximium benefits from information systems, both its flow and use throughout the organisation must be properly managed. The success of the implementation will ultimately be measured by how effectively this change is managed. Change management must begin with an understanding of the nature of change itself. Chapter 12 considers IS/IT strategy implementation from an application and project management perspective while chapter 13 considers the change process from an organisation theory viewpoint.

There are other topics which one might argue should be included in this book, for example, the IT organisation, getting value for money from IS/IT investment, or managing benefits. We believe that the ones included are those appropriate to the objectives and context of this volume. However, the reader will be pointed elsewhere to other sources when necessary. It must also be remembered that we are trying to keep this book at a high level and help managers (and aspiring managers) in developing an IS/IT strategy.

## 1.10 Conclusion

The organisation of the 1990s is an information-based enterprise requiring a comprehensive convergence of IS/IT and business strategy. Before you embark on the remainder of the book perhaps a few points to keep in mind:

- *Information should be regarded as a key resource.*

- *No corporate strategy is complete if there is no IS/IT strategy.* This should be obvious by now.

- *IS/IT is too important to be left solely to the IT professionals.*

- *Planning for IS/IT should be an important and integral part of the firm's competitive strategy development.* IS/IT must be planned for strategically.

- *IS/IT can be used to create substantial and sustainable competitive advantage.*

- *Keep abreast of how other companies are using IS/IT around the world.* Remember that innovative applications in another industry may be just the key to permit you to get a jump on your competitors.

- *Cultivate a culture that considers IS/IT issues as it does general business issues.* IS/IT permeates the whole organisation and it is now an integral part of the competitive makeup of industries. An appropriate environment must be established within the organisation to reorientate the treatment of IS/IT.

- *Technological choices are essentially business decisions.* Technology is just a means to an end.

- *Filter out buzz words.* They are the IT industry's way of confusing the business community. Managers do not need an indepth knowledge of technical details but an understanding of the technologies' capabilities, the opportunities they present, and the issues that they raise.

# Notes

1    M.J. Earl, *Management Strategies For Information Technology*.  Prentice Hall International, 1989.

2    A survey by Northwestern University revealed that only 10% of US companies (based on 125 companies from the Fortune 500 list) reported IS/IT as a strategic issue for the company.  This survey is reported in G.M. Hoffman, Why have information technology.  *Information Management FORUM*, (Management Review), American Management Association, September, 1989.  The recent study by MIT Sloan School of Management *Management in the 1990s* research program reported similar findings; see M. Scott Morton, editor, *The Corporation of the 1990s: Information Technology and Organization Transformation*, Oxford University Press, New York, 1991.

3    *Information Technology Review 1991/92*.  Price Waterhouse.  See also K. Grindley, *Managing IT at Board Level: The Hidden Agenda Exposed*.  Pitman, London, 1991.

4    For further discussion of the information age see J. Naisbett, *Megatrends*, Warner Books, New York, 1982; N.D. Mayer and M.E. Boone, *The Information Edge*, McGraw-Hill Book Co., New York, 1987; and P.A. Strassmann, *Information Payoff: The Transformation of Work in the Electronic Age*, The Free Press, New York, 1985 .

5    P. Drucker, The coming of the new organization, *Harvard Business Review*, *January-February*, 1988, pp. 45-53

6    This was a term first defined by Shoshana Suboff. See her book *In the Age of the Smart Machine: The Future of Work and Power*, Basic Books, New York, 1988.

7    S. Davis and W. Davidson, *2020 Vision*. Simon and Schuster, 1991.

8    R.E. Cole,  Target information for competitive performance.  *Harvard Business Review*, May-June 1985, pp. 100-109.

9    See, for example, J.B Rochester, Using information systems for business and competitor intelligence. *I/S Analyzer*, **28**, 5, 1990.

10    See, for example, A.M. McCosh and M.S. Scott Morton, *Management Decision Support Systems*.  Macmillan Press Ltd., London, 1978.

11    See, for example,  R.J. Mockler and D.G. Dologite, Developing knowledge-based systems for strategic corporate planning. *Long Range Planning*, **21**, 1, pp. 97-102.

12    The characteristics were observed in a study of 150 cases by John Ward, of the Cranfield School of Management.

13    R.D.Galliers, Information technology strategies today: the UK experience. In M. Earl, ed., *Information Management: The Strategic Dimension*.  Clarendon Press, Oxford, 1988, pp. 179-201.

14    Ernst and Young (1990) *Strategic Alignment Report: UK Survey*.  Ernst and Young, London.

15    This example is taken from T.H. Davenport, M. Hammer and T.J. Metsisto, How executives can shape their company's information systems. *Harvard Business Review*, March-April, 1989, pp. 130-134.

16    K.B. Clark, What strategy can do for technology.  *Harvard Business Review*, November-December, 1989, pp. 94-98.

# Additional reading

### Strategic management

Henderson, B.D., *Henderson on Corporate Strategy*. Abt Books, Cambridge, Mass, 1979.
Johnson, G. and Scholes, K., *Exploring Corporate Strategy*. Prentice-Hall, 1988.
Porter, M.E. *Competitive Strategy*. Free Press, 1980.
Thompson, A. and Strictland, A., *Strategic Management: Concepts and Cases*. Business Publications Inc., 1987.

### IS/IT and management

Applegate, L.M., Cash, J. and Mills, D.Q., Information technology and tomorrow's manager. *Harvard Business Review*, November-December, 1988, p. 128-136.
Jarvenpaa, S. and Ives, B., Information Technology and Corporate Strategy: a view from the top. *Information Systems Research*, 1, 4, pp. 351-376.
Keen, P.G.W., *Every Manager's Guide to Information Technology*. Harvard Business School Press, 1991.
Leonard-Barton, D. and Kraus, W.A., Implementing new technology. *Harvard Business Review*, November-December, pp. 102-110.
McFarlan, F.W. and McKenny, J.L., *Corporate Information Systems Management: The Issues Facing Senior Executives*. Richard D. Irwin Inc., Homewood, Illinois, 1983.
Parker, M.M and Benson, R.J. with Trainor, H.E., *Information Economics*. Prentice-Hall, New York, 1988.
Rockart, J.F. and Short, J.E., IT in the 1990s: managing organizational interdependencies. *Sloan Management Review*, 30, 2, 1989, pp. 7-17.

### IS/IT and strategy

Bakos, J.Y. and Treacy, M.E., Information technology and corporate strategy: a research perspective. *MIS Quarterly*, June 1986, pp. 107-118.
Benjamin, R.I., Rockart, J.F., Scott Morton, M.S. and Wyman, J., Information technology: a strategic opportunity. *Sloan Management Review*, Spring 1984, pp. 3-9.
Cash, J.J. and Konsynski, B.R., IS redraws competitive boundaries. *Harvard Business Review*, March-April 1985, pp. 134-142.
Cecil, J. and Goldstein, M., Sustaining competitive advantage from IT. *The McKinsey Quarterly*, 4, 1990, pp. 74-89.
McFarlan, F.W. Information technology changes the way you compete. *Harvard Business Review*, May-June 1984, pp. 98-103.
Sprague, R.H. and McNurlin, B.C., editors, *Information Systems Management in Practice*. Prentice-Hall, 1986, pp. 49-70.
Ward, J., Griffiths, P. and Whitmore, P., *Strategic Planning for Information Systems*. Prentice-Hall, 1990.
Wiseman, C., *Strategy and Computers*. Dow Jones-Irwin, 1985.

# 2

# The Strategic Dimension

*War is too important to be left to the generals.*
George Clemenceau

In the first chapter we clearly took the view that IS/IT decisions are too important for management to delegate completely (or indeed abdicate) to the IT professionals in the organisation. As IS/IT has become increasingly strategic in nature, the role it plays in organisations has changed and it has become a key strategic decision at both senior management and board room level.

The objective of this chapter is to provide an overview of the strategic challenges that business organisations will face in the nineties, how they are likely to respond to those challenges and the role of IS/IT. In so doing we will first examine the background as to why IS/IT has become more strategic in nature. Before looking at specific technologies it is important to know: *what are the key business issues facing organisations*? With this in mind we will look at the key challenges that organisations will face in the 1990s in the areas of strategy, people, technology, and operations. Having identified some of these challenges we will look at how organisations are likely to respond. One of our key proposals is that successful organisations will be those that embrace the concept of business integration in order to survive and prosper. Business integration involves looking at strategy, people, technology and operations and the interdependencies between them. We will examine how companies can put this concept into practice and the role IS/IT will play.

## 2.1 Why has IS/IT become more strategic in nature?

Organisations will put forward a number of reasons as to why they have invested in information technology. The most common include: the need to sustain and improve competitive position, to increase revenue or reduce costs or to improve flexibility and responsiveness. While these are important many organisations are driven simply by the *need to survive* in a highly competitive marketplace. Thus while it could be argued that banks installed automated teller machines (ATMs) to increase customer service the reality is that once one bank had installed ATMs competitors were left with little choice but to match that investment as the price that had to be paid to stay in the market. While it may be difficult to quantify the benefits of investing in IT the downside of taking no action is often starkly apparent. Information technology has become increasingly strategic for a number of reasons:

* The cost of maintaining existing systems and the significant investment in time and money required to develop new systems. The long term nature of IT investment and the time it can take to develop a new system demands that organisations strategically plan their requirements.

* IS/IT has an increasingly important role to play in corporate strategy as it significantly impacts the choice of options open to a company and plays an important role in the effective implementation of a corporate strategy.

* IS/IT affects the process of strategy development as it provides more information to managers through the use of expert systems and executive information systems (EIS).

* IS/IT permeates the way organisations are structured and managed. Executive information systems, for example, impact the vertical flow of information through an organisation. Top management have greater access to information and a reduced reliance on middle management to source that information. Horizontally, telecommunication networks allow information to flow easily and quickly between different departments and divisions. IS/IT has the potential to integrate different parts of the organisation and provide more information to managers.

* As well as affecting internal organisation IS/IT also impacts the organisation's interfaces with the external environment. This is having an affect on the organisations long term relationship with customers and suppliers. Inter-organisational systems, facilitated by electronic data interchange (EDI) for instance, create closer links between organisations and their suppliers and facilitate more efficient inventory management and allows a just-in-time (JIT) approach to re-

ordering (see chapter 7). This in turn affects the production strategy of the supplier.

- While representing a significant hardware and software investment IS/IT also involves making a significant investment in people and in the way they do their work (see chapter 13).

The importance of IS/IT to organisations is likely to increase. In the next section we will look at key challenges which will influence its development.

## 2.2 What are the challenges of the nineties?

Before we can fully understand the role IS/IT will play in organisations we need to understand the business environment that they face in the nineties. The focus is not just on how developments in technology will affect companies but also on how the other components of a business - its strategy, its people, and its operations - are changing.

**Trends in strategy**

*Global marketplace*
The concept of globalisation is not new and has been with us for many years as organisations have relocated plants to avail of lower workforce costs. What is new is the concept of the global marketplace and the rate at which it has developed and the complexity now involved as organisations have to think and act beyond national boundaries. As can be seen from figure 2.1 increased domestic and global competition are seen as the key reasons to accelerate product and process development. Even as organisations grapple with how to best take advantage of the European market its boundaries are expanding. Over 320 million consumers in the European Community can be extended if we include other members of EFTA and the Commonwealth of Independent States. The recent emergence of the North American trading block to rival the EC represents a challenge to organisations trying to maintain a global presence.

For some organisations the response is reactive as they face international competition in their home country for the first time. As we move into the nineties a global company will not be defined as one that does business internationally but one that provides a consistent level of high quality products and services in every market in which it operates.

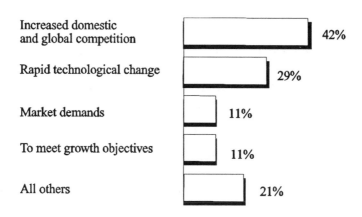

Increased domestic
and global competition — 42%

Rapid technological change — 29%

Market demands — 11%

To meet growth objectives — 11%

All others — 21%

**Figure 2.1** Key reasons to accelerate product and process development.
Source: *California Management Review*, Winter, 1990.

### Strategic alliances

The eighties saw organisations increasingly turning to strategic alliances and reshaping the traditional notion of competition. The car and computer industries in particular have been characterised by joint ventures and alliances to share manufacturing facilities in the case of cars and to access technology and markets in the case of computers. The trend is unlikely to be reversed as organisations realise that the resources required to compete on a global scale frequently exceed those available to any one company.

### Outsourcing

The concept of outsourcing is built around identifying the core activities that an organisation can perform competitively and subcontracting out other parts of the business process that it has no competitive advantage in. Traditionally organisations would subcontract out low value activities like catering and cleaning but increasingly companies are outsourcing other activities. There is a rapidly growing trend to outsource network and data centre management due to the risk and cost of maintaining systems. The outsourcing of IT is sometimes referred to as *facilities management*. It involves selling portions of an organisation's IT functions to an outside contractor and buying back the services based on consumption levels and agreed service levels.

**The people dimension**

The 90s will see information expanding at a rate never seen before in history and the growth is exponential. According to Daniel Bell, the Harvard sociologist, the communications revolution is driving our progress towards a true "post industrial society" where information and knowledge will replace capital and labour as our primary resources. The challenge for companies will be in managing this information and coping with changes in the workforce.

*Importance of people*
From the 1960s to the 1980s the information systems industry focused on technology first and people second. In the 80s came the realisation that any technical solution must recognise the people dimension. People do not learn automatically how to use a system to its full potential. There is a significant training investment required and a need to design solutions around how people actually do their jobs. In order to fully utilise human resources, organisations must leverage their workforce to perform at a higher level of productivity. The goal is a competitive workforce with three characteristics:

| | |
|---|---|
| Knowledgeable | A workforce that knows more because they are educated, informed and have continuous access to training. |
| Productive | A workforce that can do more because they are given the right tools and technology. |
| Motivated | A workforce that wants to do more because they are highly motivated and committed. |

*New skills*
One of the paradoxes facing developed countries is how the growing need of business for skilled new entrants to the workforce can be reconciled with long term unemployment in many countries. This can be partly explained by the shift in the skills required by the modern workforce as information technology and new ways of doing business create demands for particular kinds of skilled professionals. At a country level we see governments increasingly recognising the importance of planning its human resource strategy and developing people with the key skills required. At the organisational level a shortage of these workers will profoundly affect its ability to reap the benefits of information technology and effect organisational change.

*Ability to change*
As organisations become more adept at managing technological change it will increasingly be those that actively manage the people dimension that will gain the competitive edge. This involves building consensus within the organisation during times of change to ensure that the workforce is committed to the process. Chapter 13

addresses the change dimension in relation to implementing an IS/IT strategy in an organisation.

*Organisational impacts*
One of the key impacts of IS/IT is the effect it is having on the way organisations are structured. For example the growth of communications networks provide the potential to integrate human resources across traditional internal and external boundaries. Within organisations IS/IT is breaking down the traditional barriers between departments and business functions. Marketing and production for instance can no longer operate as discrete units as the need to share information between them grows. The role of middle management is under pressure as IS/IT facilitates the vertical flow of information through the organisation as executive information systems give senior management better access to information.

Externally organisations are becoming linked through the use of EDI (see chapter 7) and common systems such as those used in the airline industry for reservations and those linking insurance companies and their brokers in the insurance industry. All of the above create the need to integrate hardware and software technologies, and are driving the move towards *Open Systems* (see chapter 5).

**The impact of technology**

When we look at technology in a broader context and not just at IS/IT we can see how it is driving change in organisations and industries. Schumpeter emphasised in his *Theory of Economic Development*[1] that technology and the process of innovation are important change agents in the structuring of industries and competition.

*Revolutionising industries*
The successful exploitation of new technologies has been a source of tremendous opportunity for many companies and a significant threat to those who have not adapted. In the nineties we should begin to see the emerging technologies of genetic engineering, and developments in materials such as superconductivity and advanced composites, to name but a few, beginning to realise their potential. The effect that technological discontinuities can have on companies and even industries is illustrated in table 2.1 when we look at the changing fortunes of organisations in the semi-conductor industry.

It is interesting to note that none of the leaders in 1950 are present in 1982. Note the growth in the importance of Japanese organisations. As technology changed, a number of organisations failed to make the successful transition to the new technology.

| Indu-stry Rank | 1950 (Vacuum tubes) | 1955 (Transistor) | 1960 (Semi-conductor) | 1970 (Semi-conductor) | 1975 (Semi-conductor) | 1975 (IC) | 1980 (LSI) | 1982 (VLSI) |
|---|---|---|---|---|---|---|---|---|
| 1 | RCA | Hughes | TI | TI | TI | TI | TI | Motorola |
| 2 | Sylvania | Transition | Transition | Fairchild | Motorola | Fairchild | Motorola | TI |
| 3 | GE | Philco | Philco | Motorola | Fairchild | National | National | NEC |
| 4 | Raytheon | Sylvania | GE | GI | RCA | Intel | Intel | Hitachi |
| 5 | Westinghouse | TI | RCA | GE | GE | Motorola | NEC | National |
| 6 | Amprex | GE | Motorola | RCA | National | Rockwell | Fairchild | Toshiba |

**Table 2.1** Changing fortunes in the semi-conductor industry.
Adapted from Richard Foster *Innovation: The Attackers Advantage.* Macmillan, London, 1986.

The S-curve as developed by Foster (see figure 2.2) provides a useful way of illustrating how, for each new product or process, improvements in performance over time have to be matched by increasing effort to achieve those improvements.

**Figure 2.2**   The S-Curve: the infancy, explosion, then gradual maturation of technological progress.

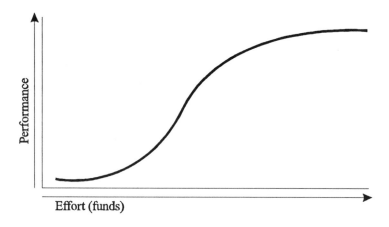

Source: Adapted from Richard Foster, *Innovation: The Attackers Advantage.* Macmillan, London, 1986.

The challenge for management is recognising the limits of its current technology, developing a technological direction and managing the associated technological change. Where the future involves adopting a new technology they have to manage the transition process.   The strategic implications are important not only in high technology industries but in most industries.

*How is technology affecting competition?*

As well as creating new industries and revolutionising existing industries technology has the potential to significantly improve an organisation's competitive position within an industry.  As we move into the 1990s technology will continue to change the dynamics of competition at an ever increasing rate.  For example, investment in manufacturing technology can reduce the cost of production in many industries and allow for greater flexibility.  The development of marketing databases facilitates the identification and cultivation of closer relationships with customers.

In chapter 3 we look more closely at the the impact which IT has on competition while in chapters 5 to 11 we examine the major information technologies.

## Operations/business processes

As well as trends in strategy, the people dimension, and the impact of technology it is important to look at how businesses will organise themselves to produce goods and services.  In many ways the success of Japanese companies in global markets is more a factor of how they organise themselves to produce goods cost effectively than to major strategic insights.

*Business process re-engineering*

Many IT investments have been unprofitable because they concentrated on automating existing inefficient processes rather than fundamentally re-examining how they perform those business processes.  Business process re-engineering questions the validity of existing ways of organising work and is concerned with redesigning the organisation around fundamental business processes.

The emphasis on *processes* rather than events or activities is crucial.  A business process is a set of activities that cuts across functional boundaries in order to realise a business objective.  Processes have two important characteristics:

*they have customers*, that is, processes have defined outcomes and there are recipients of outcomes.  Customers can be internal or external to the organisation.

*they cross organisational boundaries*, that is, they normally occur across or between organisational functional units.

While the concept is perhaps more developed in manufacturing organisations which have implemented processes like just in time (JIT) and total quality management (TQM) to improve the way they produce goods, it is rapidly spreading to service industries.  In the insurance industry, for example, it involves re-examining how insurance policies and claims are processed through the system.  The elements of business process re-engineering are illustrated in the case of Barclays Bank (see box 2.1).

*Time compression management*
One of the key sources of competitive advantage in the nineties will be time compression or the ability to deliver faster than competitors.  Competition through time can improve competitiveness in a number of ways.  Costs for instance can be reduced by increasing inventory turn and reducing the cost of carrying stock.  One of the basics of  time compression management is the need to do things right the first time through improved quality.  Time compression management is being driven by a number of elements:

- Faster Delivery
  As customers increase their demands for goods and services to be delivered in shorter time frames, organisations have to respond with faster delivery times. Where organisations are moving to JIT they  require suppliers to deliver to order in very short times.

- Shorter Product Cycles
  To be successful time has to be compressed out of other processes besides delivery.  The speed with which organisations can develop and get products to the market is an important competitive weapon; as illustrated in figure 2.3 payback and profitability can be increased by extending the front end of the traditional product life cycle.

---

**Figure 2.3**  New product life cycle.

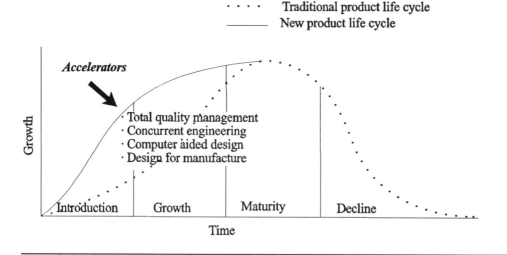

The flexibility that comes from business process change is often an organisation's best weapon against fierce competition. British-based Barclays Bank is a prime example of an organisation that is reengineering its business processes to counter the competitive forces that are threatening its profitability.

In a newly deregulated banking environment, Barclays finds its customer base being attacked by building societies (savings and loans) offering attractively-priced checking account products. Barclays has responded by offering interest on its checking accounts to its six million personal customers at a potential cost of more than $100 per customer a year. How, then, to recoup some of this outlay?

Barclays' answer was to create a new sales-driven culture for the bank. Taking advantage of the trend toward personalized products and customer service, Barclays is concentrating on segment marketing: cross-selling their wide range of financial products to customers.

This new orientation is having profound ramifications for the makeup of Barclays' workforce. Some three-fourths of the staff and office space in each branch have been devoted to back office matters; only one fourth has dealt directly with customers. The bank is reversing this proportion, converting each of its 2,500 personal and small business branches from a processing centre to a sales office.

This shift required training 40,000 people in sales, sales planning, and sales management - not only in the branches but throughout the bank. The two year sales training initiative is concentrating on teaching the customer staff face to face selling and consulting techniques. In the branches where this training has occurred thus far, sales performance has increased significantly.

In parallel with the sales training effort, Barclays is developing a new customer information system made up of both a database drawing on customer files and sales support tools. The sales support system will provide a suite of functions, from marketing analysis software to sales tracking tools. Barclays' managers in every branch will be able to segment a customer base and target a marketing campaign to that group, drawing on market analysis tools.

The bank's two-pronged response - the change to a sales culture and the new information system - synchronize well. Ideas from the new sales people are making the new system more complete and the sales people in turn are welcoming the new system. Each element is working to support the other.

**Box 2.1** Creating a new business culture: Barclays Bank.
Source: Andersen Consulting, *Trends in Information Technology*, Second Edition,. McGraw-Hill, 1992.

A successful time-based strategy must look at all of the different business cycles that make up the production of a good or service. The following quote from George Stalk, which is illustrated in figure 2.4, describes the essence of time-based competition:

*Because time flows throughout the system, focusing on time-based competitive performance results in improvements across the board. Companies generally become time-based competitors by first correcting their manufacturing techniques, then fixing sales and distribution, and finally adjusting their approach to innovation. Ultimately, it becomes the basis for a company's overall strategy.*[2]

**Figure 2.4** Current trends: time-based strategies.

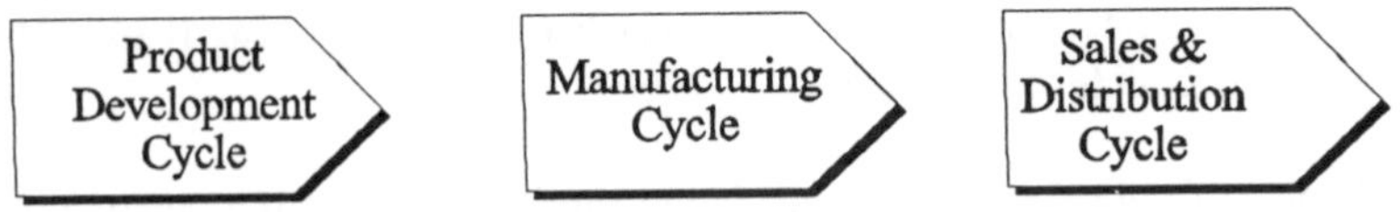

*New product development/design for manufacture*

As the process of design and manufacturing products in technology-driven industries becomes increasingly complex, the need for new approaches to product development becomes even more pressing. There are a number of approaches to bridging the traditional demarcation between marketing, engineering, manufacturing and design including design for manufacture, concurrent engineering, and simultaneous engineering. Using cross-functional teams, the objective is to integrate design and engineering with the manufacturing process, ensuring coordination. Indeed, often customers are involved. By focusing early in the design process, potential problems or breakthroughs are identified. The benefits of focusing on the development processes are illustrated in figures 2.5a and 2.5b.

## 2.3 Winning strategies for the nineties?

Given the challenges facing organisations we need to ask ourselves what will characterise the successful business enterprise of the nineties? To remain competitive in the 90s organisations will have to be flexible, quicker to market, focused on customer values, cope with rapid change, and in partnership with customers, suppliers and competitors.

**Figure 2.5a** Are we focused on the right cost drivers?

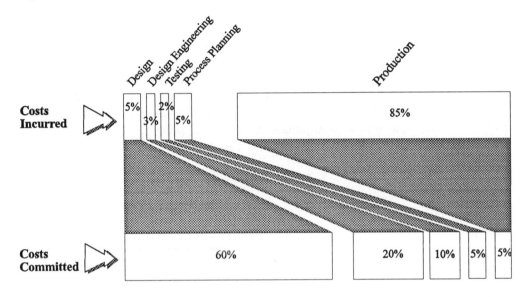

**Figure 2.5b** The price of change.

| Development Phase | Typical cost for each change |
|---|---|
| Design | $1,000 |
| Testing | $10,000 |
| Process planning | $100,000 |
| Test production | $1,000,000 |
| Final production | $10,000,000 |

Source: Dataquest data, presented in *Business Week*, April 30th, 1990.

*Flexible*
The old rigid structures and hierarchies of the past are no longer adequate and are giving way to more flexible organisation structures. IBM is a classic example of a large centralised organisation which is finding itself increasingly under pressure from smaller more focused competitors. Its response has been to reorganise into smaller more flexible organisational units.

*Quicker to market*
Increasingly companies are realising that, as product life cycles are becoming compressed, speed to market is a key source of competitive advantage. In the pharmaceuticals industry companies are under increasing pressure to speed up the development of new drugs to capitalise as fully as possible on the window of opportunity that exists before patents expire. The dramatic results of time to market strategies are illustrated in figure 2.6.

**Figure 2.6** Superfast innovators.

|  |  | Development time | |
|---|---|---|---|
| COMPANY | PRODUCT | OLD | NEW |
| Honda | Cars | 5 years | 3 years |
| AT&T | Phones | 2 years | 1 year |
| Navistar | Trucks | 5 years | 2.5 years |
| Hewlett-Packard | Computer printers | 4.5 years | 2 years |

*Focused on customer values*
Marketing has been with us as a business function since the early fifties but in some respects is only starting to come into its own. The major emphasis in IS/IT for large paper-driven industries like the banks and insurance companies has been on transaction-based systems. Technology is now providing the means to realistically segment markets and target customers according to their needs. This is switching the emphasis away from transaction processing to customer service oriented systems.

*Able to handle rapid change*
The nineties will be characterised by change and will require organisations to adapt to new market structures and reinvent the way they have traditionally done business. As is illustrated in figure 2.7 the key success factors are rapidly changing. In the fifties and sixties US companies dominated the electronics industry with innovative new

products. The Japanese established their position in the electronics and automotive markets by coupling best technology with low cost. The pressure now is to couple best technology with least cost and in the least amount of time.

*Innovative*
Successful companies will be characterised by innovation across the full spectrum of their business activities. This is not limited to new product development but includes developing new marketing strategies, opening new channels of distribution, segmenting customers in new ways, streamlining logistics, developing new organisational structures to complement their existing strengths. Innovation needs to permeate all functions and all aspects of the organisation.

---

**Figure 2.7** Key success factors.

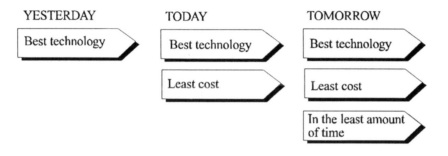

---

*In partnership with customers, suppliers and competitors*
Increasingly companies are forging closer links with customers and suppliers. A manufacturing company cannot move to just in time production without working closely with its suppliers. Electronic data interchange can facilitate these links but is driven by the core business need to integrate more closely with customers and suppliers. Globalisation is pushing many companies into partnership with competitors in the form of joint ventures and alliances in order to complement their own strengths and weaknesses.

In the sixties Igor Ansoff proposed that to be successful organisations needed to be both effective and efficient. They need to do the right things in terms of developing a successful strategy (*effectiveness*), and to implement it successfully at an operational level (*efficiency*). When we plot these (see figure 2.8) we can characterise successful companies as those that successfully reconcile both. The losers and runners up are the companies that can only move on one axis.

**Figure 2.8**  Efficiency and effectiveness.

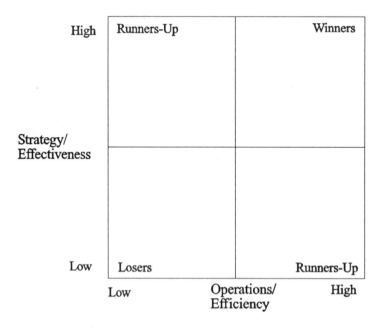

While the diagram is useful it needs to be extended to take account of two other factors.  Firstly, moving to the winning quadrant has to be achieved relative to the competition.  It is not just a question of having a more effective strategy and efficient operations than the competition but developing them faster than the competition, i.e. it is time based.  Secondly and perhaps more importantly this position can only be attained through the people in the organisation and making use of technology.

The winning organisations will be the ones who best deal with efficiency and effectiveness, do it in the least possible time, and integrate the people in the organisation with the technology.  In the next section we will look at what companies have to do to achieve this.

## 2.4  How to put business integration into practice

One of the lessons from the 1980s is that concentrating on one element such as information technology is not enough to gain competitive advantage.  For the organisation to be both efficient and effective and to move into the winning quadrant it must integrate strategy, people, operations and technology.  The objectives of business integration are illustrated in figure 2.10. Information technology on its own if it does not take into account how the business operates will only layer technology upon technology. One of the key concepts behind business process re-engineering is the need to examine an organisation's business process and simplify the processes before applying technology. Applying information technology to existing processes can often only exaggerate the problem by automating existing poor practice. Similarly the application of IS/IT must support the organisation's strategic direction.

**Figure 2.9** Winning in the nineties.

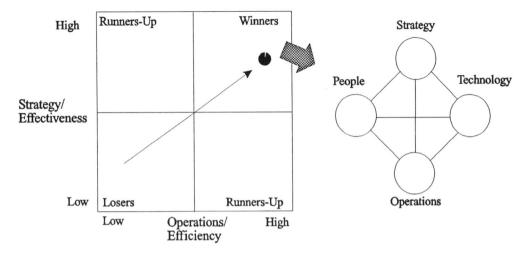

To successfully put business integration into practice requires asking some tough questions (see figure 2.12). There are also a number of key principles which need to be followed in order to successfully reap the benefits of business integration.

*Focus around results*
One of the disadvantages of modern information systems can be that they can provide too much information and performance measures. Any business has to have well defined performance measures that are significant, measurable and easily compared with previous performance to track progress.

*Set far-reaching goals and measure improvements*
Traditional approaches to managing performance have been to look for continuous improvement on a yearly basis. This is usually obtained by fine tuning the existing way a company does its business. A challenge to the organisation to make a significant improvement can force it to fundamentally rethink the way it operates. A

defence manufacturing company in the UK was faced with the immediate challenge of providing missiles on very short notice for the Gulf War. Using its traditional manufacturing techniques it would have been unable to meet demand in the tight timescales demanded. By fundamentally reorganising its manufacturing processes and implementing JIT techniques it was able to reduce delivery time from 2 years to just under six months.

**Figure 2.10** Objectives of business integration.

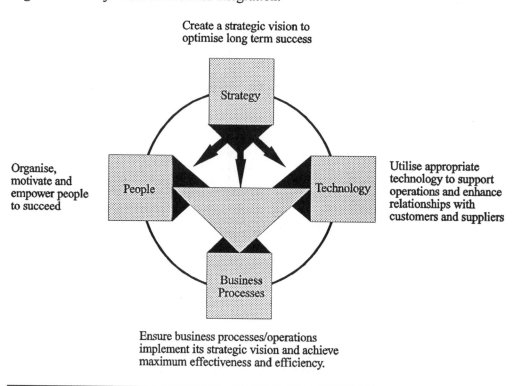

Create a strategic vision to optimise long term success

Organise, motivate and empower people to succeed

Utilise appropriate technology to support operations and enhance relationships with customers and suppliers

Ensure business processes/operations implement its strategic vision and achieve maximum effectiveness and efficiency.

Figure 2.11 illustrates how competitive benchmarking can be used to measure performance. This involves identifying the key elements for success in an industry, measuring how the industry or individual competitors perform against these criteria and then plotting your own organisation's performance. The process should be extended by looking at performance in other industries.

**Figure 2.11** Competitive benchmarking.

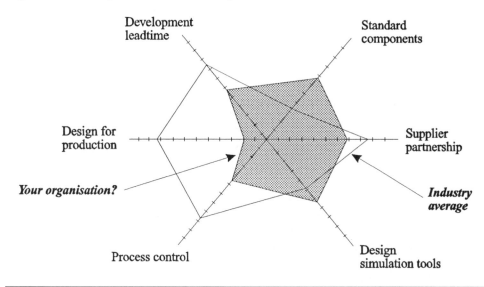

*Quality at the source*
One of the key concepts of any quality system or ethos is the concept of getting it right first time. This often involves reducing or even removing quality departments and driving home the quality message at the lower levels of the organisation. The benefits of proactively promoting quality is that it applies to all areas of the business and is relatively independent of the particular strategy chosen.

*Continuous improvement*
This is a very Japanese idea. As one prominent Japanese industrialist is quoted as saying "business is like shaving, no matter how well you do it one day you still have to do it again the next morning". This means that no matter how effectively an activity seems to be performed it is important to continue to identify ways of improving it.

In a Japanese context it is often the sum of many small incremental improvements that have proved so effective. It is important to realise, however, that over time the law of diminishing returns sets in and it may be necessary for a radical change in how the operation is performed, perhaps within the context of a business re-engineering initiative.

---

**Figure 2.12** Tough questions to be answered.

- *Strategy*
  Is it explicitly stated in the form of a unified comprehensive and integrated plan?
  Does your strategy relate the strategic advantages of the firm to the challenges of its environment?
  Will it ensure that the basic objectives of the enterprise are met?

- *People*
  Does your organisation structure reflect the way work is actually performed?
  Do all of your people:
  > Clearly understand what is required of them?
  > Have all the tools they need readily accessible to them?
  > Know how your organisation defines success?
  Is authority aligned with responsibility?
  Are rewards based on clearly defined performance standards?
  Do your people have the knowledge and skills to do the job?

- *Technology*
  Is technology leveraging the skills of your workforce?
  Are you utilising appropriate technology?

- *Operations/processes*
  Are your business processes aligned with your strategic vision?
  When was the last time you critically evaluated the effectiveness of your business processes?
  How does your effectiveness compare to:
  > Your competition?
  > The best in the world?
  What percentage of your peoples' activities adds value to your products or services as perceived by your customers?
  Do you have an effective Quality Management Program?

---

*Top management involvement*

Experience has shown that very little change occurs in organisations without the involvement and support of top management. Top management has the ability to define the agenda within organisations and articulate a vision of the future. They also have a key role in providing leadership and defining where resources are to be allocated. Their position in organisations gives them a unique opportunity to view the organisation as a whole and to effect necessary changes.

*Value driven*
This involves aggressively determining the value activities that are performed in the company and removing non value added activities. In banks, for example, this can mean shifting human resources out of transaction processing activities and into revenue generation activities like sales and marketing. It can also involve outsourcing activities which the firm has no advantage in performing. Porter's value chain can provide a useful tool for identifying the key value activities that companies perform and will be dealt with in more detail in chapter 4.

*Balance*
It is important that none of the elements of business integration are either over-emphasised or neglected. Thus a technological solution which ignores the human dimension or how the business actually operates is likely to be unsuccessful. This is clearly illustrated by the case of General Motors who in the eighties made an enormous investment in technology without corresponding improvements in competitiveness. Their CEO, in hindsight, recognised that too little attention had been paid to getting all levels of the organisation involved in the process.

*Customer perspective is the only perspective*
In approaching business integration it is important to keep in focus how changes will affect your customers and that change is customer rather than company driven.

*Empower people and energise for change*
This involves giving people throughout the organisation the opportunity to contribute to the process and to work more effectively. It entails devolving authority and responsibility further down the organisation and flattening the hierarchy. People are given the opportunity and resources to do their work more effectively and creating an environment which fosters openness and a willingness to change.

*Communicate a vision*
One of the key elements involved in successfully pursuing business integration is the concept of having an overall corporate vision. The corporate vision should communicate what the organisation is trying to achieve in the future and how it is going to achieve it. Senior management will have to provide and articulate this vision and some of the characteristics required of such a leader are illustrated in figure 2.13.

---

**Figure 2.13** Some of the characteristics of the global transformational leader.

*They identify themselves as change agents.* Their professional and personal images revolve around making a difference and transforming the organisation for which they are responsible.

*They are courageous individuals.* They are prudent risk-takers, individuals who take a stand. They have healthy egos and do not need constant reinforcement in difficult situations.

*They believe in people.* They are powerful yet sensitive to other people and ultimately work toward the empowerment of others.

*They are value driven.* They are able to articulate a set of core values and exhibit behaviour that is congruent.

*They are life-long learners.* They are able to see and talk about mistakes they have made as learning experiences.

*They have the ability to deal with complexity, ambiguity, and uncertainty.* They are able to cope with and frame problems in a complex, changing world.

*They are visionaries.* They are able to dream and to translate those images so that others share them.

Adapted from *Signals: The Magazine for Business from Ameritech*, Volume 2, Issue 4, Winter 1990.

---

## 2.5  The role of IS/IT

The importance of the business integration model is the interdependencies of strategy, people, technology and operations. Used improperly technology can waste a lot of money and divert managements attention and even increase overall costs. Treated in isolation it is unlikely to significantly improve performance but properly applied IS/IT can enable dramatic improvements in business performance. Some of the ways in which IS/IT can enable performance improvements are illustrated by the example of the Swiss Options and Financial Futures Exchange (SOFFEX) outlined in box 2.2.

*Strategy*
In the case of SOFFEX IS/IT had a major impact on how the exchange developed a competitive strategy for the nineties. Most importantly, the exchange was driven by a very clear strategic vision which was enabled by the appropriate use of technology. Rather than take an incremental approach and improve its existing way of doing business the exchange implemented their vision of becoming 'the first totally automated exchange in their world'. Another example of how companies have used IS/IT to implement a strategic vision and create new opportunities are the Life Assurance companies use of portable PCs to take business out of expensive branches and directly to the customers.

*People*
IS/IT is enabling progressive organisations to leverage more effectively the skills of their people. They can be facilitated in a number of ways through the use of electronic mail, voice mail, electronic conferencing and networks to allow access to companywide information. Increasingly, organisations will draw on knowledge networks to process information that originates both inside and outside the organisation. Similar to the nervous system in the human body, these knowledge networks will link, coordinate, and monitor the different elements within an organisation. The use of client-server technology and workstations allows the access of information from all parts of the organisation.

*Operations/business processes*
IS/IT has underpinned the development of many changes at the operational level for organisations. Used in conjunction with business process re-engineering it can reduce clerical effort in labour intensive industries. Interactive voice response systems which are being piloted by some UK banks will reduce the number of people required to respond to basic requests for information on such things as account balances. In traditionally paper-driven industries like insurance and banking new technologies such as imaging should enable significant reductions in paper flow. Again, SOFFEX provides a good example of the benefits of questioning existing business practice and fundamentally re-examining business processes.

*Technology*
IS/IT also has a role to play in developing new technologies. The speed and quality of new engines and designs in the automotive industry is significantly improved by the use of computer-aided design (CAD) technology. The increasing speed of change in information technology puts a premium on making good technology investments. Options for stretching your technology investment include:

- Write off the investment faster to reflect shorter technology lifetimes. Ten years ago, major computer manufacturers were on a five- to seven-year product cycle. This gave companies a three- to five-year window to achieve a payback. Now, some computers are on an 18-month lifecycle, and larger systems are down to three and four years.

- Skip some generation of technology by not upgrading. Instead, choose a platform - the combination of hardware and operating system on which applications operate - that the organisation can live with for a while, skip the next one, and then "leapfrog" early to the next platform.

  Not every old system needs to be replaced. Mainframes are still appropriate for many high volume systems that require centralisation and control. These kinds of applications will not disappear, nor will mainframes.    As inappropriate applications are moved off mainframes, these machines will operate more as special-purpose computers.

- Create systems that can survive multiple technology shifts by taking an architectural approach.  Just as architects designing a skyscraper must rely on standard parts to achieve a sound structure, systems designers can use the same approach.

The business vision that is enabled by information technology often allows organisations to alter the competitive landscape in radical ways.  The development of the Swiss Options and Financial Futures Exchange (SOFFEX) is an example of such market transformation.

In the mid-1980s, the three regional Swiss stock exchanges used a trading approach known as "ring trading", in which each stock is traded in rotation one at a time, before moving on to another stock.  Whatever merits this technique has, its most serious limitation is that it does not allow the development of derivative products, such as financial futures and options contracts.  Because most of the major European economies were developing such products, the Swiss financial community's position within the European business world was threatened.

A traditional response to such a challenge would have been to meet the market on its own terms, duplicating the basic procedures and technological capabilities of the marketplace.  Clearly the trading procedures would have to be revamped.  But the project team formed to meet the challenge in Switzerland had a greater vision, fuelled by leading edge technologies and unrestricted by aged business processes.  Their vision: the first totally automated exchange in the world.

Today, someone "visiting" the Swiss Options and Financial Futures Exchange is in for a surprise.  SOFFEX has no trading floor, no pits with traders waving paper.  In their place is a real-time system whereby exchange members buy and sell from workstations in their member firms offices.  The exchange system matches buys and sells and notifies the parties of trades, all electronically.

SOFFEX is actually a cluster of computers linked to three communications centres, one at each regional exchange; these in turn are interconnected by a backbone network.  Member banks link to one of the three centres.  In addition, the exchange links to the Swiss National Bank for direct payments to and from SOFFEX and member bank accounts.

SOFFEX distributes its prices and receives prices of its underlying instruments via an electronic wire service.  The member banks' accounting systems are also connected and automatically are sent updated information when a trade is executed. All members and accounts can be monitored to ensure they are handled properly. Paper based records are eliminated and there are no unmatched trades on SOFFEX.

How successful has SOFFEX been in realising the vision? Within six months after beginning operations, it had already reached its two-year goal of handling 9,000 contracts per day. After one year it was one of the top 20 futures and options exchanges in the world. Within two years it had its first 100,000 contract day and had become the world's eleventh largest options exchange.

**Box 2.2** Envisioning new opportunities in the marketplace: The Swiss Options and Financial Futures Exchange.
Source: *Andersen Consulting, Trends in Information Technology*, Second Edition. McGraw-Hill, 1992.

## 2.6 Conclusions

As we move into the mid-1990s IS/IT is going to continue to become more important strategically and spending is unlikely to decline. IS/IT has become too important to the survival and competitiveness of organisations for this to change. The nature of the investment in IS/IT should however reflect the business environment and challenges of the nineties. Some of these challenges will include global competition, strategic alliances, importance of a flexible and skilled workforce, the increasing rate of technological development, business process re-engineering and time compression management.

The consequences of this are:

- *Winning organisations in the 1990s will have the following characteristics: flexibility, speed to market, customer focus, innovation and cooperation with customers, suppliers and competitors.* They will also have to reconcile the need to be both effective and efficient.

- *Understanding what is meant by business integration and the links between strategy, people, technology and operations is critical in determining the role of IS/IT.*

- *The ability to manage change and the people dimension are central to implementing business integration as is the need for top management involvement.*

- *An overall vision must be articulated and must be driven by business issues.*

Over the last twenty to thirty years we have seen enormous changes in the way we live our lives and conduct our business. Much of this change is as a result of developments in IS/IT and the rate of change is unlikely to slow down.

In today's environment an organisation's decline begins the moment it stops transforming itself in response to these changes. For organisations that fail to respond it is only a question of how deep the decline will be and how long it will take. IS/IT does offer significant opportunities to survive and prosper to those organisations that are willing to invest the time and effort in utilising what IS/IT has to offer. Other chapters in this book will shed some light on how IS/IT can be used to an organisations advantage.

## Notes

1    J.A. Schumpeter, *The Theory of Economic Developement*. Harvard University Press, Cambridge, Mass., 1934.
2    G. Stalk Jr., Time - the next source of competitive advantage. *Harvard Business Review*, July-August 1988, pp. 41-51.

## Additional reading

### General

Andersen Consulting, *Trends in Information Technology*, Second edition, McGraw-Hill, 1992.
Ansoff, I. H., *Corporate Strategy*. Penguin, Hammondsworth, 1968.
The Economist Intelligence Unit, *The Management Challenge of Information Technology*. Special report No. 2125, April 1991.
Flatten, P.O., McCubbrey, D.J, O'Riordan, P.D., Burgess, K., *Foundations of Business Systems*. Dryden Press, 1989.
Foster, R., *Innovation: The Attackers Advantage*. Macmillan, London, 1986.
Porter M.E., *Competitive Strategy*. New York, The Free Press, 1980.

### IT and new organisational forms

Buttler Cox Foundation, The role of information technology in transforming the business. *Research Report 79*, January 1991.

Dean, J.W. and Susman, G.I., Organizing for manufacturable design. *Harvard Business Review*, January-February 1989, pp. 28-36.
Drucker, P.F., The coming of the new organisation. *Harvard Business Review*, January-February 1988, pp. 45-53.
Jacob, R., The search for the organisation of tomorrow. *Fortune*, May 18th 1992, pp. 66-72.
Kochan, T.A. and Useen, M., eds., *Transforming Organisations*. Oxford University Press, New York, 1992.
Snow, C.C., Miles, R.E., and Coleman, H.J., Managing 21st century network organisations. *Organisational Dynamics*, Winter 1992, pp. 5-20.

## Business re-engineering

Bartlett, C.A. and Ghoshal, S., Matrix management: not a structure, a frame of mind. *Harvard Business Review*, July-August, pp. 138-145.
Davenport, T.H. and Short, J.E., The new industrial engineering: information technology and business process redesign. *Sloan Management Review*, Summer 1990, pp. 11-27.
Hammer, M. Reengineering work: don't automate, obliterate. *Harvard Business Review*, July-August, 1990, pp. 104-112.
Rockard, J.F. and J.E. Short, IT in the 1990s: managing organisational interdependence. Sloan Management Review, **30**, 2, 1989, pp. 7-17.
Scott Morton, M. S., ed., *The Corporation of The 1990's: Information Technology and Organisational Transformation*. Oxford University Press, Oxford, 1991.

## Competing through time

Kotler, P. and Stonich, P.J., Turbo marketing through time compression. *The Journal of Business Strategy*, September-October, 1991, pp. 24-29.

## Strategic alliances

Hamel, G., Doz, Y.L. and Prahalad, C.K., Collaborate with your competitors and win. *Harvard Business Review*, January-February 1989, pp. 143-154.
Henderson, J.C., Plugging into strategic partnerships: the critical IS connection. *Sloan Management Review*, Spring 1990, pp. 7-18.
Nakamoto, M., Plugging into each other's strengths. *Financial Times*, 27th March, 1992.
Ohmae, K., The global logic of strategic alliances. *Harvard Business Review*, March-April 1989, pp. 143-154.

## Benchmarking

Main, J., How to steal the best ideas around. *Fortune*, October 19, 1992, pp. 86-89.

Walleck, A.S., O'Halloran, J.D. and Leader, C.A., Benchmarking world-class performance. *The McKinsey Quarterly*, January 1991, pp. 3-24.


## Outsourcing

Apte, U. and Winniford, M.A., Global outsourcing of information systems functions: opportunities and challenges. In M. Khosrowpour, ed., *Managing Information Technology in a Global Society*. Idea Group Publishing, 1991, pp. 58-67.

Bettis, R.A., Bradley, S.P. and Hamel, G., Outsourcing and industrial decline. *Academy of Management Executive*, **6**, 1, 1991, pp. 7-16.

Rochester, J.B., Taking an objective look at outsourcing. *I/S Analyzer*, **28**, 8, 1990.

# 3

# Using IS/IT to Gain Competitive Advantage

The emphasis which is exerted on information technology in organisations has changed. Early IS/IT systems resulted in increasing productivity and decreasing costs. Later still, systems were used to intergrate diverse operations horizontally. While this did provide competitive advantage at the time, since the early 1980s how IS/IT is used has fundamentally changed. Information is now treated as a corporate resource and competitive weapon, and the focus now is on exploiting IS/IT for competitive advantage. The systems which characterise this era have not replaced traditional MIS systems, but are in many cases derived from them. Being competitive in the 1990s will depend on the effective use and application of information technology to manage the information resource.

In this chapter we examine how IS/IT can be used for competitive advantage. We begin first by looking at the concept of competitive advantage. We then consider how IS/IT can influence a firm's ability to be competitive in the market place. This has implications for identifying potential opportunities. The concept of the applications portfolio is introduced for accessing the contribution of IS/IT applications to the business. The chapter concludes by considering how an organisation might sustain its competitive advantage.

## 3.1  Competitive advantage

Most of the work on competitive advantage has originated from the work of Professor Michael E Porter of Harvard Business School. Porter has written two books, *Competitive Advantage* and *Competitive Strategy*,[1] that discuss how a firm can create and sustain a competitive advantage in its industry. He defines competitive advantage as growing

> *...fundamentally out of the value a firm is able to create for its buyers. It may take the form of prices lower than competitors' for equivalent benefits or the provision of unique benefits that more than offset a premium price. Competitive advantage is at the heart of a firm's performance in competitive markets. After several decades of vigorous expansion and prosperity, many firms have lost sight of competitive advantage in their scramble for growth and pursuit of diversification. Today the importance of competitive advantage could hardly be greater.*

Competitive advantage is gained when an organisation moves into a position where it has an edge in coping with competitive forces (see below) and in attracting buyers for its products and services. Since the late 1970s many progressive organisations have recognised the potential of IS/IT in the pursuit of competitive advantage. The kernel of using IS/IT for competitive advantage is its use in either the product or service, or in the channels of distribution and supply, or to change the basis of competition against rivals.

A firm's *competitive strategy* operationalises competitive advantage and deals with management's competitive approaches for achieving market success, its offensive moves to secure a competitive edge over rival firms, and its defensive moves to protect its competitive position.[2]  Porter proposes three basic or generic strategies for achieving competitive advantage:

- Overall low-cost producer in an industry
- Seeking to differentiate one's product in some way from that of a rival.
- Focusing on narrow market niches as either a low-cost producer or through differentiation.

Figure 3.1 illustrates these generic strategies in terms of competitive scope and advantage.

**Figure 3.1** Three generic strategies.

**COMPETITIVE ADVANTAGE**

|                          | **Lower Cost**        | **Differentiation**     |
|--------------------------|-----------------------|-------------------------|
| **Broad Target**         | Cost Leadership       | Differentiation         |
| **Narrow Target**        | Cost Focus            | Differentiation Focus   |

**COMPETITIVE SCOPE**

Source: M.E. Porter, *Competitive Advantage: Creating and Sustaining Superior Performance*, The Free Press, New York. Used with permission of The Free Press, a division of Macmillan Inc., copyright 1985 M.E. Porter.

*Overall cost leadership*

Overall cost leadership is the strategy used by firms that are low-cost producers. They increase profits and market share by driving operating costs well below those of competitors. The competitive advantage derives from allowing the firm to compete on price or to reinvest the extra profit it generates. Therefore, it is the consequence of low cost that confers the competitive advantage.

*Differentiation*

A differentiation strategy is to produce a unique product or service with attributes that are valued by buyers. If they are willing to pay a higher price and if costs are under control, then the price premium should lead to higher profitability.

*Focus*

The focus or 'niche' strategy involves the selection of a segment or group of segments in the industry and meeting the needs of that segment better than competitors. Focus strategies can involve either being the lowest cost producers serving that segment or differentiating to meet the particular requirements of the segment in a way that allows a premium price to be charged.

Each of these strategies involves a different route to competitive advantage. Focus strategies seek competitive advantage in a narrow market segment; while cost leadership and differentiation strategies seek advantage in a broad range of industrial segments. As we shall see later IS/IT can support these strategies. It can change the nature of the industry's products or services, the markets of the industry, and/or the existing economies of production.  Let us first look at how a firm can gain an advantage by using IS/IT.

## 3.2  Gaining an advantage through IS/IT

By applying IS/IT in a novel way it is possible to gain a competitive advantage over competitors.  Probably the most widely cited example of the application of IS/IT for competitive advantage is the American Hospital Supplies Company (AHS) who established direct IS/IT links with their customers by giving them terminals linked directly to their computer systems.  By connecting directly to an order-entry system, AHS eliminated the effort required to order supplies and differentiated itself from its competitors.  The system allows purchase orders to be placed by less-skilled, lower-paid clerks instead of purchase agents, reduces customer-service problems, cuts order-entry costs, and provides more flexibility to customers in the time and process of order submissions.  In the period 1978-1983, AHS's revenue grew at 17% per annum (versus an overall decline in the size of the industry sector) and AHS achieved a return on sales which was four times the industrial average. The system was also a strong force in driving a division of a major Fortune 500 competitor out of the market.  Such performance is made possible by the communication element of IT which permits the establishment of applications which operate between companies, so called interorganisational systems (IOS).  Further examples are outlined in box 3.1.

So how does IS/IT provide a competitive advantage?  As we have seen in chapter 2, Porter and Miller[3] propose that the influence of IS/IT has been so far reaching as to alter fundamentally the rules by which firms in an industry compete with each other. They contend that it is changing the nature of competition in three particular ways:

- changing the industry structure
- creating new industries and businesses
- IS/IT is being used as a direct lever to create competitive advantage.

### Changing the industry structure

By using IS/IT in the pursuit of competitive advantage, organisations attempt to externally disturb the competitive forces that shape an industry.  An industry's profitability is not determined by what the product looks like or whether it embodies high or low technology: it is determined by the structure of industries.

We can analyse the effect of IS/IT within an industry by using Porter's Five Forces model.[4] This model, which is a widely used tool of competition analysis in business strategy formulation (see chapter 1), depends on a sophisticated understanding of the rules of competition. The underlying premise is that an organisation exists within an industry and to succeed it must effectively deal with the competitive forces which exist within that industry. These rules of competition are embedded in five competitive forces: the entry of new competition, the threat of substitute products, the bargaining power of buyers, the bargaining power of suppliers, and the rivalry among existing competitors. This is illustrated in figure 3.2.

**American Airlines**
American Airline's SABRE system, a sophisticated on-line reservation system, was one of the first business applications of a data communications system and represented a major breakthrough that provided American with several competitive advantages. Work on SABRE began in the early 1960s, and in its initial form kept accurate and up-to-date inventory of all seats on all flights. In 1963, the year SABRE debuted, it processed data relating to 85,000 phone calls, 40,000 confirmed reservations, and 20,000 ticket sales. The system enabled American Airlines to reduce the number of staff required to handle reservations, increase the number of passengers on a flight without fear of overbooking, and provide travellers with a guaranteed seat.

By the mid-70s, the system was much more than an inventory-control system. Its technology provided the base for generating flight plans for aircraft, tracking spare parts, scheduling crews, and developing a range of decision-support systems for management. SABRE and its associated systems became the control centre through which American Airlines functioned.

In 1976, American installed SABRE in travels agents shops. It has, since then, added new services to the database (hotels, rail, rental cars), built powerful few features to help travel agents offer better service, increased the installed base of SABRE terminals, and created a training and support infrastructure.

Today SABRE is no longer a proprietary reservation system and the subsidiary that is responsible for the system is now the most profitable business unit of American, with a turnover of about $550m in 1991 in spite of the Gulf war and the recession-induced slump in air traffic. It takes bookings for about 1.6 billion flights daily and deals with 20 times that many enquiries on 740 airlines.

**Merrill Lynch**
In the US, Merrill Lynch launched its cash management account back in 1978. This combines traditionally separate banking products such as line of credit, cheque, investment and equity accounts into a single monthly statement, with idle funds being swept automatically into a high interest account. The new account

attracted $1 billion of assets in the first year. Today, Merrill Lynch manages $85 billion, and still has almost 70% of the market. Merrill Lynch set out to permanently change the shape of the financial market place by taking several existing but separate services and stringing them together through information technology to create a new service that shattered the traditional boundaries between banking and securities industries.

**McKessons**
The company provided pharmacists and druggists with hand-held data entry terminals to record replacement stock details, and the information is down-loaded over the telephone lines direct to McKessons' computers. McKessons fills the order overnight and delivers it the next day in bokes arranged to match the shelf divisions of the retailers' store. Druggists who signed up with the service, called Economost, typically doubled or tripled their order volumes. In many cases, they began to rely exclusively on McKesson. The total service helps retailers' stock, price-label, rotate and display merchandising according to Marketing reports generated.

In another area of its business, McKesson provides a service via pharmacists to process the insurance claims for 23 million medical insurance customers' prescriptions. The system processes the claims via prescriptions completed and sends them to 150 Healthcare insurers for reimbursing.

**7-Eleven**
7-Eleven, with 3,900 convenience stores, is Japan's largest food retailer, and is separately owned from the American company of the same name. Mostly owned by franchise-holders, 7-Eleven has the highest profitability and return on equity among Japanese retailers. The parent, a subsidary of a Japanese retailer, owns only about 5% of the stores, a figure which is declining. However, 7-Eleven owns a sophisticated computer network which collects sales data and orders goods directly from the distributors.

Each store is equipped with a point-of-sale (POS) system. When something is purchased, the POS records its brand name, the manufacturer, the price, and details about the buyer. Sales of products can then be plotted against the time of day, day of the week.

7-Eleven, the parent company, can aggregate data from many stores. It then collates and sells this data to manufacturers about the sales of their own products. These statistics also allow 7-Eleven to advise their franchise holders on what to sell and when - important considering the average shelf space of only 100 square feet and over 3,500 products. The shelves are filled with a mix of goods according to the time of day.

**Box 3.1** Some examples of firms using IS/IT for competitive advantage.

**Figure 3.2** The five competitive forces.

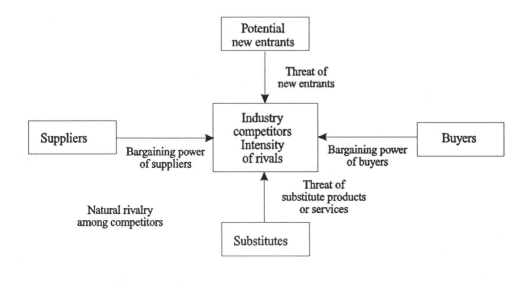

The collective strength of these five forces determines the ability of firms in an industry to earn, on average, rates of return on investment in excess of the cost of capital. They thus determine industry profitability because they influence the prices, costs, and required investment. By using IS/IT in the pursuit of competitive advantage firms attempt to disturb these forces. Let us now explore each of these competitive forces and examine the impact that IS/IT can have on each of them.

*Suppliers*
Raw materials, labour, machinery and capital are necessary inputs to the firm's production process. However, these are supplied by various interest groups within the industry. The strength of these suppliers can significantly affect an industry's potential profit. If they can exert a major influence on firms in an industry they can increase these firm's costs by extracting a higher price for their goods and services. The application of IS/IT can have a major impact on the power of suppliers.

In applying computer-aided manufacturing and robotics, a manufacturing firm can reduce its labour costs. The application of just-in-time (JIT) depends on cultivating a good supplier relationship and IS/IT greatly enhances the information flow between firms and suppliers. For example, Ford Europe is in the process of linking to suppliers to reduce the inventory of parts and to decrease the time to delivery by eliminating paper. Automated bills of material and vendor systems make it easier for buyers to evaluate sources of materials and make or buy decisions. In chapter 7 we explore EDI links between suppliers and buyers.

*Buyers*
Powerful customers can also exert a competitive influence over suppliers and can bargain away any potential profits from the firms in the industry. Further, if the number of buyers for the outputs of an industry are small, they can affect the profit that can be derived. They can cause firms to undercut each other in order to get the buyer's business and they can use their power to extract other benefits from firms like improved quality improvements, credit, etc.

By building in *switching costs*, that is the costs associated with buyers changing suppliers or to substitute products, it makes it more difficult and costly for buyers to switch suppliers. By placing order entry terminals in hospitals, AHS made it more difficult for them to change suppliers. With electronic home banking, banks hope that once a customer is familiar with their system they will be reluctant to change to another bank.

IS/IT also permits vast quantities of information relating to buyers to be collected and analysed. This proves useful in determining which buyers are most attractive and which are costing the business money and helps in determining their service level for each buyer.

*New entrants*
New entrants to a market bring new production capacity, the desire to establish a secure place in the market, and sometimes substantial resources with which to compete.[5] As new firms enter a market they have the potential to extract some of the industry's profit. Unless demand grows faster than new entrants enter a market, average profitability will decline.

The major structural components of an industry that exclude or at least affect the potential for new entrants to an industry are called *entry barriers*. The objective is to discourage other companies from entering a market as new competitors by establishing a level of service or value to the customer that will be expensive or difficult for the new entrant to replicate. They may be based on cost, service, reputation, technology or some other characteristic that is important for the success of the industry. The most common barriers to entry are:

- *Economies of scale*. These are the cost advantages that accrue through having large-scale operations.

- *Brand preference and customer loyalty* make it difficult for a new entrant to attract customers away from their existing suppliers.

- *High capital requirements* make it expensive for competing firms to enter the industry.

- *Access to distribution channels.* By controlling the access mechanisms to the market place it is difficult for firms to get their products to the customer.

- *Legislation and government policy*: patents, tariff and non-tariff barriers, etc.

Manufacturing firms can achieve economies of scale by successfully applying IS/IT in the production of its products. Any firm wishing to compete with such firms must be at least as productive. Further, computer-aided design and computer-aided manufacturing (CAD/CAM) systems have a major impact on the lead time for product development, customisation, and delivery.

IS/IT often requires large investment in complex software. The large investment made by American Airlines in its SABRE system was one of the reasons that Peoples Express and Braniff Airlines went bankrupt. Both made a strategic decision not to invest in technology. However, they quickly realised that not only were they in a catch-me-up situation but they could not afford the level of investment in IS/IT that was required to be competitive. The US Department of Transport is scheduled to examine computerised reservation systems industry rules because it is worried about the potential advantages ownership of such a system gives.[6] New airlines face higher barriers in an already capital-intensive industry.

While entry barriers are structural components, *entry deterrents* are tactics or processes that an industry or firm can invoke to make potential entrants reconsider. Patents, access to raw materials, and capital requirements are just some examples of entry barriers.

*Substitution*
Substitution represents the buyer propensity to substitute one firm's product for another product. The strength of competition from substitutes is affected by the ease with which buyers can change over to the substitute. The ease of changing is usually governed by the buyer's switching costs - the one-time costs facing the buyer of switching from use of one product over to a substitute. If the substitute becomes more attractive in terms of price, performance, or both, then some buyers will be tempted to move their custom to a competing firm. With high switching costs, competing products must offer a major cost or performance benefit. Substitution can also represent an offensive opportunity for a firm to increase its own market by offering its products as substitutes to another buyer.

Flexible manufacturing systems (FMS) have made it quicker, easier, and cheaper to incorporate enhanced features into products, thus influencing the threat of substitute products. CAD/CAM permits customisation of a product in a way not possible before.


*Rivalry among competitors*
This is arguably the most powerful of the five competitive forces. Market growth, number of competing firms in the industry, or commodity like products are just some of the factors which effect rivalry among competitors. Each firm employs its own style of competitive strategy in an effort to jockey for better position and gain a competitive edge. IS/IT presents major opportunities for firms to facilitate the degree to which, and methods with which, they deal with rivals. Offering buyers something that competitors cannot duplicate easily or cheaply gives a firm not only a market edge but also a unique competitive capability.

Order processing and customer billing systems have greatly increased rivalry in many distribution industries. In the airline industry, IS/IT permits fares to be altered frequently and for different fares to be charged on the same route.

Technology now underpins most new services provided by financial institutions. In retail banking, it has become very expensive to have branch office presence in prime locations. IS/IT in the form of automated teller machines (ATMs) reduced significantly the costs associated with having a high street presence. The Midland Bank launched its First Direct banking initiative in 1989. This was the UK's first bank to open 24 hours, 7 days of the week. It has no branches or local staff as all transactions are handled over the telephone. Customers can pay bills, arrange personal loans, order foreign exchange, etc. In order to make this service possible a sophisticated computer and communication system had to be designed to enable each First Direct clerk to have all information on every customer at his/her fingertips.

We saw in the previous chapter that *strategic alliances* with both competitors and others in the industry value system are key strategies adopted by many organisations since the late 1980s.[7,8] For example, sharing IS/IT resources, such as building societies sharing ATMs, permits them to reach a critical mass without the large investment and associated risks. Bank One of Colombus Ohio forged an innovative alliance strategy with Comp-U-Card, a computerised shopping service. Together, they pioneered Super Visa, a credit card issued by Bank One, that Comp-U-Card offered as an incentive to get new customers. For Comp-U-Card it enhanced its offering to competitors and meant they didn't have to bear the risks associated with launching their own credit card. For Bank One it increased its base of credit card customers who, in many cases, availed themselves of other financial services provided by the bank.

Figure 3.3 illustrates potential uses of an interorganisational system to combat competitive forces.


**Creating new businesses**

IS/IT can affect competition by creating new businesses, often from within a company's existing operations. Reuters, Telerate, and Dun and Bradstreet have responded to industry needs for increased information by setting up on-line information services. Reuters now generates over 70% of its revenue through real-time information products such as up-to-date news and stock prices.

In the previous chapter, we saw that in response to globalisation and rapid technological change *outsourcing* has become a popular strategy for many organisations. This strategy entails organisations focusing only on the things which it does particularly well: the so called *core competences*. Everything else is outsourced to specialist organisations. Given the rapid change and increasing complexity of IT many organisations contract specialist IT companies to manage their IT investments. There is a rapid trend towards outsourcing network and data centre management due to the costs and risks of maintaining these systems. This presents the opportunity for businesses to provide such an IT management service to organisations.

The pace and change in global logistics has been largely dictated by communication and IT systems. These have enabled the logistics industry to provide a new generation of logistical services. Federal Express is the dominant player in the parcel delivery service sector. In order to grow the business it backed up its skills in moving packages about with a computer system that can tell a customer exactly where his shipments are at any given moment. This ability has won new kinds of business. Federal Express now manages much of IBM's spare-parts inventory. Recently, they agreed a logistics deal with Laura Ashley, the international fashion group.

Some organisations now sell information that is a by-product of their operations. The use of bar-code scanners in supermarkets has turned these stores into market research laboratories. Not only is the data useful to the supermarket itself, for example, effects of advertising campaigns, but they can sell this information to other organisations. Retail outlets like 7-Eleven monitor product sales data for clients. For a monthly fee, customers are advised on shelf arrangements and potential upgrades, related to product choice. Reuters collect data from banks and other financial services firms, analyse it and sell it back to clients.

**Figure 3.3** Potential uses of an interorganisational system to combat competitive forces.

| Competitive force | Implications | Uses of an IOS |
|---|---|---|
| **New entrants** | New capacity | To provide: Entry barriers, greater economies of scale, switching costs, product differentiation, limited access to distribution channels |
| | Need for substantial resources | |
| | Reduced prices or inflated incumbents' costs | |
| | | To control market access |
| **Buyers** | Lower prices | To influence buyers: Differentiation, switching costs |
| | Higher quality | |
| | More services | |
| | More competition | |
| **Suppliers** | Higher prices | To reduce switching costs |
| | Reduced quality and services | To encourage competition |
| | | To threaten backward integration |
| **Substitute products** | Limited potential return | To improve price and performance |
| | A ceiling on prices | |
| | | To redefine products and services |
| **Traditional rivals** | Competition on price product, distribution, and service | To improve cost effectiveness |
| | | To control market access |
| | | To differentiate product and company. |

Source: J.I. Cash, Jr. and B.R. Konsynski, IS Redraws Competitive Boundaries. *Harvard Business Review*, March-April 1985, p. 139.

## IS/IT as a lever for achieving competitive advantage

In many of the examples cited above IT has been used by firms as a lever to achieve competitive advantage. In so doing, they also affected the structure of the industry, for example airline reservation systems. However, not all systems that create competitive advantage change the industry structure. IS/IT can be applied directly to achieving competitive advantage by giving organisations new ways to outperform their rivals. It can also be used either as a weapon to combat competitive forces or to act directly in support of the business strategy.

At the beginning of this chapter three generic strategies for achieving competitive advantage were presented. These strategies can be supported by IS/IT. IS/IT can support the overall cost leadership strategy by permitting major cost reductions or cost containment, particularly in clerical and other support staffs. IS/IT can also help achieve better utilisation of resources, decrease in inventory, reduction of shrinkage and waste in raw material use etc. Advanced manufacturing technologies permit a firm to become more flexible in its production and therefore more responsive to customer needs. This can perhaps enhance differentiation and permit a premium price to be charged for its products.

At its Whitburn Scotland factory, Levi-Strauss uses a line-balancing system to manage the smoothing of production. This is part of the company's objective to create a global real-time production control system. By planning production in terms of time Levi-Strauss ensured that the peaks and valleys of production activity are spread over time. One of the features of the system enables workers to calculate their income by piecework. It also allows them to schedule themselves, thus leaving management more time to concentrate on non-supervisory work.[9]

Digital Equipment Corporation's XCON (eXpert CONfigurer) is a knowledge-based system for determining computer configuration. The system substantially reduces the time required to fill orders and increases the design accuracy of the finished system. This not only results in decreased costs but enhances DECs image.

Steetley Building Product's Parkhouse brickworks produces 16 million bricks each week in a fully automated plant. The order handling system is used to increase flexibility by scheduling brick production. Inventory build-up and backlog have been virtually eliminated. Architects can connect their building designs and interpret the building requirements into the Steetley's brick design system. The customer's system and the producer's system connect with Steetley's manufacturing process to produce accurate, volume-balanced orders.[10]

During the 1980s Fritto-Lay gave their 10,000 route sales people handheld computers. This made them more productive and automated the inventory and ordering process.

During the last few years, the company has subscribed to several sources of competitive data generated by supermarket scanners and market surveys. Today, its executives can inquire on the performance of products in particular markets or geographical areas.[11]

Campbell Soup Company has used IS to refine its marketing analysis. Campbell collects sales data from neighbourhood markets and can therefore build accurate models of market dynamics at intimate levels of customer interaction for both its own and competitive products as well as correlate them with corresponding promotional activities in specific markets. This marketing approach yields detailed and timely information about products and actions that are most profitable.[12]

Figure 3.4 illustrates how IS/IT applications must be specifically chosen to support the generic strategy of the firm.

We can summarise some of the major competitive strategies a firm can adopt by using IT as follows:

- establishing entry barriers
- affecting switching costs
- differentiating products/services of a company
- limiting access to distribution channels
- ensuring competitive pricing
- decreasing supply costs and easing supply
- increasing cost efficiency
- using information as a product itself
- building closer relationships with suppliers and customers.

The assessment of potential IS/IT application areas requires a degree of creative thinking as well as analysis of business options. We address this issue in chapter 4 and present a framework to aid in this process.

## 3.3 Applications portfolio

Most organisations have different investments in IS/IT. These are likely to be of varying degrees of age, currency in technology and relevance. These applications make different contributions to the business. Some applications represent an area of great strategic importance, while for others they will play a cost-effective and useful but distinctively supporting role.

**Figure 3.4** Potential IS/IT application areas.

Generic Strategies

|  | **Low Cost** | **Differentiation** |
|---|---|---|
| Product Design and Development | • Product engineering systems<br>• Integrated systems to manufacturing<br>• Professional workstations<br>• Electronic mail<br>• Computer aided design (CAD)<br>• Custom engineering systems | • Project control systems<br>• R&D databases |
| Operations | • Processing engineering systems<br>• Inventory management<br>• Process control systems<br>• Labour control systems | • Computer aided manufacture for flexibility<br>• Quality assurance systems<br>• Systems to suppliers<br>• Quality monitoring systems for suppliers |
| Marketing | • Streamlined distribution system<br>• Modeling capabilities<br>• Centralized control system<br>• Econometric modeling systems<br>• High service level distribution system | • Sophisticated marketing system<br>• Market databases<br>• IT displays and promotion<br>• Telemarketing<br>• Competition analysis systems |
| Sales | • Sales control systems<br>• Advertising monitoring system<br>• Systems to consolidate sales function<br>• Strict incentive-monitoring systems | • Differential pricing systems<br>• Office-field communication<br>• Customer-sales support<br>• Dealer support systems<br>• Systems to customers |
| Administration | • Cost control systems<br>• Quantitative planning and budgeting systems<br>• Office automation for staff reduction | • Office automation for integration of functions<br>• Environment scanning and nonquantitative planning systems |

Source: G.L. Parsons, Strategic information technology. In E.K. Somogyi and R.D. Galliers, editors, *Towards Strategic Information Systems*, Abacus Press, 1987, p. 198.

The *applications portfolio*, which is similiar to the product portfolio approach proposed by the Boston Consulting Group, treats applications as "products" and classifies applications according to the contribution they make (or may make) to the business within the actual and expected competitive environment of the organisation. This grid aids in positioning IS/IT within an organisation and relates dependence on IS/IT to the impact of IS/IT on the business. Four types of applications can be defined: support, key operational, strategic, and high potential. These are illustrated in figure 3.5.

**Figure 3.5** Applications portfolio: the contribution of IS/IT to business.

| Strategic | High potential |
|---|---|
| | |
| **Key operational** | **Support** |
| | |

| | |
|---|---|
| *Support* | Applications which improve management effectiveness but are not critical to the business. The benefits they deliver are mainly economic. Examples may include accounting systems, payroll systems, and spreadsheets. Applications due to legal requirements would also be placed in this quadrant. |
| *Key operational* | Operational type applications that are critical to sustain the existing business. In fact, if these systems are not in place the organisation will suffer serious disadvantage. Such applications generally support core business activities. Examples may include inventory control, production control, and order management. |
| *Strategic* | Applications which are critical to future business success. |
| *High potential* | Innovative applications which may be of future strategic importance. Expert systems, imaging multimedia would probably be included here. |

Similiar applications can occupy different portfolio positions in different organisations. This is likely to depend on the business strategy of the organisation and to some extent on the industry within which the organisation competes.

Applications can also drift between quadrants. For example, ATMs were strategic applications ten years ago, now every bank must have them if it is to maintain market share. They have thus moved into the key operational sector. Homebanking is probably in the high potential quadrant, having great potential but still uncertainty about the form it will take or how competitive benefits can be produced.

There are three driving forces causing this drift to occur:

- the match between the potential of IS/IT and the firm's operations and strategy
- the strategic choices which senior management make about IT (e.g. whether to exploit IS/IT to improve productivity, to move into new businesses, etc.)
- changes unfolding in the firm's competitive environment.[13]

While competitive advantage systems may be totally independent, they are more likely to have some dependence on existing systems. It is therefore important to evaluate the coverage of business functions by existing systems and their contribution to business objectives. It may be that they provide a valuable basis on which a competitive system can be built. This analysis may also reveal areas where IS/IT is not being used effectively.

## 3.4 Managing the applications portfolio

Given that the applications portfolio classifies an application according to the contribution it makes or may make to the business gives us a clue as to how the portfolio should be managed. However, in many organisations all applications are managed in a similiar fashion. Clearly, strategic applications providing a large contribution to the business need different management practices, support and policies than support applications. Thus an application's position in the portfolio helps us identify appropriate management practices. An application should be managed in relation to the contribution it makes to the business. Let us look at management strategies for each of the quadrants.

*Strategic*          Given that the objective of these systems is to lever IS/IT to deliver and sustain business advantage, strategic applications require the commitment and involvement of senior management. Very often these systems require large investments and thus central coordination of requirements is paramount. Investments will often be evaluated based on business benefit rather than on return-on-investment criteria.

*High potential*            Applications in this quadrant need an environment that
                            accepts risk.  It involves expenditure on research and
                            development that may not produce positive results: the theme
                            is therefore experimentation.  Given that applications are high
                            risk, the underlying assumption is that today's high potential
                            applications may create competitive advantage in the future.
                            Senior management need not be too involved, however they
                            must endorse the concept and commit funds and resources.

*Key operational*           Investments in key operational applications are primarily to
                            avoid  business  disadvantages.    Risk  reduction  is  the
                            cornerstone  of  any  management  strategy  to  manage
                            applications in this quadrant.  It is important that systems in
                            this  quadrant  be  reliable  and  robust,  thus  only  proven
                            technology should be used.  All user requests must be capable
                            of  being  satisfied  which  requires  excess  capacity  to  be
                            available to respond to urgent needs.  Centralised control of
                            the IT resource is demanded.

*Support*                   Given the support nature of applications in this quadrant,
                            direct  senior  management  involvement  is  not  usually
                            necessary.  However, policy guidelines will normally be set
                            requiring  tight  budgetary  control.    The  justification  for
                            investments in this quadrant is financial, perhaps using cost-
                            benefit analysis or discounted cash flow.

## 3.5  Sustaining the advantage

A sustainable advantage is a capability of one competitor that cannot be duplicated by
another.   "First mover" strategies, such as those of American Hospital Supplies,
American Airlines or McKesson's Economost, are successful not because these
companies achieve sustainably better IT capabilities, but because they are able to
convert a temporary IS/IT advantage into sustainable forms of competitive advantage
such as scale, customer loyalty and brand image.

However as technology proliferates it becomes even harder for someone to carve out a
unique, defensible position.

- Information technologies (except for application systems) are almost
  universally supplied by vendors to user companies, and are freely available
  to all competitors in an industry.

- Application systems, while custom developed by larger user-companies, rarely confer advantage in themselves.

Being able to sustain competitive advantage is very important. If many businesses take advantage of IT at the same time, the heaviest investors tend to loose.

Information technology is expensive and complicated and the risk factor inherent in building large proprietary systems high. Today, first mover success stories aren't as common as five years ago. Cecil and Goldstein[14] suggest three reasons why IT by itself fails to deliver a sustainable competitive edge:

- Peer competitors generally start with equivalent application knowledge
- Differences in IT development capabilities among competitors can usually be evened out by vendors.
- Larger scale rarely translates into a cost advantage.

It is interesting to note that most single-source electronic sales channels, in later years, evolved into electronic markets offering competitors' products as well - a trend which changed the competitive landscape of conventional marketing and distribution patterns, in those industries, for ever. SABRE, for example, initially took shape in response to American Airlines inability to monitor its inventory of available seats manually and to attach passenger names to booked seats. Today, SABRE is neither a proprietary competitive weapon for American Airlines nor a general distribution system for the airline industry. It is an 'electronic travel supermarket', a computerised middleman linking suppliers of travel and related services, including Broadway shows, packaged tours, and currency rates to retailers like travel agents and directly to customers like corporate travel depertments.

There is a view that technology cannot be management's primary solution because it is every competitors' potential solution. Perhaps this quote from Max Hopper, who was the Director responsible for the developement of the SABRE system is salutory:

> *I do not mean to diminish the pivotal role of information technology in the future or to suggest that technology leadership will be less relevant to competitive success. Precisely because changes in information technology are becoming so rapid and unforgiving and the consequence of falling behind so irreversible, companies will either master or remaster the technology or die. Think of it as a technological treadmill: companies will have to run harder and harder just to stay in place. ... Organisations that stay on the treadmill will be competing against others that have done the same thing. In this sense, the information utility will have a leveling effect. In essence, technological skill is what qualifies a company to play; without it, they can't hope to compete.[15]*

However, no business advantage can last forever. Using IS/IT alone will not guarantee success; creative applications and ingenious use will continue to provide opportunity for competitive advantage.[16] Similarly, Kim Clark argues that new technology is not sufficient for competitive advantage.[17] She argues that advantage goes, as it always has, to superior strategy and execution. No matter how widely available technology becomes, the management process will continue to provide a source of competitive advantage to some firms and a competitive disadvantage to others. In the next chapter we look at the IS/IT planning process and how potential opportunities can be identified.

## 3.6 Conclusions

Traditionally, IS/IT has taken a largely passive role in the overall competitive strategy of many firms. However, we have seen that IS/IT has affected the competitive environment within which firms compete. Not only does it change the industrial structure but sometimes spawns new industries. Competitive advantage has been the cornerstone for developing competitive business strategies. IS/IT can be used in the creation of competitive advantage permiting a firm to follow the generic strategies of cost leadership, differentiation, or focus.

- *IS/IT competitive opportunities are a weapon of business strategy.*

- *Technology alone is rarely sufficient to gain a durable competitive advantage.* Technology is only a facilitator.

- *Assess the role of IS/IT in the industry and the firm, and identify potential application areas.* This analysis may point to areas where organisational relationships need to be reconsidered in order to exploit the new way in which IS/IT can enable the business to operate or be managed.

- *Be creative.* IS/IT by itself will not guarantee success; creative application and ingenious use will continue to provide opportunities for competitive advantage.

- *Manage applications in relation to the contribution they make to the business.*

- *Don't forget to use IS/IT to enhance what the organisation already does best.* Remember what Peters and Waterman said: 'stick to the knitting'.[18]

# Notes

1   M.E. Porter, *Competitive Strategy*, Free Press, 1980; *Competitive Advantage*, Free Press, 1985.
2   A.A. Thompson and A.J. Strickland, *Strategy Formulation and Implementation: Tasks of the General Manager.* 4th Edition, Richard D. Irwin, 1989, p. 81.
3   M.E. Porter and V.E. Miller (1985) How information gives you a competitive advantage. *Harvard Business Review*, July-August, 1985, pp. 149-160.
4   Called the Porter Model after its developer Michael Porter of the Harvard Business School.
5   M.E. Porter, How competitive forces shape strategy. *Harvard Business Review*, March-April, 1979, pp. 137-145.
6   Daniel Green, Airline ticket shops bridge the Atlantic, *Financial Times*, March 9th, 1992.
7   G. Hamel, Y.L. Doz and C.K. Prahalad, Collaborate with your competitors and win. *Harvard Business Review*, January-February, 1989, pp. 133-139.
8   K. Ohmae, The global logic of strategic alliances. *Harvard Business Review*, March-April, 1989, pp. 143-154.
9   C. Cookson, A good fit on the factory floor. *Financial Times*, June 6, 1990, p. 15.
10  D. Bradshaw, Building blocks of efficiency. *Financial Times*, August 30th, 1990.
11  R.J. Crutchfield, Getting a leg up by using handhelds. *Datamation*, January 1, 1987.
12  Campbell's marketing bites into MIS, *Information Week*, June 20th, 1988.
13  These driving forces have been proposed by Michael Earl in *Management Strategies for Information Management*. Prentice Hall, p. 7.
14  J. Cecil and M. Goldstein, Sustaining competitive advantage from IT. *The McKinsey Quarterly*, Vol. 4, 1990, pp. 74-89.
15  M.D. Hopper, Rattling SABRE- new ways to compete on information. *Harvard Business Review*, May-June, 1990, pp. 118-125.
16  See responses to Hooper's article in Letters to the Editor, *Harvard Business Review*, July-August, 1990, pp. 176-182.
17  K.B. Clark, What strategy can do for technology. *Harvard Business Review*, November-December, 1989, pp. 94-98.
18  T.J. Peters and R.H. Waterman, *In Search Of Excellence.* Harper & Row 1982.

# Additional reading

Cole, R.E. Target information for competitive performance. *Harvard Business Review*, May-June 1985, pp. 100-109.
Feeney, D., Creating and sustaining competitive advantage with IT. In M.J. Earl, ed., *Information Management: The Strategic Dimension.* Clarendon Press, Oxford, 1988, pp. 98-117.
Ives, B. and Learmonth, G., The information system as a competitive weapon. *Communications of the ACM*, **27**, 2, 1984, pp. 1193-2001.

McFarlan, F.W., Information technology changes the way you compete. *Harvard Business Review*, May-June 1984, pp. 93-103.

Runge, D.A and Earl, M.J., Gaining competitive advantage from telecommunications. In M.J. Earl, ed., *Information Management: The Strategic Dimension.* Clarendon Press, Oxford, 1988, pp. 125-145.

Ward, J., Griffiths, P. and Whitmore, P., *Strategic Planning for Information Systems.* Prentice-Hall, 1990.

# 4

# Strategic IS/IT Planning

It should be clear by now that the achievement and continuance of competitive advantage in the 1990s will depend on the effective use and application of information technology. For most organisations the era of competitive insulation, effortless growth, guaranteed market share is over. All organisations are now facing international competition from a range of other companies who wish to gain or consolidate market share. Deregulation and the opening up of international markets have forced changes in cost structures and in competitive positioning. For many organisations information technology is seen as a main source of future competitive opportunities. For other organisations the lack of IT is a major disability in responding to changing demands. Better use of IT is usually a cherished aspiration with little or no effective action to gain the real competitive benefits. We have already seen that over the past two decades, IT has been applied to the mechanisation of core processes and operations (e.g. inventory control) as well as to the primary support functions (e.g. personal finances). The 1980s saw the broadening of IS/IT into business origination (e.g. marketing and sales), strategic and financial planning as well as direct support to customers and supplies (e.g. electronic data interchange). The 1980s also saw IS/IT as a component of new products and services and a means to enhance the delivery of old products and services through new channels. In the 1980s, IS/IT took the first steps towards becoming a fundamental part of business itself.

Success and survival in the 1990s will depend on building on this foundation - both business and IS/IT - to introduce new products and services and to attract and retain new customers. It will also depend on the effective control and progressive reduction of the costs of doing business. Organisations which ignore the cost/income ratio that arises from out-dated or ineffective systems and over-staffed, cumbersome organisational structures will find themselves at a severe competitive disadvantage.

## 4.1 What is an IS/IT strategy?

We saw in chapter 1 that, in general, strategic planning involves the building of a structured framework to identify the main components of anticipated business needs (the *what*) and possible solutions (the *how*), identifying and evaluating different approaches to arriving at these solutions (alternative strategies) and producing a comprehensive, costed plan and timetable (the plan) for the preferred strategy.

Accordingly, an IS/IT strategy involves creating a structured framework for information systems (IS) needs (the *what* - as expressed in information requirements and business applications) together with information technology (IT) solutions (the *how* - including technology solutions such as hardware and software, as well as the technology infrastructure such as communications networks). This is illustrated in figure 4.1.

Typically, the current IS/IT framework (where we are in terms of IS/IT) is matched against a target framework (where we want to be in terms of IS/IT) and different migration paths are assessed (alternative strategies). The needs of the IT organisation itself are assessed. An IS/IT *implementation plan*, including a project plan, costs, benefits and timetable, is prepared to put the preferred strategy in place, together with the business case for adopting such a strategy.

The scope of such an exercise must be carefully controlled and should be driven by the high priority business and IS/IT opportunities that will focus the IS/IT planning effort and will lead to business benefits. In developing an IS/IT strategy it is imperative that these IS needs are matched against business objectives. Otherwise an IS/IT strategic plan can progress on too broad a front, with insufficient effort in the high priority areas and lead to severe disappointment. Figure 4.1 illustrates a framework for IS/IT planning.

An IS/IT strategy should chart the appropriate use of technology in the organisation and should define the relevant information, data and applications required in that organisation. It should identify the appropriate level of resourcing and should generally guide investment in IT over a period of time - usually 3-5 years - towards the achievement of specific systems and business objectives.

**Figure 4.1** IS and IT strategies

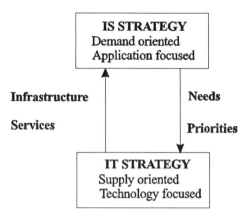

Adapted from M.J. Earl, *Management Strategies for Information Technology*, Prentice Hall, 1989, p. 63.

The **general objectives** of IS/IT planning are:

- Use information systems for competitive advantage and business support.

- Achieve cost effective investment for measured benefits.

- Control IS/IT expenditure and obtain incremental value for money.

- Protect existing IS/IT investment and reduce maintenance costs.

- Obtain user and IS/IT management commitment to making IS/IT work.

- Prioritise the application of limited IS/IT resources towards meeting important business needs.

The **role of management** in this process is paramount. Management is at the centre of the information systems planning process because it is management in an organisation that must:

- Steer the IS planning process and take overall responsibility for the process.

- Identify the specific IS/IT opportunities.

- Agree priorities, approve requirements and identify benefits to be delivered.

- Approve and plan the overall resourcing required, including the one-off and ongoing costs.

## 4.2  A brief history of IS/IT planning

The history and cycle of IT planning teaches several lessons.  One can view IT planning as having evolved in **five main stages** over a 20 year period:

- **Stage 1 - data processing led planning** - where the data processing function led the planning for information systems primarily in order to support the operational, transaction processing environments that existed in larger and medium size organisations.

- **Stage 2 - applications planning** - where a more applications orientated approach which viewed the various application systems as a portfolio, was adopted to cover both the operational systems and the emerging range of support (e.g. financial and management) systems.

- **Stage 3 - information systems planning methodology** - approaches which typically looked at the information, data, applications and technology architectures or blueprints and used these blueprints to derive an applications systems development plan.

- **Stage 4 - user driven systems planning** - which arrived with the introduction of personal computing and end user tools from the early 1980s onwards.  The growing usage of departmental solutions and the emerging need to link such solutions in an effective manner has led to the need for some structure in the user driven systems planning.

- **Stage 5 - synthesis** - which brings all aspects of the preceding stages together in  a combination of 'top down' and 'bottom up' approaches to IT strategy planning that - in effect - tailor an appropriate approach to IT planning for the industry, the market sector and for the organisation.

Many organisations stop at a combination of stages 3 and 4 where a methodology driven approach to IS/IT planning has been complemented by a user driven approach. Few organisations have reached the organisational maturity to evolve to Stage 5 - synthesis - where they can derive their own approach to IS/IT strategy planning to meet their own needs, bringing together the appropriate components of the various approaches.

The critical issue for management's attention is that strategic information systems implies winners and losers and not just relative performance. Accordingly, the identification and adoption of the most appropriate approach to information systems planning for an organisation is critical, and is one of the major decisions that the IT function will have to make.

## 4.3 Why is IS/IT planning so vital?

Having an IS/IT strategy is essential for a number of reasons - some obvious, others less so. Firstly, information technology continues to be expensive. The main long term cost driver in information technology is the level of sustained systems development that leads to operational systems. In other words, the more systems development that an organisation undertakes, the more systems it introduces to an operational status, and the greater the ultimate IT costs - both maintenance and operational - that are incurred. Progressive reductions in unit cost terms (of such items as PCs, workstations and software solutions) are largely offset by greater demand for, and subsequent supply of, such solutions.

Secondly, there is a continuously changing business environment. This business environment means that the high pressure demands on systems development to create new applications, maintain old applications and to provide value for money will continue.

Thirdly, technology itself is changing and technology opportunities will arise because of the requirement to take advantage of new technology. The role, the strategy, the components and the costs of new technologies indicate that there will always be a technology-driven level of opportunity that will be responsive to perceived needs. This will often be a 'solution looking for a problem' in the early stages, but usually matures into a viable product set (i.e. *move from turnaround to strategic as per the applications portfolio*) that delivers solid business benefits.

## 4.4 At what organisational level should IS/IT planning be conducted?

It is important that IS/IT planning be conducted at the appropriate level in the organisation. We mentioned in chapter 1 that typically IS/IT planning tends to be carried out on a piecemeal basis. Each department or functional area develops its own plans for IS/IT investment. The IS/IT strategy (if it could be called that) was simply an aggregation of these separate plans. For the larger conglomerate-type organisation

IS/IT strategy may have been formulated at the corporate level and each business unit was expected to implement it. (See figure 4.2.)

If we return for a moment to how business strategy is formulated, it is widely accepted that overall corporate strategy addresses the composition of an organisation's portfolio of business units. Each individual business unit within the corporate stable has its own strategy. A similiar situation should exist for an IS/IT strategy. This ensures that those who implement the eventual strategy are actually involved in developing that strategy.

A business unit can be defined as *a component of an organisation that sells a distinct set of products or services, serves a specific set of customers and competes with a defined set of competitors*. To determine the business unit, it is usually necessary to take an external view of what the organisation does, not how it is structured to do it. Thus, an organisation structured along geographical lines with five regions may have only three business units corresponding to the product ranges it sells.

## 4.5  Strategic planning - the business foundation

Before one can select the most appropriate approach to IS/IT planning for an organisation the initial question is to ascertain how mature the organisation may be in terms of its own strategic business planning.

Broadly speaking, there are **four main categories** of sophistication of business planning:

- *Financial planning* - which sets and meets budgets.

- *Forecast based planning* - which predicts the future.

- *Externally orientated planning* - which factors in strategic thinking.

- *Strategic management* - which creates a vision of the future.

The first phase - **financial planning** - involves the creation of a proper annual budgeting and cost control focus for each of the main business functions. The second phase - **forecast based planning** - involves the use of forecasts to predict the future to assist in changing or meeting budgets. The third phase - **externally orientated planning** - involves a strategic analysis (usually on a once-off basis) to factor in various external business components. The fourth phase - **strategic management** - involves creating a sustainable vision of the future which is maintained and updated periodically through a well developed strategic planning framework and a strategic planning process focusing on the next 3-5 years, as well as on shorter term strategic goals within the immediate 1-2 year horizon.

---

**Figure 4.2** Appropriate level for conducting IS/IT planning.

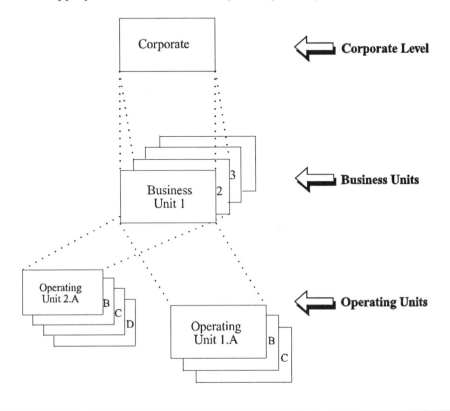

---

Depending on the maturity of the organisation and its approach to strategic business planning, different approaches to information systems planning will be both practical and appropriate.

A solid business foundation should include a thorough appreciation of:

- *The current situation* - including the application system portfolio that exists already, its effectiveness, its contribution to business aims, the overall profile of information systems, an assessment of user satisfaction, and of specific value for money.

- *The triggers for planning* - including the drivers behind the 'urge to plan'. This is often a mixture of strategic needs together with an urge to control expenditure and obtain value for money from IT. Very often, the triggers for planning are more focused on the 'today' issues with information systems and strategic views of information systems and less on the more important strategic nature of the potential technology solutions.

- *Expectation and objectives* - expectations from, and objectives of, the IS/IT planning process must take into account the business strategy of the organisation, the organisation structure itself and the motivation of the various individuals - both user and IT - who are involved. Most IS/IT failures come from a lack of expectation and objective setting during the planning for an IS/IT strategy. Hence the 'business basics' must be established at the beginning, involving a clear statement of the

> business strategy and objectives, and
> IS/IT opportunities

that will underly the IS/IT strategy. This will also help to ensure that the IS/IT strategy will produce not only 'good technology' but also good business vision.

To put this solid business foundation in place, it is best if an organisation has moved forward towards strategic management of the business, which creates the environment for longer term planning. Nonetheless, there are specific approaches to IS/IT planning that can be adopted to fit with the sophistication of the business and financial planning of the organisation.


## 4.6 Identifying IS/IT opportunities

An opportunity is an attractive area for strategic action where an organisation can successfully deploy its resources to gain and perhaps sustain a competitive advantage. The identification of IT opportunities can be one of the most difficult tasks in developing an IS/IT strategy.

Some organisations use traditional systems analysis or information requirements analysis techniques to identify opportunities. However, such techniques tend not to have a strategic perspective. Identifying IS/IT opportunities requires a more prescriptive framework which focuses on an organisation's specific business context and activities. There are a number of techniques which meet this requirement to include a strategic focus including:

- the five forces model
- critical success factors
- the value chain
- the value system.

While the identification of opportunities is a creative activity, these techniques can help in stimulating ideas and potential areas where IS/IT might be used.

**Five Forces model**

Michael Porter's model of five competitive forces, which was introduced in chapter 3, helps managers' clarify their business strategy and discuss where IS/IT potentially may yield competitive advantage in terms of defending the firm against these forces or influencing them in its favour. It can also help formulate strategic choices for firms in terms of whether it should be a 'first mover' or innovator in IS/IT or alternatively a 'follower' or imitator.

McFarlan[1] lists five questions which managers should ask themselves in assessing the potential impact or otherwise on their organisation:

- Can IS/IT build barriers to entry?
- Can IS/IT build in switching costs?
- Can the technology change the basis of competition?
- Can IS/IT change the balance of power in supplier relationships?
- Can IS/IT generate new products?

The assessment of potential IS/IT application areas requires a degree of creative thinking as well as analysis of business options. Box 4.1 presents a number of questions that might prove useful in identifying potential IS/IT options.

**Critical success factors**

Critical success factors (CSFs) are *the limited number of areas in which results, if they are satisfactory, will ensure successful competitive performance for the organisation.*[2] To identify a firm's CSFs, the business objectives for the business unit must first be determined. Objectives are specific targets for the business which the business wants to achieve within a particular time scale. The factors critical to success in meeting these objectives are the CSFs. This approach takes into consideration what management want the business to achieve in the short, long, and medium term. Figure 4.3 illustrates the CSF approach to identifying IS/IT opportunities.

1. *Suppliers*- Can we use IS/IT to:
   - gain leverage over our suppliers (improve our bargaining power or reduce his)?
   - reduce buying costs?
   - reduce the suppliers' costs?
   - be a better customer and obtain a better service?
   - identify alternative sources of supply?
   - improve the quality of products/services purchased?
   etc.

2. *Customers*- Can we use IS/IT to:
   - reduce customers' costs and or/increase their revenue?
   - increase our customers' switching costs (to alternative suppliers)?
   - increase our customers' knowledge of our products/services?
   - improve support/service to customers and/or reduce the costs of existing services?
   - discover more about our customers and their needs?
   - identify new potential customers?
   etc.

3. *Competitors*- Can we use IS/IT to:
   - raise the entry costs of potential competitors?
   - differentiate (or create new) products or services?
   - reduce our costs/increase our competitors' costs?
   - alter channels of distribution?
   - identify/establish a new market niche?
   - form joint ventures to enter new markets?
   etc.

**Box 4.1** IS/IT opportunity analysis - questions.
Source: J. Ward, P. Griffiths, and P. Whitmore, *Strategic Planning for Information Systems*. Prentice-Hall, 1990, p. 214.

---

Sometimes managers find it difficult to articulate and indeed differentiate between objectives and CSFs. As a guide, objectives normally begin with the word 'to' ...to do something. CSFs are prefixed with the word 'by' ...by achieving this or doing that.

**Figure 4.3** The critical success factor approach to IS/IT planning.

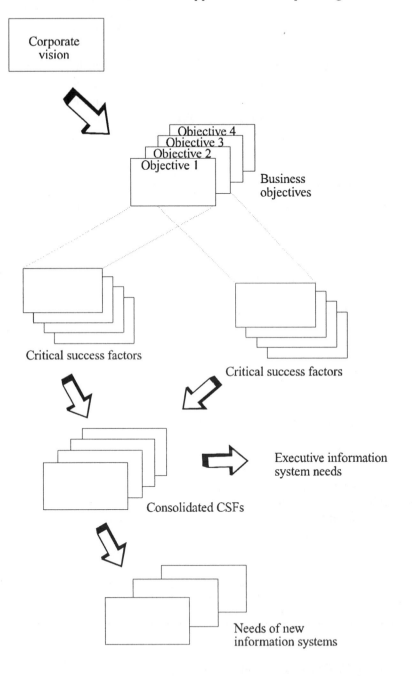

Typically, an organisation will have 6-10 objectives and each objective will have 4-6 CSFs. Once the CSFs have been identified, we then ask how can IS/IT help to achieve the CSFs and what is the impact that existing systems will have on the CSF? Figure 4.4 illustrates an example of deriving CSFs from business objectives.

Critical success factor analysis is normally carried out in a workshop setting, perhaps with somebody from outside the organisation acting as a facilitator. One of its main advantages is that it leads to a concensus view among management of where the most beneficial IS/IT investments should be made. Potential IS/IT investments can then be evaluated as to how they can be expected to contribute to the achievement of objectives. Thus, priorities for investment can be set.

Remember that not all CSFs will demand an IS/IT solution. Sometimes IT may provide a means to monitor performance of CSFs. Othertimes, CSFs will result in improvements being made in existing systems.

---

**Figure 4.4**  Critical success factor analysis example.

*Objective:* To increase market share by 10%.

*Critical success factors:*

- by improving market penetration
- by better identifying customers
- by providing a more efficient distribution system
- by making it easier for customers to do business with us.

*Applications to meet CSF:*

- marketing database
- distribution/logistic system
- access to external database
- order management system.

These systems would then be evaluated and their potential contribution to meeting the objectives assessed. Priorities would then be set.

---

The benefits of the CSF process include:

- focusing on what management want the business to achieve

- providing an IS/IT plan based on concensus
- involving senior management in the process
- linking IT investment to business objectives.

## The value chain

Porter contends that competitive advantage cannot be understood by looking at a firm as a whole. It does, however, stem from the many discrete activities a firm performs in designing, producing, marketing, delivering, and supporting its products. These activities can contribute to a firm's relative cost position and create a basis for differentiation. A cost advantage may stem from such disparate sources as a low-cost physical distribution system, a highly efficient assembly process, or superior sales force utilisation. He proposes the *value chain* as the basic tool for analysing the sources of competitive advantage. This disaggregates a firm's activities into strategically important activities, called *value activities*. These value activities are physically and technologically distinct activities that a firm performs. They are value activities because they should add value to a product or service. Figure 4.5 illustrates the value chain.

**Figure 4.5** The generic value chain.

| Firm infrastructure | | | | | | |
|---|---|---|---|---|---|---|
| Human resource management | | | | | | |
| Technology development | | | | | | |
| Procurement | | | | | | |
| | Inbound logistics | Operations | Outbound logistics | Marketing and sales | Service | Margin |

In order to be profitable the cost of performing the value activities must not exceed the value created. According to Porter, competitive advantage occurs when a firm can

- perform these activities at a lower cost than competitors, or

- performs them in a way that permits differentiation at a premium price.

These generic strategies have already been discussed in chapter 3.

Value activities can be divided into two broad types, *primary activities* and *support activities*. Primary activities are those activities involved in the physical creation of the product and its sale and distribution to the buyer as well as after-sales service. These are the activities which add value to the product or service. Support activities support the primary activities and each other by providing purchased inputs, technology, human resources, and various firm-wide functions. Let us look more closely at these activities.

- Inbound logistics

  'inbound' activities to receive, store and distribute inputs to the product, such as material handling, inventory control, warehousing, and contacts with suppliers.

- Operations

  production activities to create the product such as machining, packaging, printing, and testing.

- Outbound logistics

  'outbound' activities to store and distribute the product to customers, including warehousing, orderprocessing, and vehicle scheduling.

- Marketing and sales

  activities associated with providing a means by which buyers can purchase the product, and be induced to do so (advertising, selling, pricing, merchandising, promotion).

- Service

  activities for providing service or maintaining product value, including installation, repair, parts and training.

- Procurement

  purchasing inputs.

- Technology development

  not just machines and processes but also expertise, procedures, and systems.

- Human resource management

  activities involved in the recruiting, training, development, and remuneration of staff.

• Infrastructure                    general management, finance, planning, quality
                                     assurance.  The infrastructure supports the whole
                                     value chain.

By analysing the value chain of the company we can see whether either the physical or
information processing component of IS/IT can transform the value chain to the
organisation's advantage.   Questions one might pose include:

- Can IS/IT contribute to performing an activity more quickly or more
  efficiently or perhaps at a cheaper cost than before?
- Can IS/IT improve information flow through the primary activities?
- Can IS/IT be used to affect how support activities assist primary activities
  (e.g. finance, budgetary control)?

The value activities are interdependent and connected by linkages.  Linkages exist
when the way in which one activity is performed affects the cost or effectiveness of
other activities.

From an IS/IT perspective, the value chain is a valuable way of identifying where
better information and systems are needed, especially to show where integration
through systems could provide potential advantage over competitors (or reduce current
disadvantage).  The main benefit of value chain analysis is that it identifies the main
information needs and flows that reflect what the business actually does (or would like
to do), as opposed to how it is organised to do it (the organisation structure).


**The value system**

While IS/IT may be used in the performance of value activities or in linking these
activities, the value chain of a firm is itself part of a larger industry value chain: called
the *value system*.

The value system is made up of our value chain, competitors' value chain, suppliers'
value chains, and customers' value chains.  It is a representation of the movement of
goods and services from the source of raw materials through to the 'final' customer.
Information is continually being exchanged throughout the value system.  Orders are
sent to suppliers; invoices are sent to buyers; information about delivery is sent to
buyers; information is sent to customs for customs clearance; forecasting information
is often sent to suppliers, etc.

By analysing the value system, an organisation attempts to identify potential areas
where it might be possible to exchange information electronically with others in the

value system. Figure 4.6 illustrates where potential linkage, such as those linking buyer and seller, might be made.

---

**Figure 4.6** Linking value chains.

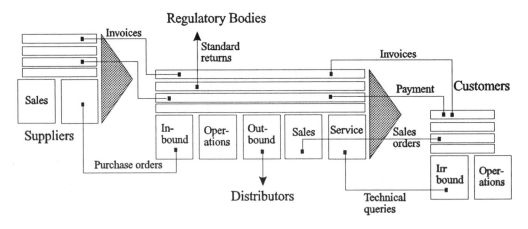

---

Systems permitting such external linkages are known as *interorganisation systems* (IOS). The technical aspect of such systems is known as *electronic data interchange* (EDI). Given the importance of interorganisational systems, chapter 6 is devoted to looking at interorganisational systems and exploring the strategic issues they raise.

Figure 4.7 summarises the opportunity identification process.

## 4.7  Approach to strategic IS/IT planning

Strategic IS/IT planning can be approached in four main phases as follows:

- *Phase 1 - Confirm business objectives and identify IT opportunities.* Produce initial information systems architecture.

- *Phase 2 - Analyse current needs, issues and produce strategy scope.* Produce an applications portfolio analysis to determine priorities.

- *Phase 3 - Produce architectures or blueprints for the five main IT strategy components - information, data, applications, technology and organisation (IDATO).* Determine alternative strategies to migrate to the target blueprints and decide on a preferred strategy.

- *Phase 4* - *Complete the strategy and consolidate the outputs.* Develop an implementation plan, an organisational development plan, a cost/benefit summary and a management summary.

**Figure 4.7** Identifying IS/IT opportunities.

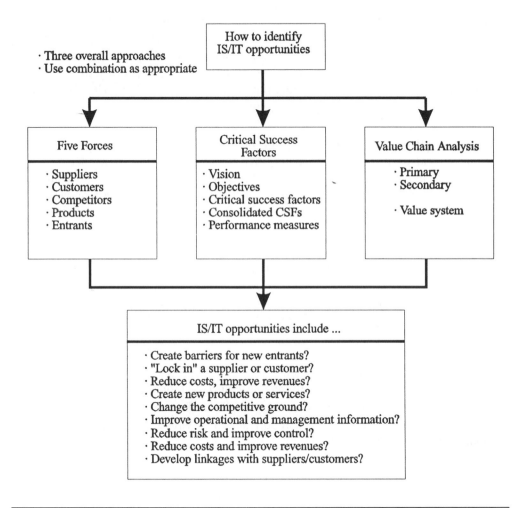

These phases are illustrated in figure 4.8. Let us now explore each of these phases in more detail.

**Confirming business objectives and IT opportunities**

The objective of this first phase is to link specific business aims and IS/IT opportunities to an initial information architecture or a high level work or blueprint of information, data and applications. Phase 1 should answer the question - why undertake an IS/IT strategy?

During Phase 1, the main focus is on the 'top down' approach, on strengths, weaknesses, opportunities and threats, on the real potential for IS/IT opportunities and on the linkage of business strategy to these opportunities. Typically, the initial fact finding work on requirements and IS/IT opportunities is appropriately undertaken for each main segment of the business and the organisation. We have already looked at some of the techniques to identify IS/IT opportunities.

This leads to the production of an **initial information architecture,** which will usually include a statement of high level information requirements, functions and their breakdown, information flows between functions, and information systems area (logical groupings of functions). A model of the main elements of data to support the current and future information needs is also produced.

**Analysing current IT and defining strategy scope**

The objectives of this second phase are to review how the existing organisation is served by IS/IT, to assess the IT environment itself and to focus on strategy by defining target applications.

An initial assessment of the organisation itself with regard to IT is undertaken, including the impact of IS/IT on organisation boundaries, functions and responsibilities. Typically, any existing plan for reshaping the organisation in the light of new products, services or support activities will be covered in terms of the potential IS/IT impact.

Normally the current IT environment itself is reviewed including the application systems profile, technology platforms and delivery for solutions (e.g. databases, development environments), current and planned development projects, staffing, skill levels and experience as well as the nature of the IT organisation itself. A view can be taken on the gap that may exist between the current ability of the IT environment to support the information systems architecture set out in Phase 1.

Most importantly during Phase 2, a view is taken on the *scope of the IS/IT strategy* exercise. There is a trend towards much more focused IS/IT strategies, with prioritisation of the areas for attention based on the relative contribution that an application system will make towards strategic goals and the CSFs, the likelihood of real IS/IT opportunity, a preliminary view of costs and benefits and the urgency of the needs. This focus is often driven by a differentiation between long term and short term goals.

**Figure 4.8** The four phases of strategic IS/IT planning.

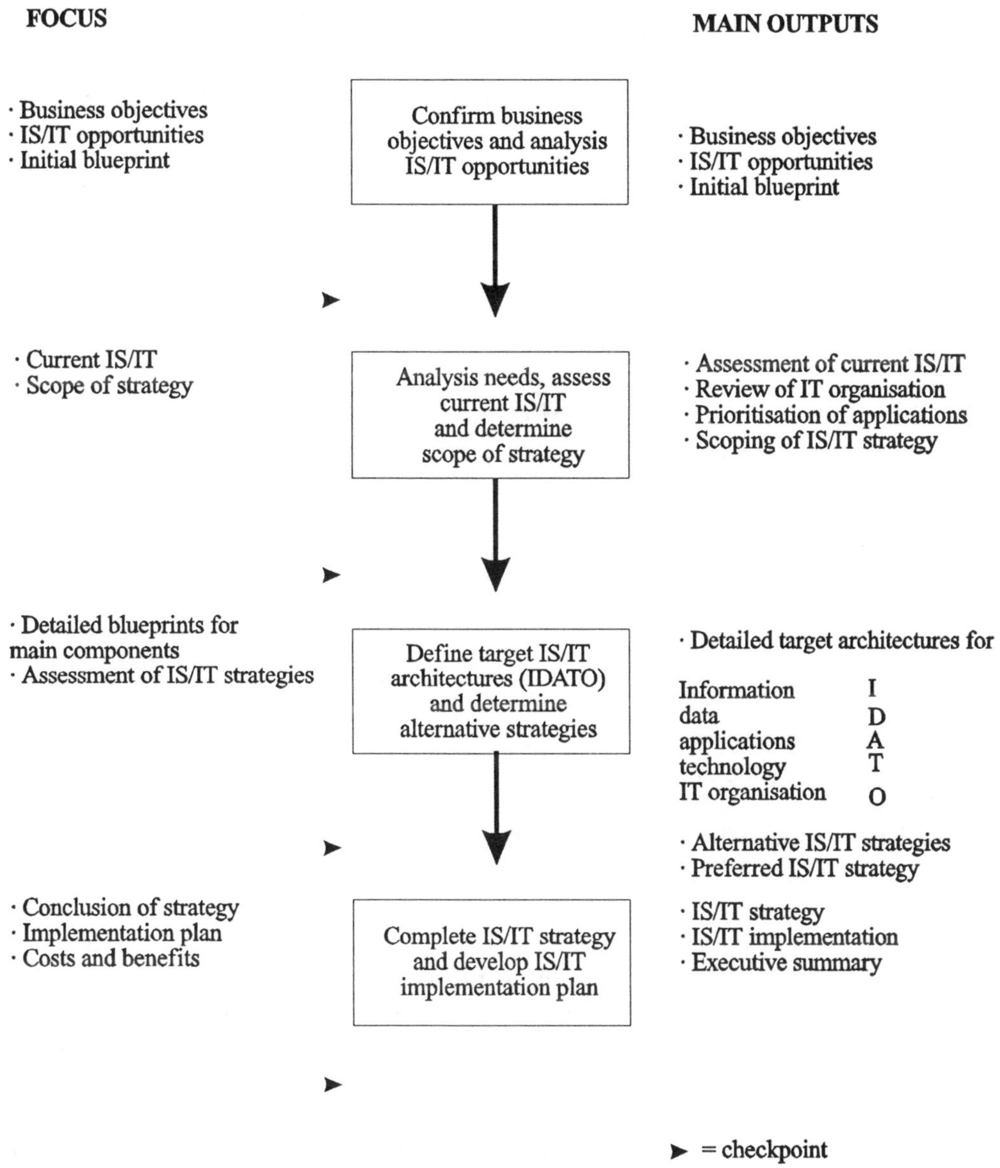

**FOCUS**     **MAIN OUTPUTS**

· Business objectives
· IS/IT opportunities
· Initial blueprint

Confirm business objectives and analysis IS/IT opportunities

· Business objectives
· IS/IT opportunities
· Initial blueprint

· Current IS/IT
· Scope of strategy

Analysis needs, assess current IS/IT and determine scope of strategy

· Assessment of current IS/IT
· Review of IT organisation
· Prioritisation of applications
· Scoping of IS/IT strategy

· Detailed blueprints for main components
· Assessment of IS/IT strategies

Define target IS/IT architectures (IDATO) and determine alternative strategies

· Detailed target architectures for

Information    I
data           D
applications   A
technology     T
IT organisation O

· Alternative IS/IT strategies
· Preferred IS/IT strategy

· Conclusion of strategy
· Implementation plan
· Costs and benefits

Complete IS/IT strategy and develop IS/IT implementation plan

· IS/IT strategy
· IS/IT implementation
· Executive summary

► = checkpoint

One means to achieve this prioritisation is an analysis of the target applications (set out in the information system architecture in Phase 1) focusing on the system objectives, key information, data, processes and interfaces, strategic implications and benefits expected, together with likely implementation options. This prioritisation can be shown in the format of the applications portfolio matrix introduced in chapter 3. This matrix categorises applications based on the contribution they make to business objectives. In summary these are

*strategic*                   applications which are critical to future business success

*key operational*             business operation applications that sustain the existing business

*support*                     applications which improve management effectiveness but, in themselves, do not sustain the business

*high potential*              innovative applications which may be of future strategic importance to either current or future operations.

This prioritisation sets the strategy boundaries and the likely implementation sequence required for the various components of the information systems architecture.


**Developing target IS/IT architectures (IDATO) and alternative strategies**

The aim in Phase 3 is to develop the detailed architectural components of the IT strategy including the information, data and applications required, together with a technical architecture and an IT organisational structure. In addition, alternative migration approaches to achieve the target architectures are considered and evaluated, and a preferred strategy is chosen.

Phase 3 puts in place the *five main* architectures or blueprints of an IS/IT strategy of information, data, applications, technology and the IT organisation (IDATO).

The IS component - the information, data, and applications blueprints - will normally be produced together, organised by each major grouping of applications that will clearly link objectives, goals, CSF's, user requirements (information and functions), and data needed to support the user requirements together with broad implementation options and assessments of costs and benefits.

The IT component - the technology blueprint - will span the major applications areas and will usually cover hardware, operating and systems software, communications, data storage and management, development environments and toolkits, together with the overall integration requirements and an assessment of costs. It should address the main technical issues and areas for concern including (for example):

- communications infrastructure
- processor strategy
- portability
- standards
- overall product strategy of IT suppliers.

In the following chapters we look more closely at these and other technological issues.

The *IT organisation blueprint* will focus on the IT function and its overall development as an organisation unit to achieve the required delivery capability to support the IS/IT strategy. During Phase 3 staffing and skills gaps will be identified, together with an initial view on staffing levels, and on how the IT function might be resourced.

Accordingly, the five main target architectures or blueprints set out a structured framework for the future. The main task in phase 3 is to consider the various different routes to achieving these target architectures and to choose the most appropriate route as a basis for the IS/IT implementation plan in phase 4.

Typically, one or more alternative strategies are defined to achieve the target. Architectures are defined and evaluated from both a technical and business point of view (e.g. costs, benefits, timescales, and risk) against criteria that reflect the objectives, needs, IS/IT opportunities and priorities defined in Phases 1 and 2. Where possible, one preferred strategy is agreed and taken forward to act as a basis for the IS/IT plan in Phase 4.

## Developing an IS/IT strategy implementation plan

The objective in Phase 4 is to develop an implementation plan for the selected IS/IT strategy and to conclude the IS/IT strategy planning exercise.

Phase 4 will initially finalise all the outputs from each of the previous three phases and conclude on the blueprints of information, data, applications, technology and IT organisation. Transition or migration approaches for each main grouping of architectures (IDA, T, & O) will be determined and a detailed implementation plan will be produced covering the various projects to be undertaken, their sequence, resourcing needs, costs, benefits, timescales, criticality and strategic impact. A business case will be made for the IS/IT strategy with a solid analysis of business potential, likely return on investment, benefits - both tangible and intangible - and all known costs and assumptions clearly stated.

Lastly, the outputs are brought together to create the three main end products:

(1) *IT strategy* - including aims; objectives; CSFs; information system architecture and priorities; target IDATO blueprints; migration or transition approaches to achieve the applications, recommended technical architecture and IT organisation structure;

(2) *IT strategy implementation plan* - including implementation plan and timetable; resource requirements; costs and benefit projections; business case and assumptions;

(3) *Executive summary* - covering the main findings, conclusions and recommendations.

## 4.8 Conclusion

In summary what makes an IS/IT strategy planning project a success? There are six 'do wells' that characterise a successful IS/IT strategy planning project:

- *Scope, aims and expectations.* The IS/IT planning project must be scoped correctly in the context of clearly articulated aims and manageable expectations. What is the focus - short term or long term? What areas of the business will be excluded? What will the end products be? Many IS/IT planning projects fail because of poor management of expectations and lack of clarity on the quality, depth and solidity of the two main end products - the IS/IT strategy and the IS/IT strategy implementation plan.

- *Understanding of present situation.* It is essential to understand in detail the present situation in terms of business strategy, application systems, existing and planned systems developments, user assessment of satisfaction, etc. A thorough knowledge of the real state of existing IT (and how it is perceived) is a fundamental building block which - surprisingly - is sometimes overlooked by IS/IT strategy teams that are too much focused on 'visions of the future'. Current systems are often surprisingly adaptable to achieving tactical or short term objectives, once their capabilities are fully understood, and should always be reviewed by the planning team.

- *Senior management sponsorship and involvement.* An IS/IT strategy has to involve senior management in all the main four phases because senior management, ideally top level function heads and executive management, become the owners of the end results. They have to set overall policy, objectives, priorities, and - most importantly - have to decide on the allocation of scarce resources. Senior management will need to be involved at steering committee level, ideally with one overall project sponsor.

- *Credible IS/IT strategy project team.* IS/IT strategy planning is highly skilled, specialist work, requiring a mix of functional, industry, technical, IS/IT planning, business planning, project management and methodology related skills. Depending on the size and nature of the IT function in the organisation, there may be in existence a system architecture unit who develop and maintain the architectures (or blueprints) for information, data, applications and technology. Such a unit is accordingly the custodian for much of the knowledge and expertise required in this area. Nonetheless, senior management, business function heads, industry experts, professional IS/IT planners should be involved in creating the correct team with the right background.

- *Thorough approach.* An IS/IT strategy must be thorough and complete within the agreed scope. It is better to complete a thorough IT plan within a narrow scope than attempt to do 'too much' and risk the project. An IT plan should always progress from the initial Phase 1 (business objectives and IT opportunities) down towards the detailed outputs of Phases 3 and 4. It is not uncommon for some organisations to attempt a form of Phase 1 (often disguised as a 'visioning exercise') involving a series of workshops that attempt to involve a far too wide range of managers in a very broad process. Few of these exercises lead to meaningful prioritisation and to the depth of solid IS/IT planning at the architecture level that is required to develop a productive and implementable IS/IT strategy.

- *Implementation focus.* An IS/IT strategy must be practical and implementable. While 'leading edge' technology delivers business benefits if correctly planned and implemented, 'bleeding edge' solutions usually lead to disaster (and to the demise of those IT planners responsible). Implementability is not only cost effectiveness in connection with existing and planned future business systems. It also encompasses the assessment and taking of measured risks in connection with 'leading edge' technology. Many of the risks with 'leading edge' technologies relate to their fundamental impact on the way in which an organisation will do business (and its ability to absorb such change) rather than any inherent level of technical risk. A good example is the use of imaging technologies where many proven and effective solutions exist, but where the level of business process and organisational redesign may be such as to pose a threat to the success of application of imaging solutions, depending on the nature and complexity of the organisation.

# Notes

1    F. Warren McFarlan, Information technology changes the way you compete. *Harvard Business Review*, May-June, 1984, pp. 89-103.
2    J. Rockart, Chief executives define their own data needs. *Harvard Business Review*, 1979.

# Additional reading

## General

Earl, M.J., Information systems strategy formulation. In R.J. Boland and R.A. Hirschheim, eds., *Critical Issues in Information Systems Research*, John Wiley & Sons, pp. 157-178.
Kantrow, A.M., The strategy-technology connection. *Harvard Business Review*, July-August, 1980.
McFarlan, F.W. and McKenny, J.L., *Corporate Information Systems Management*. Dow Jones Irwin, Homewood, Illinois, 1983.
Nolan, R.L. and Gibson, C.F., Managing the four stages of EDP growth. *Harvard Business Review*, January-February, 1984.
Nolan, R.L., Managing the crisis in data processing. *Harvard Business Review*, March-April, 1979.
Raghunathan, B. and Raghunathan, T.S., Information systems planning and effectiveness: an empirical study, *OMEGA International Journal of Management Science*, 19, 2/3, pp. 125-135.
Seddon, D., Experiences in IT strategy formulation: Imperial Chemical Industries plc. In M.J. Earl, ed., *Information Management: The Strategic Dimension*, Clarendon Press, Oxford, 1988, pp. 147-156.
Sprague, R.H. and McNurlin, B.C., *Information Systems Management in Practice*. Prentice-Hall, 1986, pp. 71-109.
Ward, J., Griffiths, P. and Whitmore, P., *Strategic Planning for Information Systems*, Prentice-Hall, 1990.
Wiseman, C., *Strategy and Computers*, Dow-Jones-Irwin, Homewood, Ill.

## IBM Systems Planning

IBM, *Business Systems Planning: Information Systems Planning Guide*. IBM, GE20-0527-4, July, 1984.

## Five forces analysis

Cash, J.I. and Konsynski, B.R., IS Redraws competitive boundaries. *Harvard Business Review*, March-April, 1985.

Porter, M.E. How competitive forces shape strategy. *Harvard Business Review*, March-April, 1979, pp. 137-145.

Porter, M.E.,*Competitive Strategy*. Free Press, 1980.

## Critical success factors

Boynton, A.C and Zmud, R.W., An assessment of critical success factors, *Sloan Management Review*, Summer, 1984.

Earl, M.J., *Management Strategies for Information Technology*. Prentice Hall, 1989, pp. 70-73.

Shank, M.E., Critical success factor analysis as a methodology for MIS planning, *MIS Quarterly*, **9**, 2, 1985 pp. 121-129.

Shank, M.E., Boynton, A.C. and Zmud, R.W., Critical success factor analysis as a methodology for MIS planning, *MIS Quarterly*, **9**, 2, 1985.

## Value chain analysis

Porter, M.E., *Competitive Advantage*. Free Press, 1985.

Porter, M.E. and Miller, V., How information gives you a competitive advantage. *Harvard Business Review*, July-August, 1985, pp. 149-160.

# 5

# Open Systems: Making Strategy Decisions about an Emerging Technology

In only a few years, Open Systems have come from being a peripheral debate in the IT industry to being a major issue for a growing number of IT users and professionals. More and more managers are asking *"should we move to Open Systems and if so how, and what are they anyway?"*

This chapter endeavours to answer all three of these questions. In so doing, we will be concerned with the general principles underlying Open Systems and not the specifics of various businesses or industries. The objective is to give users who are contemplating an Open Systems strategy an overview of what Open Systems are, and for those who have decided on such a strategy, a set of guidelines on implementing it. Before going anywhere, it should be clearly understood that, in formulating an information systems strategy, it is imperative to start from business needs. Systems must always serve the strategic ends of the organisation first. If this can be done equally well or more effectively using Open Systems, so much the better. However some users start from the position that they want an Open System first and make other criteria subservient to this. This is a dangerous approach and the risks involved are discussed elsewhere in this book.

What follows is therefore for those who have either thought the user needs through, and want to know whether Open Systems is an attractive option, or would like to know what the major issues are. For readers who have committed to an Open architecture or simply want to keep their options open, it provides some guidelines on actions they can take now.

## 5.1  A statement of mission

Let's start with a simple statement of mission. An Open Systems strategy may have many objectives but high on any list will be software investment protection and account control avoidance. Later on, we will look at several other reasons why an Open Systems strategy might be considered and at the likely impact of Open Systems on IT generally. Before doing so, it is useful to understand where the information technology industry is coming from. Open Systems are a child of consumer demand, not technical know-how. This is the first important fact to grasp. To understand why, we need to look at some history.

## 5.2  Why do we need Open Systems?

Most outsiders perceive the computer industry as being highly competitive. Thirty years of technological progress, delivering more and more processing power for less and less money, would certainly appear to be an example of free market competition at its best. New companies have entered (and in many cases exited) the market every year - sometimes every month. Growth  rates have been explosive. It has had all the hallmarks of a vibrant, thriving, consumer focused industry.

Unfortunately, beneath the surface, the industry was, and in some quarters still is, by no means as consumer oriented as it appeared. The nature of the competition in the market was less than healthy. In fact, true competition only really existed at the point of first sale. Thereafter, a computer company could progressively tie in a customer to the extent that, under the wrong circumstances, the relationship could, from the customer's viewpoint, become tantamount to blackmail. And while many computer companies enjoyed excellent relationships with their customers, the reality was that, when dealing with their suppliers, customers were nearly always negotiating from a position of weakness.

The reason for this lay in the unique nature of every supplier's products and in the special role of computer systems in organisations. To illustrate the first point, let us look briefly at just one aspect of it. In order to do anything useful, every computer is totally dependent on one key piece of software, its operating system. The operating system makes the computer work; without it, the machine is dead. Every useful application that runs on the computer, from payroll to process control, has to work closely with the operating system. From the early 1960s, as the industry evolved from the first practical commercial mainframes through the minicomputer era and up to the first microcomputers, each machine came with its own unique operating system, closely tied into its physical hardware architecture. Because of this, an application written for machine from vendor A would not normally run on a machine from vendor B without major modification or even a total rewrite. The concept is illustrated in figure 5.1.

**Figure 5.1** Hardware and software incompatibility.

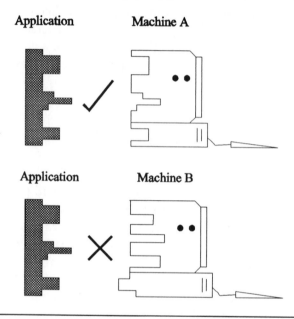

One result of this was a software market made up of vertical specialisations. Most software (there were some exceptions) ran on one and only one manufacturer's machines. Even worse, in many cases, software would only run on a particular range of machines within a manufacturer's product line. For example, an application written for, say, an IBM System/36 would not even run on an IBM 4300, never mind a Data General or an ICL machine. Likewise, a program written for a DEC PDP/11 would not run on a DEC VAX, and vice versa.

Because computer systems are deeply embedded in the day-to-day operations of most companies, an immediate consequence of this was that, unlike changing a washing machine or a car, changing computer supplier was a painful, not to say expensive, process. Changing computers involved massive conversion of programs, files and procedures as well as radical retraining of computer staff (and frequently users as well). The cost of such an operation could quickly dwarf the cost of replacing the machine itself. Add to that the risks involved and changing supplier became an intimidating prospect. The reality was that having selected a given hardware supplier, the user was dependent on the software available on that supplier's machine, a situation known graphically as vendor lock-in. A company with even a modest computer system had to be either desperate or rich before it could even contemplate changing its hardware supplier. Change only happened if the incumbent supplier went into liquidation, couldn't supply essential products or services or if relationships had deteriorated to breaking point.

## 5.3  The demand for standards

It is not surprising that users grew increasingly agitated about this state of affairs and, as always, where there is a demand for a new way of doing things, someone will supply it. Largely in response to growing consumer demand, the concept of Open Systems, systems which were not unique to one supplier, was born in the early 1980s and has steadily gathered momentum ever since.

The underlying idea was not new. Several bodies, notably the American National Standards Institute (ANSI), had been striving for standardisation in various areas of IT since the early 1960s. IBM, which dominated the world market up to the early 1980s, also had its own view of "openness", i.e. conformity to IBM's own standards such as Systems Network Architecture (SNA). But what has come to be called the Open Systems movement had, and continues to have, both broader and more fundamental aims than earlier (and less ambitious) attempts at standardisation. The objective of the Open System movement is to revolutionise the way information systems work. A consequence of this, as noted in Chapter 1, is that Open Systems are set to become the dominant theme of the 1990s.

## 5.4  A difficult birth

The emergence of Open Systems has not been without debate. Within the IT industry, there have been vitriolic public arguments about the virtues (and vices) of Open Systems. Much of the criticism has come from those whose interests are most threatened by Open Systems, and consequently cannot be said to be objective. Much of the criticism, it has to be said, is also ill informed. On the other hand, some of the advocates of Open Systems have oversimplified the issues as well as grossly overstating both its attainments to date and potential for the future. Neither have Open Systems suppliers helped their own case by rival claims about who has the true faith and by internecine warfare, based more on commercial manoeuvring than on technical considerations or consumer interests. The latter has led to the curious phenomenon whereby traditional inter vendor rivalry has been replaced by a series of shifting alliances and counter alliances. Consortia have formed and dissolved with alarming regularity often leaving even seasoned industry observers bemused.

## 5.5  The standards maze

The drive for standardisation has also spawned over a dozen standards bodies, each trying to codify rules or guidelines for some aspect of the technology. Table 5.1 lists the major players. Numerous small consortia have also tried to create islands of standards, usually built around a particular processor (see below under Portability).

| Organisation | Example of Standards Area Covered |
| --- | --- |
| American National Standards Institute (ANSI) | Languages |
| International Standards Organisation (ISO) | Communications |
| Institute of Electrical and Electronic Engineers (IEEE) | Networks |
| Unix International (UI) | Operating Systems/GUIs |
| Open Systems Foundation (OSF) | Operating Systems/GUIs |
| Comite Consultatif International de Telegraphs et Telecommunications (CCITT) | Telecommunications |
| Comite European de Normalisation Electronique/Comite European de Postes et Telegraphs (CENELEC/CEPT) | Message/communications |
| European Commission and the National Institute for Standards and Technology (U.S.) | Procurement |
| X/Open | Software, hardware |
| U.S. Department of Defense (DoD) | ADA, Security standards |
| Electronic Data Interchange for Administration, Commerce and Transport (EDIFACT) | Electronic Data Transmission |
| American Telegraph and Telephone Company (AT&T) | Unix System V.4 |
| International Business Machines (IBM) | IBM standards |

**Table 5.1** Key standards bodies.

To complicate matters even further, standards come in different shades. For example, standards may be:

- **De jure**, i.e. internationally recognised and permanent. Examples are FTAM, X.25, X.400, Ethernet;

- **De facto**, i.e. so widely accepted that they qualify as unofficial standards, no matter what the international bodies say. Examples are MS-DOS, Unix System V.4, TCP/IP, Novell, SNA;

- **Going to last**, this includes many de facto standards e.g. Unix, SNA, etc.;

- **Going out sooner or later**, albeit maybe much later, e.g. TCP/IP, MS-DOS, etc.

In these circumstances, it is not surprising that even those closely involved in the industry find it difficult to keep track of what is going on. It is even less surprising that many managers facing IT strategy decisions have become thoroughly confused and, in some cases, disillusioned. Surveys show that managers want Open Systems, while at the same time being uncertain as to what exactly Open Systems are, or how to go about implementing them. Managers are not helped by the barrage of opinion from vendors, industry watchers and the press in which highly technical (and often unimportant) back room arguments are fought out in emotive language. As we enter the last decade of the century, the market and technical battles raging around Open Systems that became a feature of the late 1980s, are still being fought, with little sign of a reconciliation in sight, despite the fact that most observers agree that market pressure will inevitably force vendors to compromise in the long run. We have covered this background at length to emphasise the point that, in formulating an Open Systems strategy, the first quality needed is a cool head. The Open System is a crucial stage in the maturing of the information technology industry, but it is neither a panacea nor, in its present state, the highest form of evolution that will be reached. While it is an essential technology for a wide range of users and will provide, as we will see, enormous benefits to customers (if not to suppliers), it is not the answer to every problem, as some of its more fervent advocates claim.

Nonetheless, despite all of the above, one crucial landmark should be noted. Whereas in the early eighties the debate was very much between the upstart proselytisers of Open Systems and the computer industry establishment, now all but the most reactionary industry observers agree that Open Systems are here to stay, and that they will increasingly dominate the market and the industry. The argument has therefore shifted to the best way of realising Openness and the struggle amongst suppliers to come out on the top of the pile is on in earnest. In this volatile situation, users and managers, faced with conflicting claims by rival vendors, have to try and formulate a sensible strategy for development of their Information Systems. Today, few organisations can afford not to have a position on Open Systems. But how do you choose the best strategy in a market where there is virtually open warfare between some of the players and where crucial issues still remain to be decided?

## 5.6  To act or to wait?

In order to address this question, it is important to understand some basic Open Systems concepts and vocabulary. In the remainder of this Chapter, we will examine the basic principles underlying Open Systems and suggest practical strategies that can be adopted now for those who wish to move towards an Open architecture or at least to keep their options open. Because there is still uncertainty about several issues, these strategies will, in many instances, have to be defensive and precautionary in nature. However, the alternative of sitting, Hamlet like, waiting to see what happens next, is inadvisable. It is a truism in IT that if you wait a year, there will always be something better and cheaper. Unfortunately, in the meantime you lose twelve months of progress. There are times when inaction is the best policy, but this is not one of them. The issues involved in Open Systems will continue to rumble through the 1990s; the luxury of waiting is one users cannot afford.

## 5.7  Starting points

A key element in any discussion of an IT strategy (whether open or not) is the point from which you start. Essentially, there are three positions in which users could find themselves:

- *A green field site*  This is where there are no significant existing systems or where such systems as there are, are going to be scrapped;
- *A piecemeal system*  A piecemeal system occurs when there has been no overall strategy and department/local systems have grown up in an ad hoc manner. Many of the individual systems may be good and useful in their own right and a key aspect of strategy is to retain what is best.
- *A mature system*  This is a system which has grown in a coherent and planned manner and which is functioning well, but ageing. The objective here is to retain the cohesiveness of the present system while migrating to the new environment.

An organisation's attitude to Open Systems will be very much coloured by its starting point. A green field site has a free choice but must make fundamental decisions from day one. A piecemeal system will almost certainly need a phased approach, designed to salvage the best elements of the old system. A mature system can pose problems of a different order again, especially if the technology is highly proprietary and requires total replacement. In looking at positive or defensive Open Systems strategies, it is necessary to take account not only of business needs and industry trends, but of what you already have in situ.

With these points in mind, we can proceed to review the four pillars on which an Open System is built.

## 5.8 What are Open Systems?

In a single sentence, Open Systems are about *vendor independence* and *application transparency*. This is a conceptual rather than a technical definition which is the way it should be. But to understand what vendor independence and application transparency are, and how they are achieved, we need to delve (briefly) into the technology itself.

There are numerous technical definitions of Open Systems. One straightforward working definition is that Open Systems are about four things:

- Software portability;
- Communications between machines and applications;
- How the machine looks to the user; and
- People skills.

These are sometimes called the "ilities", portability, interoperability, useability and transferability. Other "ilities" you will often see are scaleability (the ability of a system to expand) and compatibility - an aspect of portability. We will touch on both of the latter below. The first two items on the above list, portability and interoperability, are the major issues in Open Systems and most of what follows relates to them. We will start with portability.

## 5.9 Portability

People brought up in the age of microcomputers take many things for granted that older heads do not. For example, they assume that, if they buy software for one machine, it will run on any other. If I buy a copy of WordPerfect for my IBM microcomputer, then trade in the IBM for a Compaq or a Dell, I expect that the same software on the same diskettes can be copied from one machine to the next. Likewise, as I move from a 286 to a 386 to a 486 based machine, or move from **MS-DOS** version 2.0 to version 5.0, I expect that my software will continue to work.

It therefore comes as a surprise to many to know that this is not true with other types of computer. Portability is far from common in the computer world.

## Portability fundamentals

Fundamentally, portability is dependent upon operating systems and processors. All else is built on these. Take the above example. For the IBM compatible PC user, there are three aspects of portability at work as software is moved from machine to machine. These are:

- Application binary compatibility
- Scaleability
- Upwards compatibility.

Translated, this means that the interface between the software, for example WordPerfect, and the machine is identical, even if the machines are different brands, of different generations and use different versions of the operating system. Two things make this possible. The first is that IBM compatible microcomputers are based on the same processor series, in this case the Intel 80286/386/486 series. Thus the engines of all of these machines are of the same fundamental design, even if the horsepower and bodywork are different. The second factor is that they use the same operating system, MS-DOS. Both factors are important and selecting an Open System strategy involves decisions about both.

We will start with the operating system. As has already been stated, any software application running on any machine has to have a close working relationship with the operating system. Because proprietary operating systems vary widely, writing an application, for example an accounting system, that will run on several machines, effectively means having several different versions, probably a different programming team for each version, and major headaches keeping versions synchronised. While the system must appear identical to the user, it may have to appear very different to each machine. This is illustrated in figure 5.2.

**Figure 5.2** Portability fundamentals.

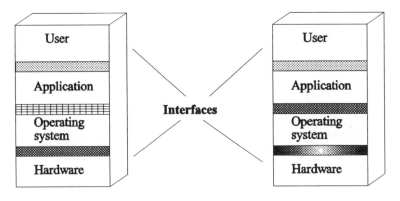

Earlier in this chapter it was stated that there were some exceptions to the general lack of portability in software in the 1970s and early 1980s. One example of an exception is the Oracle relational database and fourth generation environment which was available on a wide range of proprietary and open machines. This meant that Oracle looked the same to a user on a VAX as it did on an IBM mainframe. However to achieve this, Oracle had to have a massive team maintaining different versions which hid the operating system differences from the user.

A seemingly simple solution to this problem would be to have a common operating system which ran on all machines. This would appear to pass the problem illustrated in figure 5.2 from the applications designer to the operating system designer (see figure 5.3).

Commonality of operating system certainly simplifies the problems of moving software from one machine to another. But so called "shrink wrapped" portability, of the type described above requires something extra, something called a common Application Binary Interface or ABI. Unfortunately, an ABI requires that the *processor* be the same on all machines. Shrink wrapped portability is possible on IBM compatibles only because they all use the same family of processors and the same operating system. Microcomputer software is readily portable because the microcomputer market is dominated by two such families of processors, the Intel 80x86 series (on IBM compatibles), and the Motorola 680x0 series (on Apples).

**Figure 5.3** Using a common operating system.

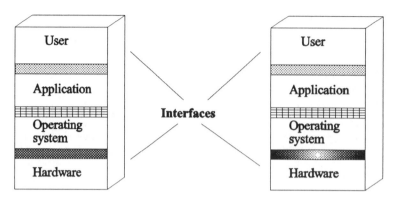

The same uniformity does **not** hold in the workstation and minicomputer world where there are a wide variety of processors on the market. These include the aforementioned Intel and Motorola chips plus many others, for example the SPARC and MIPS processors and several proprietary (in the sense that they are exclusive to one hardware vendor) products. Unfortunately therefore, achieving shrink wrapped portability currently requires a user to stay with the same processor family, which contradicts one of the key objectives of an Open System, i.e. vendor independence. Alas, to get all hardware vendors to use the same processor would require either a miracle or an act of market interference of Stalinist proportions. As neither of these seems practical, researchers and standards bodies have tried to devise other ways of achieving "near shrink wrapped" portability.

**Alternative strategies**

Two alternative strategies in this search are *Application Program Interfaces* and *POSIX*. Application Program Interfaces (APIs) seek to eliminate the processor from the equation by providing standard libraries of function calls. All you need for API compatibly is the same operating system. While this does not give the full benefits of shrink wrapped software, it does give a relatively high degree of software portability. The second initiative, POSIX, is an operating system standard (loosely based on Unix) to which any operating system can be made to comply. POSIX is, however, a lowest common denominator and, as such, enables almost any supplier, including many proprietary operating systems, to achieve compliance.

**Operating systems options**

A user can, therefore, achieve a reasonable level of portability by selecting the right operating system without being locked into a single processor. There are now two widely accepted standard operating systems, MS-DOS for microcomputers and Unix (which comes in a variety of brand names) for workstations and minicomputers. At the time of writing, a third, IBM's OS/2 Version 2.0 is bidding to join these. Others are expected to join the fight (see below).

Neither Unix nor MS-DOS would rank highly in any competition for operating systems for commercial environments. Both have serious limitations. However being the best is not necessary for commercial success. The Betamax video recorder was in many ways a better system than VHS, but the cheaper VHS recorder eventually put the Betamax out of business. At another level, the QWERTY keyboard is an appalling layout for high speed typing (it was originally designed to slow typists down because the mechanical typewriters couldn't keep up with more efficient layouts). Over the years there have been several attempts to replace QWERTY with something better, none have succeeded. Likewise, attempts to replace COBOL, a verbose and inelegant programming language, with more structured and sophisticated languages have largely failed. In the IT world, as elsewhere, products gather a momentum that is often impossible to reverse.

So the first key step in portability strategy is to select the degree of portability you want, from POSIX (low) to ABI (high). This involves making decisions about operating systems and processors and balancing flexibility against choice. This will get you to first base. However, portability strategy must take into account three other factors.

**Portability Strategy**

While processor and operating system are the fundamental planks of portability, a comprehensive strategy requires actions on three further fronts:

- Development tools
- Data management systems
- Application packages.

**Development tools**

There are a four basic strategies users can adopt with regard to development tools. These are:

- A 3rd Generation (3GL) strategy

- A 4th Generation (4GL) strategy

- A Computer Aided System Engineering (CASE) generator strategy

- A mixed strategy ("horses for courses") approach.

*3rd Generation Languages*
This strategy is based on continued use of 3GLs for development. Although it will be increasingly unusual for a long term 3GL strategy to be independent of CASE strategy (see below), the present lack of standards in the fourth generation world can mean that, in choosing a 4GL, you merely substitute software vendor lock-in for hardware vendor lock-in. This is not a problem with many 3GLs for which well established and vendor independent standards exist. However, it is necessary to choose the 3GL carefully. For example:

- COBOL and C are highly portable, well standardised languages; PL/1, ADA, BASIC fall in between.

- PL/1 and ADA have good standards but are not as portable as COBOL or C. BASIC is quite portable but notoriously non standard;

- Languages such as RPGII and DIBOL are almost totally non-portable.

Choosing a third generation strategy based on COBOL or C would therefore appear to be a fairly safe Open Systems direction. But there is a large penalty in programmer efficiency to be paid.

*4th Generation Languages*
A 4GL strategy overcomes much of the productivity shortcomings of the 3GL approach. Many 4GLs are also highly portable, although none would have more than a fraction of the usage level of the leading 3GLs. This position is unlikely to change until the next century. From the viewpoint of an Open Systems strategy therefore:

- A Open 4GL will be machine portable, have interfaces into the main RDBMS and other commonly used file structures. Examples of such languages include FOCUS, Progress and Powerhouse;

- A Closed 4GL will be proprietary, may only access its own proprietary file system and may not communicate easily with other products or packages. Examples of proprietary 4GLs are MAPPER, LINC and PACE.

Nevertheless, as an Open Systems strategy, the criticism made above is valid. All current 4GLs are proprietary. A 4GL strategy is therefore, by definition, only partially open.

*Computer Aided System Engineering*
Another way of overcoming the low productivity of the 3GL development environment is to use CASE. CASE program generators can be used to create third and even fourth generation code. Unfortunately the same charge can be levelled at CASE as has been levelled at 4GLs, i.e. all CASE tools are proprietary and standards for CASE are only in the embryonic stages. It has also been argued that, while a CASE generation strategy may be fine for single applications, they may not be a practical option when it comes to whole systems.

That said, the prognosis for open CASE standards is much better than for 4GLs. Although there are a variety of proprietary tools, CASE methodologies and techniques do not tend to vary greatly, and much of the variation there is is cosmetic (the different shapes used in diagramming techniques etc.). Even so, it is likely to be several years before CASE standards crystallise into vendor-independent toolsets.

*Data management*
The objective of an open data management strategy is to get away from proprietary and/or inflexible file systems and architectures. Here the options are good. Possible strategies are to:

- Go for a good, machine-independent Relational Database Management System (RDBMS) which is ANSI SQL compliant (e.g. Ingres, Oracle, Sybase etc.); or

- Use a good widely used file system such as C-ISAM;

In general, an open data management strategy will seek to avoid low mobility file systems such as most hierarchical DBMSs, most network DBMSs and, of course, all proprietary file systems.

Portability, and, by implication, openness, is aided by uniformity and consistency in file management structures. The more file management systems types you have, the less mobile your system tends to be.

*Packages*

Where portability is concerned, application packages present a slightly different problem. What an open package needs is machine portability and good interfaces, both to other products and to the human beings who use it. In looking at application packages, a flexible strategy is to aim for software that has several open offerings/versions of the package. To date, regrettably few application packages are, for example, based on relational data management systems or SQL. What is more important is the core language in which the package is written and how it is compiled onto the target machines.

---

Most packages currently on the market are written in 3GLs (some are actually written in 2GLs such as Assembly language!). Increasingly packages are becoming available which are written in a 4GL, often developed by the 4GL suppliers or their business partners (e.g. Oracle, ASK/Ingres and Progress). Some of these are new, some are rewrites of existing packages. It is important to know which language a package is written in as this affects its portability and ease of maintenance.

---

## Portability - summary

The overall options for portability are shown in figure 5.4.

Decisions must be made about processors, operating systems, development tools, data management and application packages. Within each of these, users have a wide choice. They are also likely to be faced with these types of choices for the next five to ten years as new technologies emerge and struggle for standardisation continues.

**Figure 5.4** Portability options.

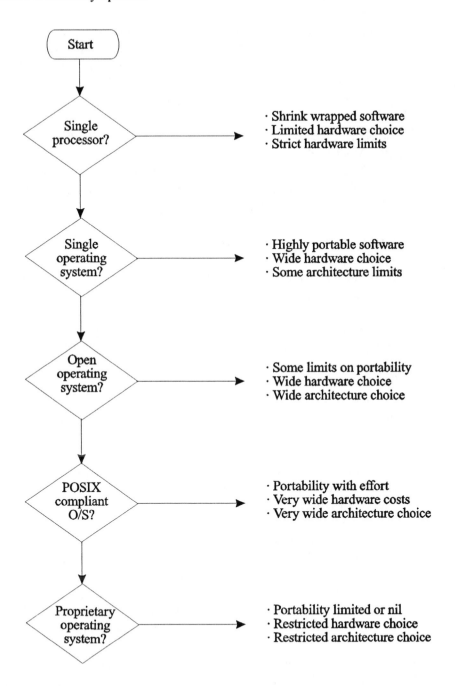

## 5.10  Communications

If software portability is the acid test of openness, communications (or interoperability to give it its precise name) is a more pressing issue for most users.  An open communications system is one where any application on any machine can communicate with any application on any other machine.  This is easily stated.  In practice, it gives rise to an intimidating range of technical issues.

To understand some of these issues, let us look at a "simple" problem.  Imagine two users A and B.  A is based in London, and B in Paris.  User A has a simple report in an Excel spreadsheet on an Apple Macintosh microcomputer in his London office.  He would like to get this into a document on B's proprietary minicomputer-based word processor in Paris.  Let us consider some of the complications.

- First the data must be extracted from Excel.

- Next, the information must be put into a format that the minicomputer will be able to understand.  To do this, the London user would probably use ASCII, a lowest common denominator for character and number representation.  Let us make the simplifying assumption that there are no strange characters used in the spreadsheet that are not in standard ASCII.

- The next problem the London user faces is to get the ASCII file to the machine in Paris.  A simple way to do this is via diskette but the Paris machine does not have a diskette drive.  The London machine does not have a tape drive so he can't use tape.  He could send it to a specialist conversion bureau but that would take too long.  Fortunately he has a modem on his machine.  The Paris machine does not have a modem but it is connected to a network on which there is a modem connected to the French PTT packet switching service.

- So A can send the file to Paris via the modem over the British Telecom X.25 service, Telecom Gold (assuming that he has an account).  This in itself raises numerous issues which we won't go into here.  In sending the file to Paris, they will be using a standard called X.25 which governs packet switching systems.  Telecom Gold passes the data to the French PTT packet switching service which, in turn, passes it to the Paris user.

- When the file is successfully received in Paris, B has to get it into his word processor.  This raises a further series of problems such as character sets and interchange formats which, again, we will ignore.  B changes the report on his word processor and now wants to send it back to London so that A can update his spreadsheet. This requires all the above steps to be repeated, in reverse. Then having received the file, A finds that, while Excel will accept an ASCII file as input, it will not "understand" the columns of numbers.

- A has therefore to import it into his word processor and doctor it, before he can read it meaningfully into his spreadsheet.

It all sounds pretty tedious, and it is. The steps are illustrated in figure 5.5.

**Figure 5.5** Sending a spreadsheet datafile from London to Paris

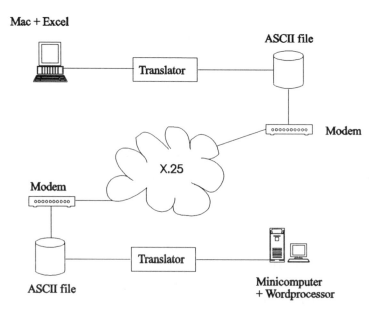

The above anecdote gives but a flavour of the problems involved. At each point in the transfer, there are conversions, protocols and logistics to be overcome, many of which we have conveniently glossed over (including the fact that the Frenchman doesn't speak English!). Yet there is no law of nature that says that it must be this way.

Open Systems communications are therefore about agreeing standards for each step of the process with a view to making it transparent to the user. This, it will easily be appreciated, is a non-trivial task and for this reason, the approach to the problem has been to break it down into isolated chunks. To do this, the International Standards

Organisation (ISO for short) has therefore developed a model which it has called the Open Systems Interconnection model, generally referred to as OSI. It is important to differentiate each set of initials!

OSI breaks the communications process down into seven layers as follows:

| Number | Layer |
|--------|-------|
| 7 | Application |
| 6 | Presentation |
| 5 | Session |
| 4 | Transport |
| 3 | Network |
| 2 | Data Link |
| 1 | Physical |

The scope of each layer and the interfaces between them are carefully defined. The importance of the model is that it isolates each layer so that issues within a layer can be resolved without constantly having to be concerned with what is happening in the layers far above and below. Each layer need only be concerned with what is happening in the layer immediately above, immediately below and in the corresponding layer on the other machine.

Within each layer, there may be several standards. To understand how this works, consider layer 1, the **Physical** layer. This is concerned with matters such as wiring. Various standards are defined within it, including the well known network topologies, Ethernet and Token ring. (Network topologies are discussed in chapter 6.) Standards in the layer define physical characteristics such as the wire width, shielding impedance, standards of insulation and so forth. All other matters relating to communications (addressing conventions, data formats, error correction techniques and so on) can be, and are, ignored by the Physical layer standards. An Ethernet cable is not concerned whether it is carrying protocols, text, SQL or images. That is an issue for another layer.

> It should be noted that, while ISO is responsible for the model, ISO also sets standards in each layer. ISO can, and has, adopted standards. It also tolerates other interim standards (see note on TCP/IP below). The grand plan is to move all open communications to official OSI standards as quickly as users will allow.

## Open communications strategy

Unlike the wars over operating system, processor and Graphical User Interface (q.v.) standards, there is more or less a consensus on communications. Several de facto and a number of de jure standards are already well established. Examples of key communications standards are:

- X.400
- X.25
- TCP/IP (Transmission Control Protocol/Internet Protocol)
- Ethernet
- Token Ring
- HDLC.

As time goes on, ISO is adopting more official standard(s) in each OSI layer. Some (X.25, Ethernet, X.400 and several others) have already been adopted. Others, notably TCP/IP are so widely used that displacing them will take time. In general, the standards in the lower layers (1-4) are well understood. Standards in the upper layers (with some exceptions, e.g. X.400) are still emerging.

An Open Systems communications strategy should therefore ensure that all planned communications systems are broadly compatible with known ISO standards and statements of direction. Use of, for example, X.25 or Ethernet is totally in line with internationally accepted standards; use of, for example, WangNet is less so.

> A special word must be said about TCP/IP. TCP/IP is the de facto standard in the Unix world for layers 3 and 4. Because it is so widely used, TCP/IP, like COBOL, and MS-DOS, has developed its own market momentum despite a number of theoretical problems. TCP/IP does not fit nicely into the OSI model (it crosses over layers which is not convenient) and has certain other shortcomings. Nonetheless, as an interim strategy for Open System communications it makes sense.

The communications world is also replete with de facto standards. Examples of such standards include the Novell networking system, Sun Microsystems's Network File System (NFS) and the terminal emulation protocol, TELNET. In theory, all of these will, in due course, be superseded by "official" standards. However, because of their wide usage, it is likely that many of these will find a place in the Open Systems world and some will, like COBOL, defy all attempts to replace them with something "better".

## 5.11 Interfaces

Interfaces are how we see and operate the computer when we sit down in front of it. When you sit down in the driver's seat of your car you expect the three pedals under your feet to be, from left to right, clutch, brake and accelerator. You take this for granted. Each time you get into a different car, you do not take time to check out the arrangement of the pedals.

It would be nice to think that every time you sat at a computer keyboard the same thing would be true. For example, that the keys would do basically the same things (e.g. press F1 for help, Esc for interrupt and so on), no matter what brand of computer you were using. Likewise, when working with a mouse and windowing system, it would be helpful to have consistency about what each icon on the screen means. As the world moves towards Graphical User Interfaces (GUIs), the latter will become the major issue in interface design.

The importance of this is highlighted by exhibit 5.1 which shows a typical Macintosh screen and its standard features. Part of the enormous success of the Macintosh is based on Apple's ruthless insistence that its developers make their packages consistent with the Macintosh standard. On a Macintosh, whether you are using a spreadsheet, an accounts package, a word processor or an expert system, common menu items (such as"print", "help", "open a new file") will appear in the same place. If I know how to use the printer in MacPaint, I can print from Excel without looking up the manual. This commonality of interface and ease of use has an impact on users which is difficult to overestimate. The time saving on learning is enormous. As a direct consequence, users use more software, make more effective use of the machine, and derive much greater benefit from the company's investment. Apple claim that the average Macintosh user uses over three times as many applications as the average user of MS-DOS. It is not difficult to see why.

Having learned from Apple, a key objective of Open Systems is therefore to achieve the same type of consistency in Open System Graphical User Interfaces. Why should the user have to learn a different way of doing things for every application he or she uses? In the absence of a single acknowledged standard setting body, individual

**Exhibit 5.1** A graphical user interface.

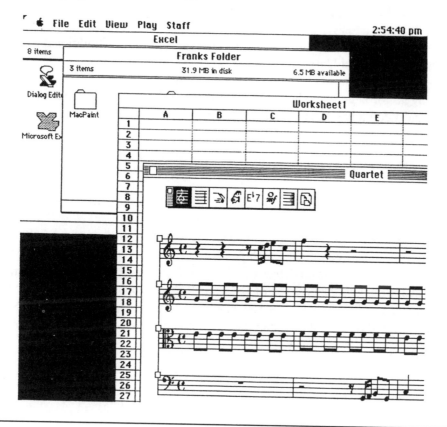

suppliers are vying to become the **MS-DOS** or Novell of the GUI. Contenders for this include:

- Microsoft's Windows NT
- Open System Foundation's/Motif
- Unix International's/Open Look
- IBM's Presentation Manager.

As GUIs are closely linked to operating systems, GUI standards are closely linked into what will happen in the world of operating systems. To the present list of contending operating systems, it is therefore necessary to add a number of systems recently released or promised for later in the decade, notably:

- The Open Systems Foundation's OSF/2
- IBM's OS/2 Version 2.0

- Microsoft's New Technology (NT)
- IBM and Apple's "Pink" operating system.

not to mention possible future developments in the more "traditional" operating systems, MS-DOS and Unix.

This struggle for supremacy has been termed the "GUI Wars". It shows no sign of abating and a definitive standard may take some years to emerge.

### Open user interface strategy

Although there is still much argument about GUIs, at least the choices are simpler than elsewhere. It is likely that, at least in the short term, the market will settle for a combination of MS-DOS/Windows and Unix (in one of its guises) plus Motif. In the medium term, other contenders include the NT version of Windows and IBM's presentation manager. Most GUIs are still relatively undeveloped in comparison to the Apple Macintosh, and the decision of IBM and Apple to cooperate on the new "Pink" operating system/GUI may bring a new challenge to the market in the mid 1990s. A GUI policy based on any of the main players is the best that users can hope for at the present.

## 5.12  People skills

All systems boil down to people in the end. From a systems viewpoint, people can be classified into four types:

- Users
- Developers
- System support
- System management.

Each of these has a different perspective and different priorities. Happily, Open Systems offers a resolution to many of the traditional conflicts between these parties.

**Users** want consistency. They would like all systems to have the same "look and feel". This reduces learning time. Users also like systems to be seamless. They do not want to have to recall on which hard disk a particular file is resident or to have to set up meaningless looking strings of header codes for different printers. Openness to the user is seen in the GUI and communications. The finer nuances of file storage technology or operating systems standards are irrelevant.

**Developers** want to master one set of skills (at least most do) and to be able to bring these from task to task. They do not want to have to work with COBOL one day, PL/1 the next nor with Unix on Monday and MVS on Tuesday. They also want to be able to recycle code, to have access to the best and most powerful tools and not to be stuck in some specialist niche which locks them into their employer!

**System support staff** and operations staff want consistency of a different sort. They do not want to have to manage several operating systems, numerous emulators and a communications system that relies on customised interfaces owing more to Heath Robinson than good engineering. Support staff want to be able to concentrate on user problems and they want routine system management to be just that, routine.

**System managers** want efficiency, cost effectiveness, ease of management and ease of recruitment. People are often the most expensive component in any information system. Cost of ownership is a key measure in all systems and the cost of people looms large in any metric. Minimising people costs requires several actions not all of which are relevant here. However Open Systems can contribute in a number of ways, for example:

- It is easier to recruit staff as the skills are common;
- Training organisations and Universities are increasingly geared to training people in Open System areas;
- Internal staff are more flexible and mobile;
- Contract staff are easier to find.
- User learning times are reduced.

On the down side, increased staff mobility means that you can also lose people more easily, but the pluses considerably outweigh this minus.

Achieving openness with people involves all the preceding elements of Open Systems strategy, portability, communications and interfaces. Whereas managers often see the immediate benefits in lower hardware costs and investment protection, the savings in user time and hassle is often the biggest benefit of any good system. It should not be taken for granted that Open Systems equates to happier users, but Open Systems will increasingly provide the means to satisfy users more effectively.

## 5.13  Conclusion - the rationale for Open Systems

By the mid 1990s, the information technology market is likely to be made up of four major segments:

- Unix and Unix lookalike based Open Systems
- Microcomputers and network systems based on MS-DOS/Novell and other de facto standards
- The IBM world
- Others.

Estimates vary, but it is likely that the breakdown will be roughly as in figure 5.6.

---

**Figure 5.6**  Market breakdown by mid/late 1990s?

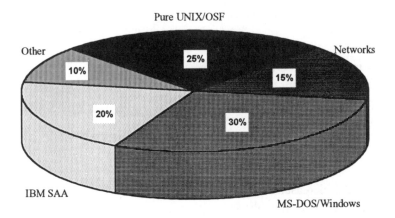

---

There are several consequences of this:

- *The cost of Open Systems will be less both initially and over time.* This is because the buyer is buying in a mass market where true competition is at work. Proprietary system costs will have to follow what is happening, but Open Systems will force the pace.

- *Very few proprietary systems will survive.* Those that do will only do so either because they have sufficient momentum to last or because they can establish themselves in a market niche.

- *The major industry developments will tend to take place in this sector first.* No single supplier of proprietary systems, not even IBM, can hope to compete with the range of products that will be delivered. Look at what happened in the microcomputer market in the 1980s.

- *Open Systems will (eventually) be much less hassle.* When you buy an electrical household appliance, you plug it into the socket and it works. Why should you not do the same with a printer. If you plug a printer into an Apple Macintosh, it immediately knows what kind of printer it is and asks you to confirm. Connecting a printer to an MSDOS machine can be a messy and complicated business requiring special scripts on the micro, fiddling with printer setup parameters and even getting a screwdriver to change the dip switch settings on the motherboard. In the 1990s, this is ridiculous. Machines should be seamless. In the 1990s, users will expect seamlessness.

There used to be a saying, probably true at one time, that nobody ever got fired for buying IBM. None of us wants to be remembered as the person who bought the Betamax tape recorder or the Video Disk player. The recurring worry for buyers of computers is *"Am I with the right computer supplier or following the right strategy?"*. Despite their shortcomings, Open Systems offer users a relatively low-risk path to the future. The way forward may still be unclear, but it is the direction in which industry is headed. Perhaps more important, it is what the customer wants, and, whatever the theoreticians and technicians may think, in this instance, the customer is right.

# Additional reading

Black, U., *OSI: A Model for Computer Communications Standards.* Englewood Cliffs, NJ: Prentice Hall, 1991.

Bluestein, W.M., Open Systems Agony. *The Computing Strategy Report*, Forrester Research, July 1991.

Comer, D.E., *Internetworking with TCP/IP, Volume I.* Prentice Hall, Englewood Cliffs, New Jersey, 1991.

Comer, D.E. and Stevens, D.L., *Internetworking With TCP/IP, Volume II.* Prentice Hall, Englewood Cliffs, New Jersey, 1991.

Datapro Reports, *ISO Reference Model for Open Systems Interconnection (OSI).* January 1991.

Datapro Research Group, Applications portability. *Datapro Reports on International UNIX*

*Systems* IU05-510. McGraw-Hill, Inc., Delran, New Jersey, September 1991, pp. 101-103.

Datapro Research Group, Migration to Open Systems. *Datapro Reports on International UNIX Systems* IU40-340-101. McGraw-Hill, Inc., Delran, N.J., January 1991.

Gartner Group, Building open applications - the key issues. *Software Engineering Strategies* K-950-588, August 7, 1991.

DTI - The Department for Enterprise, Migrating towards Open Systems. *The Enterprise Initiative: Open Systems Bulletin*. London: 1991.

Gray, P., *Open Systems: A Business Strategy for the 90s*. McGraw-Hill, Inc., London, 1991.

Hugo, I. *Practical Open Systems*. NCC Blackwell/Data General, 1991

Hyland, J.L. and Modahl, M.A., TCP/IP's renaissance. *The Network Strategy Report*, Forrester Research, January 1991.

Hyland, J.L. and Modahl, M.A., The LAN O/S race. *The Network Strategy Report*, Forrester Research, December 1990.

McCarthy, J.C., Demystifying OSF's DCE. *The Professional Systems Report*, Forrester Research, February 1991.

Nutt, G. J., *Open Systems*. Prentice Hall Series in Innovative Technology, Englewood Cliffs, New Jersey, 1991.

Rose, M.T., *The Open Book: A Practical Perspective on OSI*. Prentice Hall, Inc., Englewood Cliffs, New Jersey, 1990.

The Economist, Open Hokum. *The Economist*, 320:7725, September 21, 1991, p. 90.

The European Commission, *Guidelines for an Informatics Architecture*, Fourth Edition. Luxembourg, April 1990.

Rose, M.T., *The Open Book: A Practical Perspective on OSI*. Prentice Hall, Englewood Cliffs, New Jersey, 1990.

# 6

# Communications

From its beginnings in the mid-nineteenth century the number of different forms of electronic communication has grown dramatically. Figure 6.1 illustrates the growth to the end of the 1990s. In the future this growth will appear to stop. Not because communications has stopped growing but because the distinction between the forms will no longer be important. How you communicate will no longer depend on the technology but on what you want to do.

For the 1990s, the form of communication still has to be considered when making decisions about information systems. Telecommunications is increasingly pervading all parts of the world economy. The use of communications has been most intense in the services industries, such as finance, which are the fastest growing industrial sectors, but manufacturing has also become more dependent on telecommunications.

In this chapter we look more closely at telecommunications, particularly the convergence of analogue and digital transmission mechanisms. Future developments are placed in the context of Open Systems, which we discussed in the previous chapter. Different types of communication networks are examined and explained. The chapter concludes by looking at the issues which need to be considered in developing an organisation wide communication strategy.

**Figure 6.1** Expansion of telecommunication services from 1847 to the year 2000.

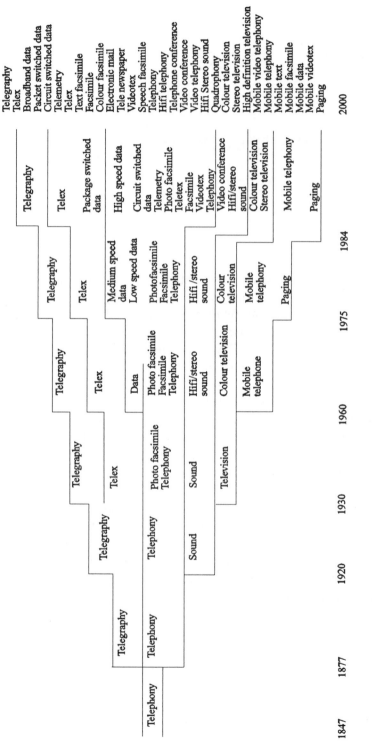

Source: *Clearing the Lines.* European Roundtable of Industrialists, November, 1986.

## 6.1  Information

Communication is the transfer of information from one place to another.  So, before we look at the means of transfer we should say what we mean by information.

Information comes in 'bits'.  A bit of information is *that required to make a choice between two (equally probable) items*.  For example the electronics of a black and white television needs one bit of information to tell it whether a particular 'dot' on the screen should be black or white.  Any piece of information can be represented by a stream of bits (a 'bitstream').

The "equally probable" comes from the fact that the television does not know beforehand whether the dot is going to be black or white but in some instances this is not true.  It is this that allows devices like videophones to use ordinary telephone lines. A telephone line does not have the capacity to carry all the information needed to show a moving picture.  However, because one picture of somebody's head looks almost the same as the previous,  a videophone can predict what the next picture will look like. So, your videophone only needs to send my videophone the changes, not the whole picture, and this is within the capacity of a telephone line.  Of course this only works if the changes are slow.  A rapid movement will defeat the videophone's attempts at prediction, as you may have noticed if you have seen a videophone.

Computers store information in devices that can be in one of two states so their storage capacity is measured in bits.  Current storage devices can store one to four megabits on a single device or 'chip'.  Within a computer, data is usually manipulated in *bytes,* either a single byte (eight bits) or two bytes (16 bits) or four bytes (32 bits).

The amount of information you need depends on what you want to know.   Some typical examples are :

| | |
|---|---|
| A bank cashpoint transaction | 1,000 bits |
| One page of electronic mail | 6,000 bits |
| One second of voice | 64,000 bits |
| One page of facsimile | 100,000 bits |
| One second of full motion video | 10,000,000 bits |

So, a bit can be part of a picture or a song or an electronic cash transfer.

It is the ability to use a computer to manipulate all types of information plus the ever decreasing cost of computer chips that is leading to the integration of voice, data, text and image.  New communication networks do not carry telephone calls or text or television, they just carry information.

However most telecommunication networks are either old or connect at some point to old networks. This places limits on the information (i.e. voice, data, video etc.) they can be expected to carry.


## 6.2  Telephone networks

A telephone network is one designed to carry human speech in a recognisable form. Its design limits are set by technology and the human ear. In practice this means sounds between 300 Hz and 4000 Hz (or 3000 Hz for some international calls) will be carried and everything else will not get through. This is why women's and children's voices, with significant elements above 4000 Hz, are more distorted by the telephone system than men's voices.

---

**Hertz**
One Hertz (Hz) is one complete vibration per second. Middle C on a piano is 440 vibrations per second or 440 Hz.

---

Modern telephone networks use digital transmission and switching. Digital signals are easier to send accurately over long distances and so give better quality voice reproduction. Digital signals can also be processed directly by modern telephone exchanges which gives very fast call connection. You may have noticed that on an increasing number of calls the distant telephone starts ringing as soon as you press the last digit of its number. You get the same quality of voice reproduction whether you are making a long distance or a local call.

With digital switching and transmission, the analogue voice signal is converted to digital form as soon as it reaches the telephone exchange. It is switched through the telephone network as a digital signal and only converted back to voice just before leaving the distant exchange. Users of the latest private exchanges may even have their voice signal converted to digital form in the handset of their telephone.

This situation can lead to some very odd results if you are trying to use the telephone network to send data (remember the example of sending data in chapter 5). Your data starts in digital form, it is converted to analogue (voice) form by a *modem* (modulator/demodulator) for the journey to the local telephone exchange. If you have listened to a data call you will have heard the 'whistling' tones generated by the modem. At the local exchange it is converted to digital form for switching. At the far end the reverse happens.

Fax is even worse. It starts with an analogue signal (the lines on your piece of paper) which is then digitised. The digital form is then converted to analogue (voice) form by a fax modem for transmission to the local telephone exchange, and so on and so on...

Since all the forms of information are switched in digital form it would seem to make sense to keep them in digital form for as long as possible: in other words get rid of the need to use modems for conversion between analogue and digital forms. This is in fact the idea behind *ISDN* (Integrated Services Digital Network). Digital signals need never be converted. Analogue signals (voice or lines on a piece of paper) are converted to digital form as soon as possible and converted back, if necessary, as late as possible. For voice this means conversion in the handset or as near as possible. For fax this could mean never being converted at all, if the lines were produced on a computer and will be viewed on a computer.

An ISDN connection is made up of two types of communication channels: *bearer channels* (called B-channels), each offering 64 kbps (kilo bits per second) capacity transmission rates to carry information; and 16 kbps *signalling channels* (called D-channels) that carry the messages that establish and control the call, including dialing the number and possible low speed data services such as security or meter reading.

At the moment there are two type of ISDN services available *Basic Rate* and *Primary Rate*. Basic Rate consists of two 64 kbps B-channels and one 16 kbps D channel. The B-channels can each can each carry a voice telephone call or data service. The D channel is used for signalling. Primary rate is aimed at business users with private telephone exchanges or large scale data transmission requirements. It consists of 30 B-channels (or 23 B-channels in the USA, Canada and Japan) and one 64 kbps D-channel (used only for signalling).

ISDN offers certain features that are not possible on conventional PSTN (Public Switched Telephone Network). They include call line identification, sub-addressing for routing calls to a particular terminal, call diversion, and three way calling.

ISDN provides the lower level services on the OSI model referred to in the last chapter. Figure 6.2 shows the functions of the various layers in the OSI model. A layered model such as OSI helps simplify the problem of using communication equipment. It allows us to mix-and-match the equipment we use and still be sure that it will work with anybody else's equipment. Layering is not a new idea, we use a layered approach to communication every time we make a telephone call - the layered telephone call example in box 6.1 explains how. Figure 6.3 show the relationship between the OSI model and ISDN standards (CCITT's I and X series). The B and D channels are shown separately along with the anticipated uses for them.

**Figure 6.2** OSI model: the functions of each layer.

| | |
|---|---|
| Application | Provides user interface to lower levels |
| Presentation | Provides data formatting and conversion |
| Session | Coordinates connection between end processes |
| Transport | Provides reliable transfer of data between end points |
| Network | Sets up, maintains and terminates connection |
| Data Link | Provides reliable data transfer across data link |
| Physical | Passes bits between devices over physical medium |

Significant among the non-voice uses of ISDN is X.25. X.25 is a standard (layers 1, 2 and 3 of the OSI model) commonly used for data networks that run alongside the telephone network. This standard is principally of interest to companies with their own data networks. Individual users still need to use the telephone network (and a modem) to gain access to X.25 networks.

**Figure 6.3** Relationship between OSI model and ISDN standards.

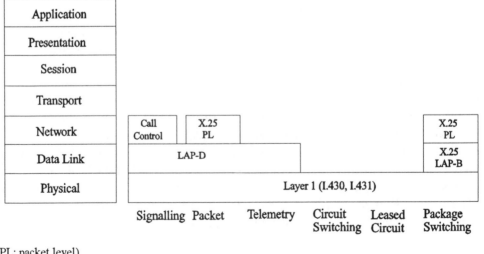

(PL: packet level)

In the course of preparing this chapter I have telephoned the editor. Though we were not particularly conscious of it we used all seven levels of the OSI model.

*Physical*
We both have telephone handsets with microphones and earpieces that are plugged in to the switched network.

*Data link*
During the call there may be crackles on the line and we will automatically adjust by raising our voices or asking the other to repeat. If it gets too noisy we hang up and try again.

*Network*
The network has a numbering (or addressing) scheme which allows me to identify the telephone that I wish to be connected to and an agreed way of starting (and stopping) the call. By exchanging signals with the network I am told that the network can accept my call (dial tone), and I tell the network the address I am calling (I dial the number) and the network tells me that it is signalling Joe that somebody is trying to talk to him (ringing tone). At the end of the call I put the telephone back on the rest.

*Transport*
I am now interested in talking to a particular person, Joe, who may or may not be the person answering the ringing telephone. To do that I exchange messages with the person answering the telephone:

Person answering: Hello, 432-1234.
Me: Hello, may I speak to Joe please.
Joe: Speaking
Me: Hi Joe, it's Ian here.

A similar exchange takes place at the end of the call so that we both know that the call is finishing rather than that we have been cut off.

*Session*
Now that contact has been made I tell Joe why I rang him and we have a conversation about it. We don't both speak at once and if one of us is speaking for a long time the other confirms that he is keeping up with occasional "Um's" and "OK's." If we do speak at once or if one of us loses track of the conversation we exchange control messages to restart the conversation, "Sorry, you first" or "I didn't follow that, can you go over it again."

*Presentation*
We both work in the same business so we know what the other means by the words used. But if we started talking about, for instance politics, we then might

totally misunderstand each other.

*Application*
Finally, the reason for the telephone conversation is to ask Joe when he needs a draft and in what format.

**Box 6.1**  A layered telephone call.

ISDN has had a shaky start and has been dogged with a number of problems:

- While ISDN has been under development the modem based technologies have advanced so far and decreased so much in cost that there is no obvious advantage to the existing user of converting to ISDN. Indeed, some modems are now capable of transmitting data at close to the speed of ISDN.

- The standards have taken a long time to emerge.

- Users expectations have faded giving way to apathy.

The problem for the phone companies trying to market ISDN is that it has no obvious single mass-market application. It can be used for video-conferencing or facsimile or low speed data transmission - but so can other types of communication lines.

## 6.3  Data networks

A data network carries data! But so can a telephone network so what is the difference? For many networks there is no difference. A typical example would be a network connecting terminals (or PCs) to a dialup information service. Here the telephone network is the data network. However the telephone network only 'knows' that it has connected two 'telephones'. In other words it only provides the bottom layers of the OSI model and strictly not even all of them.

In almost all countries, legislation means that any data network going beyond the organisation's premises has to use the telephone network for its lower levels. These data networks are referred to as Wide Area Networks (WANs).

Within an organisation's premises the data network usually takes the form of a Local Area Network (LAN). These are different from telephone networks in that they are not switched and do not have the concept of a connection. Connections are important over long distances not least so that you can be charged for the time you are connected. Within an organisation connections are less important (see box 6.2).

Establishing (and releasing) a connection between two devices takes time and involves a third device (which must be paid for). However, once the connection is established messages sent over it do not need to be individually addressed.

Connectionless communication between two devices requires a full address on each message but need not involve a third device. Each device has to 'read' the address on every message to see if it should 'open' the message.

Networks can be connectionless, for example LANs, or connection oriented, for example telephones. A corporate network linking PCs on branch office LANs to a head office database via the telephone network is a hybrid. It will also require an expensive box at the point the two types of network meet.

**Box 6.2** Connection oriented versus connectionless.

Most LANs have all the data devices (terminals, printers, PCs, mini-computers and various sorts of server) connected to a common wire. The devices are all connected all the time and send any message to every other device. Devices are expected to stick to the rules (called *protocols*) and ignore any messages that are not meant for them. (An important exception are network management devices which are designed to look at everything.)

LAN protocols have evolved from manufacturer's standards, to *de facto* market standards, to international standards. Most popular at the moment are *Ethernet*, *Token Ring* and *Token Bus* - see box 6.3 for details. These are defined by the IEEE 802 series of standards and cover levels 1, 2 and 3 of the OSI model. Originally, there was a direct relationship between the LAN protocol, the type of wire used and how the wire was laid. Now you mix-and-match to suit your needs and budget - see box 6.5 for details.

**Ethernet**
A method of networking that broadcasts messages into the 'ether' (in practice a wire of some sort). It provides rules for what to do if two devices broadcast at the same time (i.e. what to do if the messages 'collide'). Standard transmission rate is 10 Mbps but because of collisions has a much smaller capacity.

### Token Ring
A method that passes an electronic token around a ring of devices. If the token is free as it passes a device, the device may add a message. The message will then go around the ring returning to the sending device which frees the token. If the token is not free the device must wait. Standard transmission rates are 4 and 16 Mbps. Because the token passing ensures everybody gets a turn, it is better than ethernet under heavy load.

### Token Bus
A combination of ethernet and token ring. Uses a token to control message passing but with all devices connected to a common bus. Favoured for manufacturing environments where the single bus is an advantage and the token ensures each device gets a turn.

**Box 6.3** LAN protocols.

---

There are three basic wiring 'topologies' or layouts (Bus, Ring and Star) with one common variation (Star wired Ring):-

### Bus
A single common wire to which every device is connected. Typically laid around the outside of an office space. Can be laid without too much disruption. Limited in length depending on the type of wire but can be extended by using repeaters. (Repeaters are devices which boost digital signals by regenerating them.)...........

Printer                                                                    Workstation

### Ring
Like a bus but the two ends of the wire must be joined to form a ring.

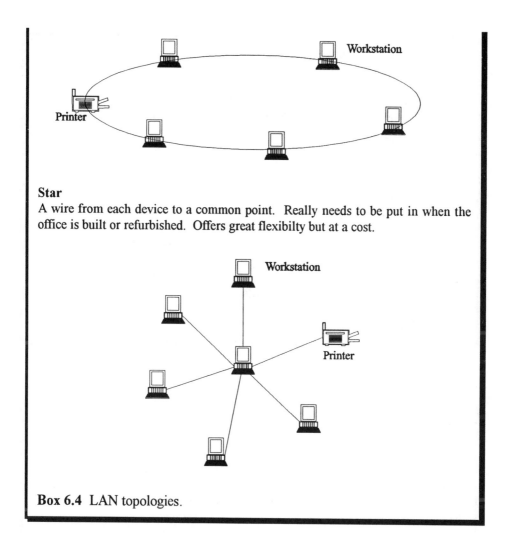

**Star**
A wire from each device to a common point. Really needs to be put in when the office is built or refurbished. Offers great flexibilty but at a cost.

**Box 6.4** LAN topologies.

LANs started small, linking a few PCs and printers. This is still a major use of LANs. However, many LANs are now anything but local and consist of interlinked networks as illustrated in figure 6.4.

A common hybrid is to have a LAN serving each floor of an office block. These floor LANs are then linked to a *backbone* LAN that connects all the floors. The backbone often uses fibre optic cable because it can be run close to electrically noisy places like lift shafts. The linking devices are called *bridges*. Similar devices called *routers* and *gateways* are used to link to networks with different protocols or to WANs - see box 6.6 for more details.

There are three basic types of wire (Twisted Pair, Co-axial and Fibre Optic Cable) with variations:

**Twisted Pair**
Otherwise telephone wire. Cheap if installed at the same time as other wiring (eg telephone) as part of the building's 'structured wiring'.

**Co-axial**
Two main sizes are thin and thick. The thick wire carries signals further without needing a repeater but cannot go around tight corners.

**Fibre Optic Cable**
Cable with several (2, 4, 6, 8 or more) optical fibres in it. Most of the cable is there to protect the optical fibres. Very good in electrically noisy environment and can carry signals a long way without needing repeaters but relatively expensive. Can support very high transmission speeds.

**Box 6.5** Wires.

---

The definitions of these terms overlap and their usage is confused even by experts.

**Bridges**
Devices that pass messages from one network to another where both networks use the same protocol. By looking at the address of the messages they can only pass on messages that are for devices connected to the other network. This means that the other network is not loaded with unnecessary messages.

**Routers**
If the device has to make a choice about which network to pass a messsage to then it is often called a router. The term can also be applied to a device that converts messages from one protocol to another to allow their transmission over another network.

**Gateways**
Devices that connect one network to a very different one, e.g. a LAN to a WAN. The term is also used to mean devices that give access to particular services often chargeable.

**Box 6.6** Bridges, routers, and gateways.

**Figure 6.4** LANs as interlinked networks.

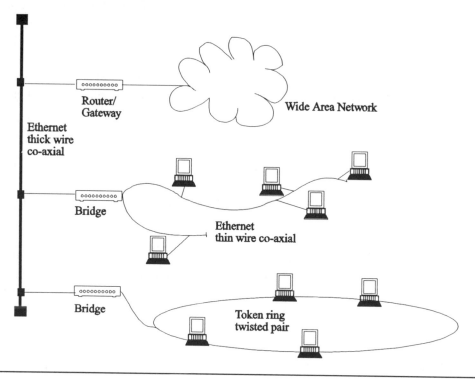

## 6.4 Broadcast vs point-to-point

Today, the majority of us receive broadcast services (television radio, videotext (e.g. Ceefax)) through the 'ether' from terrestrial or satellite transmitters. We use point-to-point services (voice telephone, video phone, facsimile, telex, data) via wires (analogue or digital telephone (ISDN)).

For those wishing to use more than the basic services this is throughly inconvenient. I do not want my roof covered in aerials and dishes each requiring its own box of electronics to decode the signal. When I make a telephone call I want to be connected to a particular person not a room where they are sometimes to be found.

It would be much more convenient to receive broadcast services by cable and point-to-point services through the 'ether'. This is beginning to happen. Some of us subscribe to cable television and so avoid the clutter. Some of us carry cellular telephones.

At the moment only relatively few people have made the switch. However this will increase as the problems of availablity and occupancy are starting to have an impact on everyday life. There is only one 'ether' through which signals can be sent but I can be connected to a virtually unlimited number of cables each of which can carry as many signals as the 'ether'. Even if I am a telephone addict most of the time I am not actually using the telephone to exchange information. Even when I am making a call I only use 30% of the capacity (50% of the time the other person is speaking and 20% of the time is pauses.) This combined with the fact that the 'ether' is everywhere means that I can share my telephone line with the rest of the world but still be telephoned anywhere in the world.

## 6.5 Where are you and where am I?

Just because you are connected to a network which is connected to the network I am connected to does not mean we can communicate!

I must know your 'address' and what you can cope with at that address. You may have a postal address (for letters), a street adddress (for visitors), a telephone number (you or your answering machine), a facsimile number (your fax or computer) and several electronic mail addresses. I know which one to use because either you told me or I looked it up in a directory.

In the past your address, including your telephone number, has been determined by your physical location. There is no technical reason why this has to be so. Provided you tell some central point where you are your address can follow you. Cellular telephones and the follow-me facility on private exchanges work in exactly this way. What we do not have yet are similar public facilities. However, proposals for the future of telephone numbers in the UK make provision for such facilities.

Modern communications also means that one can communicate from just about anywhere. From an electronic croft on a Scottish island it is possible to telephone as quickly as if one was in the same building and the PC there can be connected to the same LAN as any PC.

Of course, you may be at 39,000 feet on your way from London to Sydney!

## 6.6 Communications strategy

In the past there has been a tendency on the part of organisations to view communications as a technical issue with the only management involvement being to control costs and ensure adequate return on investment. In a heavily regulated environment without personal computers or faxes this is an understandable approach.

However, this approach is no longer appropriate. The blurring of the boundaries between the technologies and the moves towards deregulation mean that there are choices to be made that will affect the competitiveness of the organisation.

The growth of communications over the last 150 years shows no sign of stopping. The previously clear distinctions between voice, data and image are blurring. How you communicate will no longer depend on the technology but on what you want to do. So how does an organisation make the right choices.

The answer is to be as flexible as you can in your use of technology and learn how to experiment with new technologies.

Be flexible so that you do not become locked into a particular technology. This means specifying requirements at as high a level as possible, leaving you free to change the lower levels. Do not specify X.25 or ISDN to link two LANS but merely that they need linking. You can then use X.25 or ISDN or whatever gives you the greatest advantage.

Organisations find it difficult to learn. Benefits are demanded of experiments whose objective is to learn. This can make the experiment worthless as a means of learning. So, recognise technology experiments as a particular class of project that will not give a positive financial return. On the other hand they should still have fixed timescales, budgets and deliverables like any other project. In relation to the applications portfolio introduced in chapter 3, such projects would fall in the turnaround quadrant.

> In today's competitive financial market, NCB Group, the Dublin based stockbrokers - along with similiar institutions - is exercising tighter cost-controls across its operating divisions. In common with many financial houses, NCB regularly sends information and newsletters to its clients which include a wide range of Irish multinational companies, private businesses and substantial private investors.
>
> NCB is one of the first financial institutions to apply the advanced technology of AT&T's "EasyLink" services. Every Friday, two newsletters bringing clients up-to-date with key developments are sent to hundreds of companies in the UK, Europe, and the US - one deals with equity business and the other with Irish and international bond markets. A typical newsletter would run to about three pages with commentary, price changes and other data.
>
> Before the introduction of Enhanced Fax to the operation NCB used a fax card in a PC to communicate the weekly updates to its clients. Although adequate, NCB found its original system time-consuming and costly.

NCB has found that the application of AT&T's Enhanced Fax has brought cost savings and cut administrative time. The company simply keys in the list of its customers into a "mailbox" node at EasyLink, where it is stored. Since the link is held at EasyLink and not in the PC time spent on the line sending the fax is reduced considerably.

The Enhanced-Fax "broadcast" facilities uses AT&T's dedicated international fiber-optic network. The digitised transmission has an automatic error-correcting protocol which ensures a higher-than-normal quality of transmission. NCB staff no longer have to undertake a laborious Monday morning routine of manually scanning for transmissions that failed to be sent, if, for example, the receiving fax terminal was not in operation.

**Box 6.7** Stockbrokers find better way to update clients.
Source: *Financial Times*, June 18, 1992.

# 6.7 Conclusion

While the growth of communications over the last 150 years has provided an ever increasing number of options, it is the recent moves to deregulation that have allowed the consumer to choose between them. Unfortunately for the consumer now is the time that the distinction between voice, data and image are blurring.

The best advice available to the consumer, organisation or individual is to seek flexibility.

This means

- *twisted pair wiring throughout each building with at least two pairs to each workplace - one for telephone-based sevices and one for LAN-based services*
- *a star wired LAN*

- *a telephone exchange that can switch ISDN traffic (Private digital exchanges, even the most recent, do not necessarily have this capability)*

- *connecting the two with fax servers (gateways) and an X.25 gateway*

- *preferring general solutions such as scanner, personal computer and laser printer to low volume photocopiers.*

All of which means an impossibly high budget. However, there is no reason why it should not be used as the target against which compromise proposals are measured. In other words, is the saving I get adequate compensation for the loss of flexibility?

## Additional reading

Case Network Communications, *The Case Book: Computer Communications*. Case Network Communications, 1988. Available from Case Communications, Watford, UK.

Green, D., ed., *Business Guide to Communication Systems*. Pitman, 1987.

Keen. P.G.W., *Competing in Time: Using Telecommunications for Competitive Advantage*. Ballinger Publishing Co., Cambridge Mass., 1986.

Richardson, R., *Exploiting Digital Communications*. NCC Publications, 1990.

Runge, D.A. and Earl, M.J., Gaining competitive advantage from telecommunications. In M.J. Earl, ed., *Information Management: The Strategic Dimension*, Clarendon Press, Oxford, pp. 125-145.

de Woot, P., *High Technology Europe*. Basil Blackwell, 1990.

# 7

# Electronic Data Interchange (EDI)

In developing an IS/IT strategy we introduced the concept of the value system as a tool for examining the possibility of sharing or exchanging information with other organisations in the industry. Such exchange is facilitated by *interorganisational systems*: *electronic data interchange* (EDI) refers to the technical features that make such systems possible. However, as we shall see, a clear understanding of the business issues underpins any attempt to implement EDI.

This chapter sets out to explain what EDI is, why it is useful in today's business world and what sets it apart from other types of electronic communications such as electronic mail, fax, and direct computer-to-computer links. Standards are a crucial part of making EDI happen and developments in this area are examined. We look at the advantages of using EDI and the benefits, both operational and strategic, that can be expected. Organisational and management issues involved in implementing EDI are addressed. This chapter concludes by taking a brief look at developments in the emerging area of financial EDI.

## 7.1 What is EDI?

As its name suggests, EDI is concerned with the electronic interchange of data among computer systems. More specifically, EDI is defined as:

> *The transfer of structured data, from computer to computer, using agreed communications standards.*

The two key aspects of EDI that set it apart from other forms of electronic communication are:

- the information transmitted must be ***directly usable*** by the recipient's computer system without the necessity to rekey data;

- it involves a ***two or more*** organisations, or parts of an organisation, communicating with each other in a ***common agreed format***. Groups usually trade within the same industry area. Membership is normally open to anyone with the technology to connect into the network and process the data in the required format.

## Information for other computers

The first point, that the information should be directly usable by the recipient's computer system, sets EDI apart from telex, electronic mail and fax technologies. These technologies are aimed at humans who read the information and act on it accordingly.

EDI can be illustrated by the example of a supermarket chain purchasing a wide range of goods from many suppliers. The supermarket company operates a computerised stock system which keeps track of the quantity of each product in each of its outlets. The stock system detects when the quantities of product at each store fall below minimum levels. Based on its records of past stock movements and supplier/product delivery times the system determines when and in what quantities a particular product should be ordered from a supplier. Prior to EDI, the system printed purchase orders which were then mailed to the suppliers. The speed of this mail was part of the product delivery time.

With EDI the computerised stock system now electronically produces the purchase orders for each supplier in a pre-determined format. The format of this electronic purchase order is agreed between the supermarket and its suppliers. These orders are transmitted to each supplier's computer system using a telecommunications network. The supplier's computerised sales processing systems have been programmed to recognise the orders and issue the necessary instructions to have the goods produced and delivered to the supermarket stores.

In 1991, the Irish customs import and export procedures were automated using EDI technology. The new system linked together 70 customs offices and handles 2.5 million documents annually. It allows traders to submit documentation electronically and to receive clearance much more quickly than before - usually within minutes of submission.

The system was implemented on an independently managed network using open, internationally recognised, message standards. Within one year of going into operation, over eighty percent of all imports were cleared using the system and, today, every trader with a significant volume of customs entries into the Republic of Ireland has joined the system.

For the trader, the system provides a shorter and more predictable customs clearance time. For customs, the system allows officials to spend less time on routine paper handling and more time on direct customs work.

**Box 7.1** Irish customs and excise.

An alternative approach would be for the supermarket company to prepare each purchase order on a word processor, print it onto paper, and fax it to a supplier. Or if his computer system has a fax capability built in, send it directly to the supplier without having to print it out on paper. While this process involves the electronic transmission of information, it is not EDI. Even if the recipient has the capability to receive the fax and view it on screen, the contents of the purchase order will only make sense to a human operator. For this reason the information on the document would normally have to be rekeyed into the recipient's computer system.

EDI requires that the information be transmitted in a structured manner so that it can be directly used by another computer system. The example outlined above could be considered as a form of electronic mail - a direct replacement for surface mail.

### Networks of computers

The second key aspect of EDI - that it involves a group of organisations communicating with each other in a common agreed format - sets it apart from traditional computer to computer communications. These are usually set up as bilateral links between different computer systems (see figure 7.1) and may involve magnetic tape transfer or file transfer across telephone lines. For each organisation or department that you wish to communicate with, a link must be set up and maintained.

The cost of setting up and maintaining individual links to each computer system can be prohibitive and can make it difficult for new organisations to get involved.

**Figure 7.1** Bilateral links between computer systems.

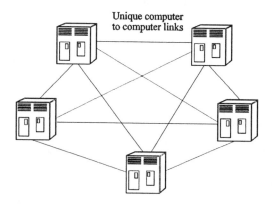

EDI, however, involves the use of a common network to which many organisations can subscribe as illustrated in figure 7.2. Messages are passed across this network in an agreed format which can be translated by anyone connected to the network.

EDI involves the use of common message structures that are suitable for computer interpretation and a network to which many organisations can subscribe. This facilitates easier and more flexible passing of information between organisations. But how does EDI work?

## 7.2 How EDI works

The concept behind EDI is very simple. Consider the case of Senderco, a company that wishes to send a message from its computer to the computer in another company called Receiverco (as shown in figure 7.3). The problem is that Senderco's computer system is completely different from Receiverco's system. So how do they do communicate?

Firstly, both companies must subscribe to a network, agree a message format that they will both use and load appropriate software on to their computer systems. This software provides translation services, EDI services and network access services which work as follows.

**Figure 7.2** EDI links between computer systems.

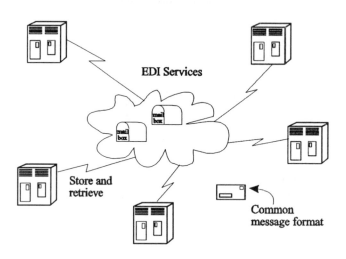

Senderco's computer system produces a message and passes it to the translation service software. This translates the message into the common agreed structure and sends it to the EDI service software. EDI services creates the commands necessary to send the message, track it, and ensure that it reaches its destination. In addition, EDI services may handle auditing and billing functions. Network access software is used to handle the actual transportation of the message across the network.

Generally speaking, EDI networks work on the principle of 'store and retrieve'. Messages are sent to 'mail boxes' that are managed by the EDI service provider. Recipients can collect messages from their mail box and translate them into their own required formats.

So in order to complete the cycle, Receiverco retrieves the message from its mail box using its network and EDI services. The structured message is then passed to Receiverco's translator where it is converted into a format understandable by Receiverco's own computer systems.

This whole process is analogous to:

writing a letter in a language such as English (*source message format*),

giving it to an interpreter (*translation services*) who translates it into a common language such as Esperanto (*common message format*), passing the letter to a secretary (*EDI services*) who puts it into a stamped, addressed envelope

giving the letter to the postal service (*network services*) for delivery.

The letter would then be delivered to the required address where another interpreter would translate it into the native language of the recipient.

---

**Figure 7.3** EDI link between Senderco and Receiverco.

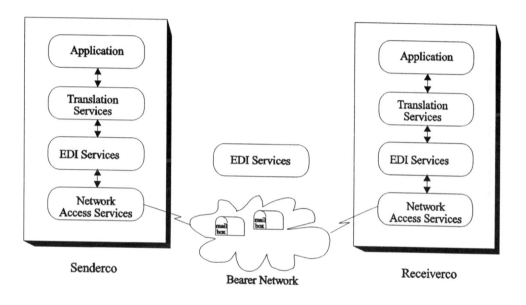

---

## 7.3 The need for standards

Standards are arguably the single most important aspect of EDI. If everybody in the world had the identical computers and identical software then EDI standards would not be required. Data could automatically be exchanged between organisations (even just by swapping floppy disks) and utilised by a range of organisations. As we have already seen in chapter 5, standards are the driving force behind the Open Systems movement.

Historically EDI was carried out by groups of companies trading within a common industry area. For example, a car manufacturer would set up EDI links with suppliers of car components. These suppliers would in turn set up EDI links with their own suppliers. And so on down the line. These groups of companies created their own message standards and often created and supported their own networks to convey the EDI messages. For example, in the car industry there is ODETTE (Organization for Data Exchange TeleTransmission in Europe); banks use SWIFT (Society for Worldwide Inter-bank Financial Telecommunications). This has led to the creation of a number of distinct national or sectoral standards groups to define the message structures.

---

There are approximately 12,000 brokers and several hundred insurance companies in the UK. Each insurance company offers a range of products. Suppose your broker is equipped with an EDI link to Brokernet, the EDI initiative for the insurance industry. The broker enters your details into a computer terminal whose screen then shows example premium quotes from a range of companies. You select a particular policy and the system asks supplementary questions. These details are then automatically sent to the insurance company and a proposal is then printed out on your broker's printer. You then sign the proposal which the broker files away. If you make a claim or change your car the EDI link enables these adjustments to be handled.

**Box 7.2** EDI in the insurance industry.

This example is adopted from: Systems are go with motor insurance pioneering the way. *Financial Times*, November 12, 1991.

---

SWIFT, for example, enables banks to send payment instructions to each other in a quick, error free way in formats each bank understands. Because these instructions come and go in easily understood formats, large amounts of automation can be applied. Rather than simply being dumped through a bank's letter box, SWIFT-type messages can be fed directly into a bank's computer systems.

The trend today, however, is for these groups to come together and to use internationally recognised message standards. The major standards setting body for commercial applications is UN/EDIFACT (United Nations/EDI for Administration, Commerce and Transport). EDIFACT comprises a set of internationally agreed standards, directions and guidelines for the electronic interchange of structured data, and in particular that related to trade in goods and services, between independent computerised systems. The other standards groupings have committed to harmonising with EDIFACT.

As with a language, EDI standards consist of grammar and a vocabulary of words. The grammar covers syntax and rules for structuring data elements in segments and in defining segments within an EDI message. The vocabulary includes a data element directory, a segment directory and a message directory. In short, standards are essential to the successful adoption of EDI.

The emergence of Value Added Network (VAN) providers, catering for many different sectors of EDI users, coupled with the adoption of internationally recognised EDI message standards, is leading to the creation of 'electronic marketplaces'. This means that companies will have unprecedented freedom to go and buy a range of products and services from around the world.

EDI VAN providers handle routing, delivery and tracking of the documents being conveyed in return for a charge. Sometimes this charge is applied to the sender alone or sometimes it is split between the sender and the receiver.

The European Commission has recognised the strategic importance of rapid and coordinated developments of EDI to improve trading relations within the community. TEDIS (Trade Electronic Data Interchange Systems) was established by the Community to promote and coordinate electronic trading within the community. The aim of TEDIS is to avoid the proliferation of closed EDI systems which are incompatible with each other and to support the use of open standards such as EDIFACT.

It must be said that not all companies are anxious to establish EDI standards. For example, when suppliers see an opportunity for 'significant' competitive advantage, it is in their interest to preempt any evolving standards and create their own proprietary protocols.

## 7.4 What are the advantages of using EDI?

EDI eliminates the paper stage of many inter and intra-departmental processes. This can lead to:

- reduced delivery times,

- increased accuracy of information,

- reductions in inventory and processing overheads,

- access to new markets.

We look at each of these in turn:

**Reduced delivery times**

In the retail industry for example, EDI can dramatically speed up the process of requesting quotations, checking stock availability, ordering stock, invoicing and payment. This can yield immediate and very tangible benefits in reducing delivery times, thus giving organisations a competitive advantage.

**Increased accuracy of information**

Increased accuracy of information reduces costs due to re-work, reshipping of goods, spoilage etc. Accurate information also leads to improved customer perceptions and avoids delays and missed business opportunities.

**Reductions in inventory and processing overheads**

Processing overheads can be reduced because EDI eliminates the need for printing, paper handling, postage and data entry. The adoption of EDI can reduce delivery times and lead to increased vertical integration among suppliers and consumers. This in turn supports just in time (JIT) resource planning and allows for reductions in inventory held, with consequent savings in overheads.

**Access to new markets**

Increasingly companies are beginning to demand EDI capabilities from their suppliers. Companies that adopt this capability early may gain access to new markets. Also as barriers to international trade come down - particularly in the EC - EDI will give access to larger and more multi-national markets.

**But there is more to EDI than performing existing business practices more efficiently.**

In chapter 2 we introduced the concept of business re-engineering. We saw that while the automation of existing business practices can yield immediate and tangible benefits, it is often the adoption of new business practices, enabled by the information technology, that creates the real paybacks and differentiates businesses from each other. Consider the following evolutionary stages of EDI within an organisation.

The first stage involves using EDI to automate some of the existing processes within a business function, for example a company that normally accepts orders by letter and keys the appropriate data into a computer system. A first implementation of EDI might allow customers to transmit orders directly into the computer system. This saves effort on rekeying data and allows for orders to be filled more quickly.

The next stage is when a company automates all of the processes in a business function. Consider again the company in the above example. If it now decides to insist that its own suppliers implement EDI links, it can change its computer systems to take advantage of the increased integration by automatically reordering stock replenishments without human intervention. This involves using software that checks the availability of stock at each supplier and makes a purchasing 'choice' based on a set of business rules. Knowing that it can replenish its own supplies quickly, the company can afford to maintain much smaller stocks onsite: facilitating just-in-time ordering and supply.

---

**Stage 1**  Automating some of the existing processes in a business function.

**Stage 2**  Automating all of the processes in a business function.

**Stage 3**  Changing the way that the business function is performed.

**Stage 4**  Performing new business functions.

**Box 7.3** Evolution of EDI within an organisation.

---

The third step involves leveraging EDI to enable the technology to change the way business is done. EDI enables organisations to change the way business functions are performed. The availability of up-to-the-minute information can enable the reduction and elimination of many of the steps that were required previously. An example of this might be a manufacturing company that moves towards 'build to order' instead of 'build to plan'. This is made possible because the manufacturing company knows that it can use EDI to reduce the turnaround time between receiving an order and manufacturing and dispatching the goods. Switching to a 'build to order' philosophy can result in significant reductions in inventory overhead and wastage due to obsolescence.

The final step in the evolution of EDI may well be in the creation of new business. Consider 'follow-the-sun' trading on the world's financial markets. EDI enables large organisations to keep their money working for them around the clock by shifting from market to market around the world. This is an example of a new type of business that simply wasn't possible before the widespread use of EDI.

A final word on the evolution of EDI. While EDI is generally associated with external communications between organisations, it may actually deliver most business benefit for internal communications among different departments within an organisation. These departments may exist within the same country or they may reside in several countries.


## 7.5  Value-adding partnerships

While it is true that a telecommunications network is usually a main feature of the implementation of EDI, technical facilities can be obtained quite easily from third party sources.    EDI is more concerned with purchasing policy, customer-supplier relationships, and an awareness of the industry at large.   There is a suggestion that EDI applications, rather than being a competitive weapon, are increasingly a necessary way of doing business.[1]

The sharing of information is probably the most significant strategic benefit of EDI.  It enables the cultivating of a closer relationships with both suppliers and customers along the value system.   Johnson and Lawerence[2] have coined the term *value-adding partnership* (VAP) to describe such relationships, which are more than just conventional EDI links.   They depend largely on the attitudes and practices of the participating organisations' management.

Effective management of the supply chain is seen as one of the key areas in increasing competitiveness in the 1990s.  By identifying key customers and working more closely with them, some organisations are striving for more stability in their markets through longer-term relationships.  A VAP is a manifestation of a strategic alliance strategy which we discussed in chapter 2.


## 7.6  Issues involved with adopting EDI

Implementing EDI in an organisation raises a number of issues.


### Legal issues

There are two sets of legal relationships to be considered:

- between trading partners,

- between users and providers of EDI services.

The first thing to consider when adopting EDI is whether it changes the legal position between two trading partners. For example, in some countries a written signature is necessary to secure a legal contract. Generally speaking however, if EDI is simply automating existing methods of doing business then there should be little impact on the underlying contractual arrangements. Where EDI is being used to do business in a fundamentally different way, then the legal and contractual obligations are affected in a much greater way. For example, if a company has up-to-the-minute information on the inventory holdings of its suppliers then it may be obliged not to disclose this information to other parties.

The other main area that needs to be considered is the relationship between users of an EDI service and the EDI service providers. It is possible for the EDI service to become the life blood of companies involved in electronic trading. Missing or inaccurate information could have severe financial consequences for these companies. However, in most cases the EDI service providers bear little or none of the responsibility for lost or corrupted messages. The main reason quoted for this is that EDI service providers charge a relatively small amount per transaction and that if they were to take on more of the responsibility then they would have to charge more for their services.

## Data protection / security

Data protection and privacy of personal data also needs to be catered for in EDI networks. Many countries now have laws governing the use and dissemination of data. In addition, companies must be in a position to ensure that data sent and received is from an authorised source and has not been tampered with in any way. Issues relating to security are discussed in chapter 8.

## Auditing and tracking

Often regulatory and taxation authorities need access to auditing and tracking information to ensure legal business practices are being adhered to and to calculate Value Added Tax. This may mean that the EDI services need to track this information in a secure way.

## Service levels

Competing EDI service providers may offer different guaranteed service levels. It is important for users of the service to ensure that the chosen provider can offer a suitable service and that they are not paying for higher service levels than their own computer systems can handle. In particular, it is important to make sure that when more than one network is connected that the overall service levels are not unacceptable.

### Organisational issues

Companies that wish to take full advantage of EDI may begin to change the ways in which they do business. This can lead to re-engineering of the business processes used in the firm. This in turn can have a large organisational impact in terms of changing job functions, eliminating certain types of job and creating new roles in the organisation.

## 7.7 Financial EDI

The advent of electronic trading is bringing pressure on banks to provide a similiar type of service. Instead of paying by cheque, organisations would issue an electronic payment instruction to their bank to take money from their account and transfer it to the account of the payee. This is the so called *closing of the loop*. Financial EDI entails issuing payment instructions and sending remittance information electronically to the bank. Figure 7.4 illustrates the movement of information between two organisations and the positioning of financial EDI. Box 7.4 outlines how one organisation is using financial EDI.

---

**Figure 7.4** Using financial EDI.

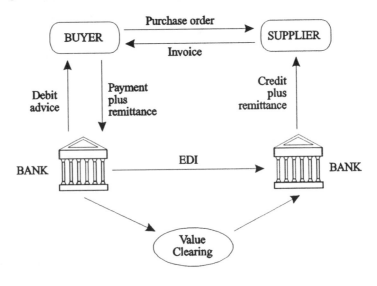

---

Norwich Health Authority purchases goods and services in large volumes, from life saving drugs to office equipment. The Authority deals with up to 5,000 suppliers. This presents major administration problems for the accounts payable department which has to generate thousands of payments and remittance advices every month. Payments are typically to a high volume of small suppliers. While commercial EDI has been embraced by a large number of their suppliers, financial EDI is being adopted by a few.

In association with Barclays Bank a financial EDI service is being promoted. NHA now transmits all its payment instruction and remittance information as EDI transactions. NHA's suppliers, if EDI users and customers of Barclays or Lloyds Bank, will receive payment and remittance information from Barclays electronically. The remaining suppliers will receive the same advice on paper, printed and mailed by Barclays.

**Box 7.4** The Norwich Health Authority settlement system.
Source: *Electronic Trader*, July-August, 1991; *British Journal of Healthcare Computing*, March, 1991.

It must be said that making payments "electronically" is nothing new. Banks have been making payments between themselves in such a manner for a long time. In the UK, the Banks Automated Clearing System (BACS) has been in existence since the early 1970s and settles volumes of regular payments. Direct debits and salary payments are all generally paid via the BACS system. For high value payments, the UK clearing banks introduced CHAPS (the Clearing House Automated Payment System) for same day settlements. SWIFT offers automated clearing for international payments.

Banks have been slow to take up EDI despite the fact that most of their business is built around complex and expensive communication systems. Corporate users have also been hesitant in asking for an EDI type service from the banks. Debate rages over whether payments by EDI offer real benefits over existing payment mechanisms, and whether the payor or payee should bear the cost.

Financial EDI is different from commercial EDI because there are three parties involved, the bank, the payor and the payee, and it is the supplier (the payee) who gains most benefit from settlements by EDI. Yet, it is the buyer (the payor) who bears the most cost but receives the least benefit. This is an inhibitor in the move towards financial EDI as it is the customer who is the driver for commercial EDI. The customer may not see much benefit in closing the loop. It is likely that this problem could be overcome with buyers and sellers building a value-adding partnership, in which both sides benefit from the various aspects of EDI in each part of the trading cycle: the purchase order, invoice, and payment.

Financial EDI presents a major opportunity for organisations to "re-engineer" how they conduct business. By that we mean that existing ways of paying can be obliterated, cutting out existing processes, not just automating existing paper-flows. The practice of self-billing is now in widespread use in the motor industry. This gets rid of the invoice altogether and therefore the need to reconcile it with the payment.

## 7.8 Conclusions

It is increasingly likely that in the future EDI will become the language of business.

- *EDI is a business decision, not a technical decision.*

- *To be successful EDI requires building closer relationships with buyers and suppliers.*

- *Use EDI as an enabler of change in how your organisation currently conducts business.*

## Notes

1    R.I Benjamin, D.W. DeLong, and M.S. Scott Morton, Electronic Data Interchange: how much competitive advantage? *Long Range Planning*, **23**, 1, 1990, pp. 29-40.
2    R. Johnson and P.R. Lawerence, Beyond vertical integration - the rise of the value-adding partnership. *Harvard Business Review*, July-August, 1988, pp. 94-101.

## Additional reading

**General**

Barrett, S. and Konsynski, B.R., Inter-organization information sharing systems. *MIS Quarterly*, December, 1982, pp. 93-105.
Business Week, An electronic pipeline that's changing the way America does business. *Business Week*, 3rd August, 1987, pp. 80-81 .
Bytheway, A. and Dyer, B., EDI: Persuading senior management. *EDI Europe: COMPAT '90*, Blenheim Queensdale Ltd., 1990, pp, 125-134.
Ives, B. and Learmonth, G.P., The information system as a competitive weapon. *Communications of The ACM*, **27**, 12, 1984, pp. 1193-1201.
Malone, T.W., Yates, J. and Benjamin, R.I., *Electronic markets and electronic hierarchies.* Centre for Information Systems Research, Working Paper 86-018, Sloan School of Management, MIT, Cambridge Mass., April, 1986.

## EDI and business strategy

Benjamin, R.I, DeLong, D.W, and Scott Morton, M.S., Electronic data interchange: how much competitive advantage. *Long Range Planning*, **23**, 1, 1990, pp. 29-40.

Dearing, B., The strategic benefits of EDI. *The Journal of Business Strategy*, January-February, 1990, pp. 4-6.

Hirschheim, R. and Adams, D., Organizational connectivity. *Journal of General Management*, **17**, 2, 1991, pp. 65-76.

Konsynski, B.R and McFarlan, F.W., Information partnerships - shared data, shared scale. *Harvard Business Review*, September-October, 1990, pp. 114-120.

Robinson, D.G. and Stanton, S.A., Exploit EDI before EDI exploits you. *Journal of Information Strategy*, Spring, 1987, pp. 23-35.

## Implementing EDI

Bytheway, A., EDI: managing the costs and benefits. *EDI 91 Proceedings*, pp. 60-79.

Parfett, M., *The EDI Implementors' Handbook*. NCC Blackwell, 1992.

## Financial EDI

Ahwesh, P.C., Who pays for risk in worldwide EFT networks. *Information Strategy: The Executive's Journal*, Spring, 1991, pp. 21-26.

Golden, C.E., Making General Motors and America more competitive through Financial EDI and EFT. *EDI FORUM*, 1990 Issue, pp. 24-30.

Hill, N.C. and Ferguson, D.M., The EDI revolution and bank strategy. *EDI FORUM*, 1991 Issue, pp 38-40.

Lamond, A. and Davis, R.H., Electronic funds transfer in the UK banking system. *International Journal of Information Management*, **11**, 2, 1991, pp. 105-125.

Laurie, B., The burning issue of supervision. *Financial Times*, 13 November, 1991.

# 8

# Information Systems Security

The last decade has witnessed dramatic developments in information technology. The personal computer has made computing accessible to business of all sizes. Technological advances have made computers more powerful and less expensive. Communications technology, which we looked at in chapter 5, has also advanced, enabling systems to be linked together within organisations, across organisations and even across national borders.

However, the most dramatic developments have been in the exploitation of technology by business. Business managers have identified information technology as being one of the critical success factors for the business, and have used IT as a weapon in the battle to obtain competitive advantage (see chapter 3).

Thus, information systems have been transformed from being the means of merely accounting for business transactions, to being the medium through which business is conducted. As a result, information systems play a central role in the operation of the business. There are many illustrations of this phenomenon:

- the banking industry is now heavily dependent on technology as a trading mechanism through its ATMs, on-line bank services, and home banking;

- in the retail sector, bar code equipment is increasingly used at customer checkout desks to speed up customer service and to enable stock records to be maintained in realtime;

- in the insurance industry, the provision of online services by insurance companies to their brokers is becoming commonplace.

These developments have resulted in much greater interconnectivity of the information systems used by business enterprises, and in greater reliance on systems and information provided by third parties. This trend is set to continue as organisations move towards electronic data interchange (EDI), which involves the replacement of paper documents with electronic documents (see chapter 7).

The consequence of these developments is that modern business is now utterly dependent on its information systems. A disruption to the core systems used by a business can have an immediate impact on its trading activities, and is likely to be directly visible to the outside world in general, and to suppliers, customers, and employees in particular.

Information systems are also more vulnerable than heretofore. The opening up of information systems through, for example, the provision of online facilities to customers and suppliers, has increased the risk of systems being accessed directly by third parties, making them more vulnerable to attack from outside. Modern information systems are also more complex to construct, operate and maintain, and as a result, there is a greater exposure to technical error and loss of skilled and highly specialised staff. New threats have emerged - such as the computer virus.

The utter dependence of business on its information systems, and the increased vulnerability of these systems to disruption, means that *security* is now a topic which should be high on every business manager's agenda.

## 8.1 The business needs for security

How serious is the security problem? Unfortunately, there are few reliable statistics to illustrate the importance of security to modern business.

Organisations are reluctant to publish details of security incidents which have occurred, partly because of the knock-on effect this may have on shareholder, customer and public confidence, and also because of the embarrassment caused by making such events public knowledge.

| Type of risk | Type of loss | | | | |
|---|---|---|---|---|---|
| | A Physical damage | B Increased cost and consequential loss | C Loss of money and goods | D Other losses | E Total losses |
| 1. Physical accident | 380 | 650 | | 50 | 1,080 |
| 2. Theft, sabotage | 35 | 30 | | | 65 |
| 3. Breakdowns, malfunction | | 1,025 | | | 1,025 |
| 4. Errors - data capture, transmission | | 660 | 120 | 20 | 800 |
| 5. Logic errors | | 300 | 20 | | 320 |
| 6. User errors | | 450 | 100 | 70 | 620 |
| 7. Fraud | | 350 | 1,250 | 100 | 1,700 |
| 8. Copying, theft of information | | 220 | 40 | 50 | 310 |
| 9. Copying software | | 1,050 | 150 | | 1,200 |
| 10. Human factors - strikes, loss of key people | | 90 | | | 90 |
| 11. Other. | | | | | |
| Total | 41 | 4,885 | 1,680 | 29 | 7,270 |

**Box 8.1** Estimated losses due to information system security breaches (France 1986). Statistics published by the *APSAIRD* organisation in France.

However, statistics prepared by APSAIRD (an association of French insurance companies) do illustrate the types of security breaches and scale of damage which can be caused. They indicate that the problem is a significant one and it is also notable that the scale of losses reported by APSAIRD has been on the increase. (See box 8.1 and figure 8.1.)

In overall terms, there are two ways in which organisations may suffer harm from breaches in the security of their information systems:

- direct loss, and

- consequential loss.

**Direct loss**

The development and operation of an information system requires a significant investment of funds and manpower. Accordingly the system is itself an asset in its own right which needs to be protected against damage, theft, destruction and other physical threats.

**Figure 8.1** Estimated losses due to information systems security breaches.

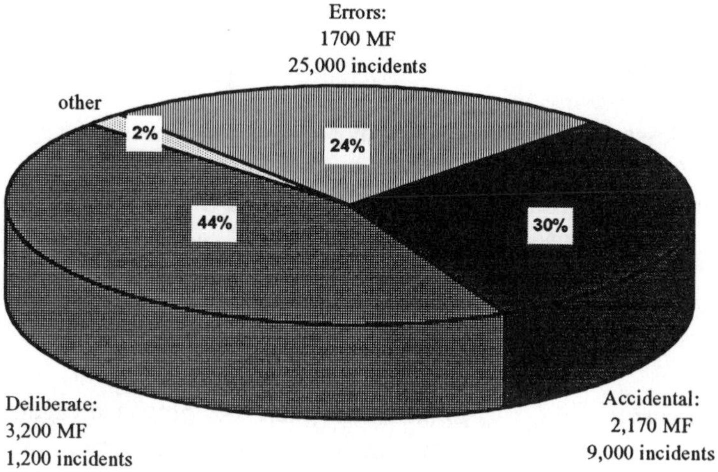

Errors:
1700 MF
25,000 incidents

other

2%

24%

44%

30%

Deliberate:
3,200 MF
1,200 incidents

Accidental:
2,170 MF
9,000 incidents

MF=Million Francs
Source: *APSAIRD*, France, 1986.

There are five main elements of the system which need to be protected:

- *Hardware*  being processors, workstations, disks, tapes and communications equipment and lines.

- *Software*  being system software (e.g. the operating system) and application software (e.g. the accounts payable application).

- *Physical Environment*  being computer rooms, communication rooms, air conditioning and power supply equipment.

- *Documentation*  being system and program specifications, file definitions, operating procedures and user manuals.

- *People*  being operators, technical and support staff, management and users.

The statistics reveal that direct losses actually only account for a very small proportion (a little over 5%) of the aggregate losses arising from security branches.

## Consequential loss

Consequential losses, however, are much more significant.

Firstly, an organisation can suffer harm if either the confidentiality or integrity of the **information** is compromised:

- *Confidentiality*    sensitive information should only be disclosed to authorised individuals

- *Integrity*    information must be protected against accidental error, and also against deliberate manipulation, for example to perpetrate or conceal a fraud.

Secondly, harm can be caused due to the services provided by an information system (the Application Services) not being available.

In summary then, there are three properties which need to be protected:

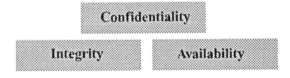

The extent to which consequential losses represent the greater part of the total losses associated with security breaches, underlines the dependence of modern business on these three properties.

However, the relative importance of confidentiality, integrity, and availability will vary significantly from business to business, and indeed from system to system. The potential business consequences of fraudulent manipulation of information in a funds transfer system, for example, are likely to be much more serious than the potential consequences which could arise within a manufacturing system.

To establish controls which provide adequate protection in a cost effective manner, management must have a clear understanding of its dependence on the confidentiality, integrity and availability of its information. To obtain this understanding, the business consequences of a security breach affecting each of the properties must be separately analysed. Business consequences may, in fact, be in three different forms:

- operational consequences, eg. the inability to deliver goods or to provide services, or the need to invoke recovery procedures;

- intangible consequences, eg. the loss of customer confidence, embarrassment, damage to reputation, increased risk of fraud; or

- financial losses arising from the operational and intangible consequences, eg. loss of profits because of reduced sales, lost interest through diversion of funds, additional staffing costs through the need to invoke recovery procedures.

## 8.2 The legal requirements for security

The legislators have started to recognise the need for security of information systems. Data Privacy legislation has been enacted in a number of European countries including Denmark, France, Germany, Luxembourg, the Netherlands, Portugal, Ireland and the UK. The legislation has been enacted because it is considered necessary to protect individuals against threats to their privacy arising from the processing of personal information on computer systems:

- the unfair collection of personal information,

- the existence of inaccurate or out-of-date personal data,

- the use of personal data for inappropriate purposes, or

- failure to preserve confidentiality of sensitive personal information.

In some countries, however, the legislation requires that organisations must have appropriate security measures in place to protect against unauthorised access to data, and against their accidental alteration, disclosure or destruction. Thus modern businesses in many countries now have a legal obligation to properly secure their computer systems, with the prospect of penalties for the entity or its officers in the event of non-compliance.

The actual provisions enacted in the different countries actually vary quite significantly. In some instances, for example, organisations must obtain explicit approval for the transfer of data outside their national borders. In others, such approval is not explicitly required. The European Commission has identified this as being a matter of concern and, at the time of writing, is working on a directive which will harmonise and increase the potency of legislation across the member states. The European Commission has also initiated research into legislation on IS/IT security across the member states, and it is likely that further directives will emerge on this topic in the future. (See figure 8.2.).

All of these developments are having a positive impact through creating a greater awareness of the importance of maintaining secure computer systems. A side effect, however, is that modern business, company directors and business managers will be obliged to comply with an increasing number of legal and regulatory requirements, and to operate within the constraints arising from these provisions.

## 8.3  Threats to information systems

Attitudes to security have been coloured by the media attention given to particular kinds of security threat. Media coverage has concentrated particularly on newsworthy incidents which have caused major disruptions to computer systems. Thus, there is widespread awareness of the havoc which fire, flooding, hacking and the computer virus can cause to computer systems.

Certainly these are major threats against which computer systems must be protected. However, it is important to recognise that a threat constitutes **any** means through which the confidentiality, integrity or availability of information or information systems can be impaired. This brings into play a plethora of threats many of which are easy to overlook. They include:

- natural and man-caused disaster

- human error

- deliberate manipulation of data and programs

- wilful destruction of computer materials and data.

The range of threats is too numerous to mention or describe (see box 8.2). Further, we have witnessed the emergence of new and potent threats, such as the computer virus, and it is likely that additional threats will become apparent as technology develops through the 1990s.

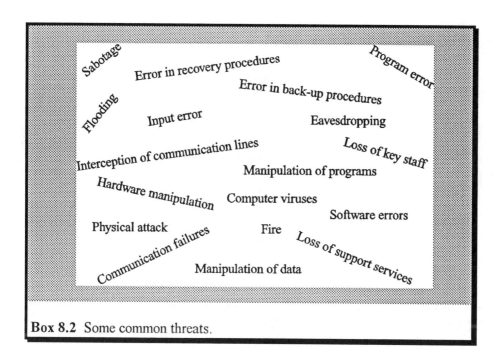

**Box 8.2** Some common threats.

Whilst it is impractical to identify all threats, it is desirable to establish a balanced set of controls which combined together:

(a) **prevent** threats from affecting the confidentiality, integrity or availability of information systems;

(b) **detect** their occurrence if they do manage to infiltrate the protective shield; and

(c) minimise the impact on the business by having appropriate procedures to **recover** from such a breach arising.

**Figure 8.2** The security environment.

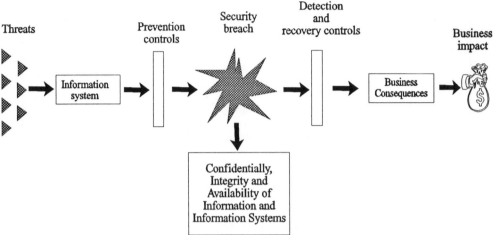

Based on a model developed by the European Security Forum in a research project entitled
*Establishing a Risk Analysis Method Which is Easy to Understand and Simple to Apply.*

Hacking has become a significant threat to computer systems. "Hacking" is the
term coined to describe intruders gaining access to a computer system through the
telephone network. Typically, the hacker uses a PC, a modem and a telephone to
contact a computer system and then gain access to programs or data by infiltrating
the password controls.

Hacking is a particular concern for computer systems which provide dial-up access
to employees, maintenance engineers or third parties such as customers or
suppliers. Techniques are available to control these threats - some involve the use
of hardware devices which are carried by the authorised user and are used to
authenticate his validity. Smart Card technology is also emerging as a more
reliable means of authenticating users. However, the simplest way of minimising
this risk is the elimination of dial-up access, or the establishment of dial back
procedures (where the operator or computer dials back the person attempting to
gain access).

**Box 8.3** Hacking.

The computer virus emerged as a threat in the late 1980s, and has developed into a serious threat to the security of information systems.

The virus is a hidden program code which is designed to copy itself without the user knowing about it. Viruses are most common in PC based systems where users frequently load new programs to their systems, often from diskettes borrowed or copied from other users, or received free-of-charge (public domain software).

At some stage, the virus is activated; in some cases this results in obscure messages appearing on the screen. In others data and programs are corrupted or deleted causing serious problems for the user.

The virus problem has escalated to the point where there are now over 1,000 of them in circulation, originating from all corners of the world.

Sensible precautions can help to minimise the risk of viruses:

- prohibit the use of non-authorised software on PCs (e.g. games etc);

- centrally control the purchase of PC software;

- install virus protection and detection software on all PCs; and

- regularly back up program and data files.

**Box 8.4** The computer virus.

## 8.4 The establishment of secure information systems

Against this background, it is more important than ever to establish secure information systems. The "House Model"[1] is one conceptual framework which can provide a useful basis for considering how secure systems can be built in any organisation.

### The bedrock

A pre-condition to the establishment of sound security is general agreement as to what the term "security" actually means. Surprisingly, until quite recently no such consensus existed and invariably discussions on the subject were at cross-purposes. However, the following definition has now received quite widespread acceptance:

*Information Systems Security is the protection of the confidentiality, integrity and availability of information processed by an information system, and of the information system itself.*

The adoption of this definition is a useful starting point for any organisation wishing to establish a suitable framework for the security of its information systems.

---

**Figure 8.3** A framework for information system security.

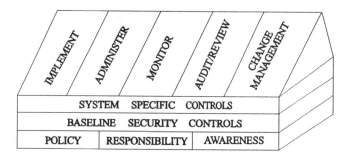

Source: *The Security of Network Systems - A Study on Behalf of the European Communities.* Coopers & Lybrand, United Kingdom.

---

**Foundation**

The first layer of the House Model represents the foundation upon which the sound security is built. There are three elements of the foundation:

- security policy

- responsibilities

- security awareness.

A *security policy* is a formal statement expressing the organisation's commitment to the establishment of secure information systems. The statement should be approved by management at the highest level, preferably the chief executive officer. The existence of such a policy demonstrates to all personnel the importance of maintaining a secure environment, and provides managers with the necessary authority to managers to implement the procedures and controls which are required. A security policy should be brief, but should include statements of *principle*, of *direction* and of *responsibility*.

**Responsibilities** for security should be allocated to specific individuals or functions within the organisation. The following matters need to be considered when allocating responsibilities:

(a) Business management should have a role in defining security requirements. Business managers are clearly better placed to assess the consequences of breaches in security, and therefore to determine the relative priorities attaching to different aspects of security.

(b) Senior management should play a role in monitoring the adequacy of security arrangements. Security is now of such fundamental importance to major organisations that it merits some consideration by very senior management, perhaps even by the board of directors.

In many organisations nowadays, a *security committee* oversees the security arrangements. Such a committee would typically comprise representatives of the major business units, the significant business functions, eg. finance, human resources, internal audit, the IT function and security personnel. A high level security committee is commended because it provides a sound mechanism for dealing with security problems which have implications across the different business units and functions. In addition, security projects may involve major capital expenditure and the security committee provides a basis for assessing such expenditure proposals in the overall corporate context.

(c) Responsibilities should be allocated to specific individuals or functions with the skills, authority and tools necessary to fulfil them.

(d) Ideally, responsibilities should be specifically allocated to cover the following aspects of security:

- research and development - monitoring the availability of methods, techniques and tools within the market to address security needs;

- the implementation of security procedures and controls;

- operations - the performance of day-to-day security procedures and controls;

- monitoring the performance of supervisory procedures on a day-to-day basis, to ensure that security procedures and controls continue to operate as intended;

- audit/review - the periodic examination of security arrangements to provide independent assurance that procedures and controls operate as intended.

A high level of **security awareness** is also a pre-requisite to establishing secure information systems.  Personnel who have access to information should be aware of the importance of security to the overall business goals, and should also have a positive attitude towards complying with the security practices, procedures and controls which have been established.

To meet this end, many organisations have initiated security awareness programmes. Such programmes involve the publication of brochures, posters and other advertising materials, the use of corporate videos and the mounting of training courses for personnel of all levels.  The use of these techniques needs to be carefully thought out. A different blend of techniques may be desirable for different target audiences and in overall terms a "drip-drip" approach is likely to be more effective than the "big bang" approach.

## Baseline controls

A control is a policy, method, procedure, device or programmed mechanism which satisfies the security requirements of an organisation.   These controls may be categorised as:

- baseline controls; and

- system specific controls.

*Baseline controls* should be installed based on prudent business management rather than on detailed cost benefit analysis.   They are the safeguards which generally accepted good practice indicates should be established regardless of the nature of the information systems, or of the underlying risks associated with the information system. They are the controls which are self-evidently sensible in any situation.

The concept of baseline controls is powerful, notwithstanding the fact that there are few formally documented and agreed checklists of what constitutes baseline controls. In the absence of such checklists, baseline controls must be implemented based on the judgement and expertise of managers responsible for security in their organisations. Typically such controls are required for the following areas:

- software development, implementation and maintenance

- hardware installation

- physical protection of computer equipment, communications equipment and lines

- logical protection of access to programs, data files and user facilities

- procedures governing operation of the computer and the usage of applications, and

- disaster recovery and business continuity plans.

Aspects of these controls impact on all areas within the organisation, for example, the computer department, the systems development department, the user department, etc.


## System specific controls

System specific controls are required to meet the specific security needs of the organisation. These are the controls, over and above baseline controls, which are necessary because the risks merit specific protection.

Organisations should use a systematic risk analysis process to determine their requirements for system specific controls. Ideally, risk analysis techniques will be used during the system's development life cycle, ie. when the requirements for the application are being defined, and during detailed design and implementation. In addition, risk analysis can provide a useful basis for reviewing the adequacy of security in respect of application systems which are already in use.

Risk analysis, however, is not widely used by commercial organisations. Whilst the requirement for risk analysis is generally accepted, existing methodologies can be time consuming, cumbersome and complicated to use and therefore difficult to justify. The author has been involved in the development of a method which is "easy to understand and simple to use". It is hoped that the emergence of more pragmatic methodologies may facilitate the more widespread usage of risk analysis in commercial and other organisations across Europe.

Risk analysis is the process through which security risks associated with an information system can be understood, thus enabling the security requirements to be properly determined. When this process is being completed the alternative control techniques must be examined and the most appropriate one selected. This typically requires some form of cost benefit analysis where the cost is the initial and ongoing cost of maintaining the control, and the benefit is the reduced impact of a potential breach in security, and/or the reduced likelihood of such an event actually occurring.

The combination of baseline and system specific controls should result in the implementation of a balanced set of controls which:

- prevents security breaches from arising

- detects, on a timely basis, such breaches when they arise

- facilitates the timely recovery from such security breaches.

### Management processes

Once a secure environment has been established, it must be adapted to take account of changes in the business environment, system changes, changes in the security environment and security incidents which may arise from time to time. Management processes must therefore be established to ensure the ongoing maintenance of a secure environment. These processes have been identified as being:

- implement

- administer

- monitor

- audit/review, and

- change management.

Thus security must be seen to be a continuous process and for this reason it is important that security considerations are incorporated into standard business practice throughout each organisation.

## 8.5 Summary

In summary, the modern business is heavily dependent on the security of its information systems. Senior managers should take positive steps to ensure that their information systems are properly protected. This will involve, inter alia, the establishment of sound structures for dealing with security - through defining security policy, clearly allocating responsibilities and maintaining a high level of security awareness. It will also involve monitoring of risks and of the adequacy of the security arrangements on an ongoing basis.

Taking security seriously will not result in all of the risks being eliminated. But it will enable the risks to be recognised, understood and appropriate safeguards put in place so that they are reduced to manageable proportions.

## Note

1   Based on a model developed by the European Security Forum in a research project entitled *Establishing a Risk Analysis Method Which is Easy to Understand and Simple to Apply.*

## Additional reading

Agranoff, M.H., Controlling the threat to personal privacy. *Journal of Information Systems Management*, Summer, 1991, pp. 48-52.
Edwards, C.E., Savage, N. and Walden, I., *IT and the Law*, 2nd Edition.  Macmillan Publishers, 1990.
Schwartz, M., Computer security: planning to protect corporate assets. *The Journal of Business Strategy*, January-February, 1990, pp. 38-41.

# 9

# Trends in Manufacturing Systems Management

*A company's manufacturing function is either a competitive weapon or a corporate millstone. It is seldom neutral...*

Quoted from Wickham Skinner, Manufacturing - missing link in corporate strategy, *Harvard Business Review*, 1969.

To be an effective weapon, manufacturing must surpass the competition in providing products to the customer. Superior performance is the result of action. The most intelligent foundation for action is a deep understanding of the entire production system combined with accurate and timely information. The understanding keeps the manufacturing weapon powerful, while the information keeps the manufacturing weapon sharp.

The purpose of manufacturing is to provide products for customers - customers who are free to select products from those offered by a range of competitors. To attract and retain customers products must be better than those available from competitors - better in terms of design, quality, or price; or better because the manufacturer can provide the product faster or more dependably than the competition. To survive the company must be able to provide these products at a profit, which means that cost must be lower than price.

To meet such stringent demands, a firm requires a great deal of information. Information about customers and their needs, information about competitors, information about available production technology, information about material suppliers, information about the work force, information about the production processes within the organisation.

The manufacturing function translates this information into products. To accomplish this, the information must be collected, transmitted, stored, recovered, understood and used. Information is used to coordinate the various activities of the firm - to tell employees what action to take and when to take it - so that each action supports the overall goal of making products for customers. To understand how information is used by a manufacturing organisation, this chapter starts with a discussion of manufacturing as an operating system and presents several historical trends in manufacturing. To develop this understanding, the impact of seven modern trends in manufacturing will be reviewed. Several lessons, drawn from the review, will be summarised in the conclusion.

## 9.1 Developing a systemic view of manufacturing

A manufacturing organisation can be modelled as an open system. The four walls of the factory and its adjoining offices provide a fairly clear system boundary. The people, machines and materials in the factory are the elements of the system. Manufacturers combine various inputs (people, information, energy, materials, and equipment) into outputs (products, information and, unfortunately, waste). The inputs and the outputs come into the system from its environment. This is illustrated in figure 9.1. Each of the inputs has dimensions of time and money. One of the major challenges in managing a manufacturing system is coordinating the activities of each of the component parts.

In manufacturing the basic material inputs are converted into physical products. The transformation of materials by the people and the equipment is usually done in a series of production processes. Each of these processes can be seen as sub-systems of the overall manufacturing system. The case in box 9.1 illustrates the example of an automobile assembly plant which is then shown as a system in figure 9.2.

**Figure 9.1**  Elements of a manufacturing system.

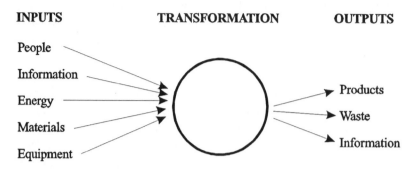

An automobile is made of many parts, made of several materials, including sheet steel, cast steel, glass, copper, plastic, rubber, and many more.  Many types of machines are needed to convert these materials into an automobile, including steel presses, welding machines, drills and conveyer belts.  Energy is needed to run the machines.

Building a car also requires people, with special skills and talents.  Some of the people are used to run the machines and transform the materials.  Other employees plan and coordinate the activities.  What to produce is determined by information about what style and colour of cars are wanted by customers.

Many of the parts that make up an automobile are produced at different production plants.  Engines may be made at one plant and transmissions made at another.  All of these component parts come together at the final assembly plant.

In the assembly plant coils of sheet steel are pressed into the steel parts which make up the frame, the floor, the side panels, the doors, the bonnet, the boot and the roof.  These parts are welded together in the welding shop and finished.  The completed body is then coated and painted.  On the assembly line all of the parts - the wiring, the lights, the dashboard, the glass, the power train, the wheels, the engine, the seats, etc. - are connected to the painted body.  In one of the last steps on the assembly line the petrol tank is filled.  At the end of the line a new automobile is driven off for its final testing.

**Box 9.1**  An automobile assembly plant.

**Figure 9.2** The automobile assembly plant as a system.

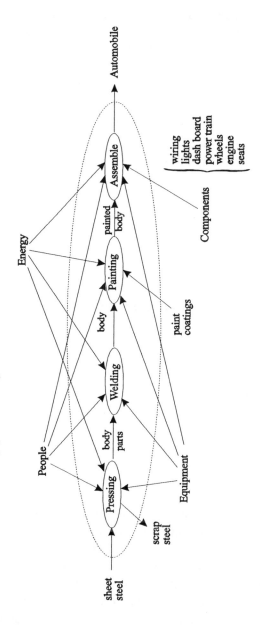

To coordinate the internal activities of the firm, the management information system must also be able to support internal information transactions. These transactions include horizontal connections between production processes and the supporting departments as well as vertical connections in the hierarchy.

Each production process is supported by various activities. For instance, material inputs need to be sourced and purchased, by a purchasing element of the organisation. Equipment must also be sourced, purchased and maintained, by engineering. People to operate the system must be hired from the labour market and trained, by the personnel department. Both process activities and supporting activities must be scheduled to meet the demand of the market. Information is needed to coordinate all these actions. Key elements of information required range from a forecast of future customer demand to a record of the current operating performance.

---

**Figure 9.3** External connections of a manufacturing system.

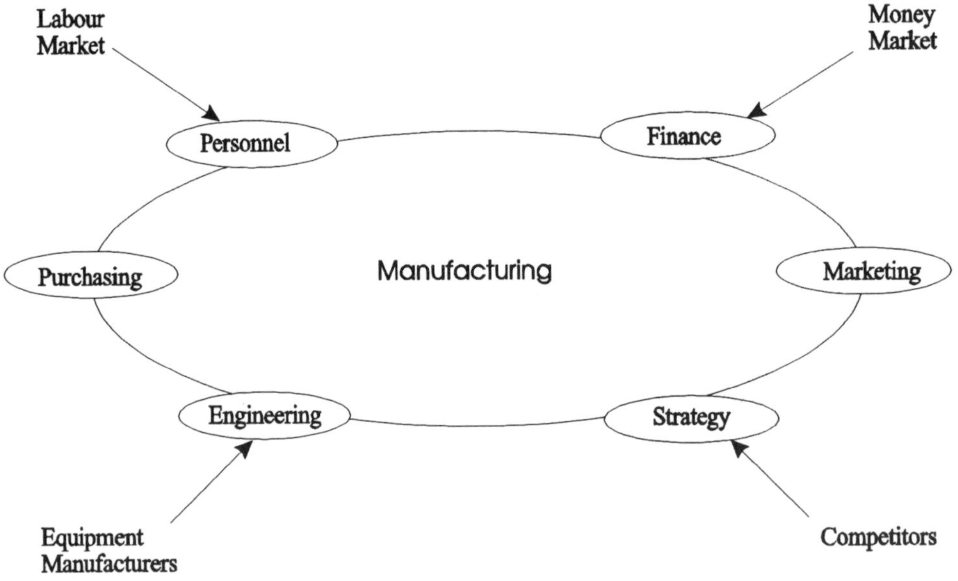

---

This network of sub-systems must be connected to the external environment. These connections can be physical, but nearly always there is an informational element. For example, materials arriving from suppliers is clearly a physical transaction. However, a great deal of information must be exchanged before the physical delivery is achieved. The material must be matched with the needs of the designs. A supplier must be found. Material engineers in the manufacturing company may need to discuss the specifications with engineers of the supplier. The information system must support the requirements of these external connections (see figure 9.3).

In most manufacturing firms, gathering and developing knowledge about the customers is the role of marketing function. They must be able to predict the direction in which their market is moving. This information must be passed to the production function, which must be flexible enough to move quickly to produce the right products for that market.

To make products the firm must gather the necessary resources. Investment must be made in the buildings and machines which make up the production system. Raw materials must also be bought from suppliers. Buildings, machines and materials must be financed. Gathering the necessary finances is the role of the finance department. To man the production system people must be hired to make the product, to run and maintain the machines and to manage the organisation. Hiring and training people is the role of the personnel or human resource department.

The production system transforms raw materials in a series of processes into finished goods. The production function is responsible for the design, control, maintenance and improvement of the production system. To do this intelligently the production system - its raw materials, its technology, its components, its people, its specifications, its history, and its performance - must be understood in great detail.

To design the best products, buy the right equipment, purchase the right materials, hire the right people, and produce the right products to meet the needs of the market, all of the parts of the organisation that perform these tasks must share timely and accurate information. Information plays a vital role.

To support the manufacturing operation, the information sub-system of the organisation, includes all means of transmitting information. It should not be limited, in general concept, to electronic transactions between various computers. The major lesson of the systemic view is the intricate and interdependent nature of the business system. The production system is a sub-system of the higher level system which is the organisation itself.

One of the major difficulties in communicating information through this network is that various elements may attach different meanings to the same piece of information. For example, for the design engineer the "cost" of a component is the price listed in the suppliers catalogue. To a material buyer in the purchasing department the "cost" is the price the supplier actually quotes to him. To the materials manager the "cost" of an item might also contain the cost of inspecting the item when it arrives and storage until it is used. A management accountant might add the time spent by the engineer, the buyer and the materials manager to the "cost" of the same item. To the customer service manager, selling the item as a spare part, the "cost" is the difference between the price quoted to the customer and the profit on the item. An information system based on a naive assumption of shared meanings for technical terms could sustain significant misunderstandings. Box 9.2 illustrates the example of a company which clearly did not match what they meant by "on time delivery" with what the customer understood by the term.

---

The customers of a small Irish manufacturer complained that they were not getting delivery of ordered product on time. Due dates were often missed. This was confirmed by looking at the shipment records; 60 percent of due dates were regularly missed.

Immediately action was taken to ensure that orders were shipped to meet the customer's due date. Within a few months 95 percent of orders left the loading dock on time. Proud of their accomplishment managers asked the customers if any improvement had been noticed.

The response was shocking. In the customers eyes the performance was marginally worse. Yes, orders were arriving on time, but line items within the order were missing. The on time shipments were incomplete.

**Box 9.2** "We weren't measuring the right thing."

---

## 9.2 Some historical trends

Current production systems are the result of several long term historical trends. These are:

- division of labour
- mechanisation
- standardisation

These trends are based in the roots of the industrial revolution.

Historically, manufacturing has been driven by the twin benefits of division of labour - specialisation and mechanisation. Division of a task into elements and the assignment of these elements to individuals allows those individuals to become extremely good at performing their element. By focusing on one element they become faster, more accurate and develop a deeper understanding of that element.

Division of the task also allows for the development of mechanical devices to help the worker or to perform an element of the task. This is the start of mechanisation, that is replacing human efforts with machines.   Most manufacturing processes are mechanised to some extent.   The degree of mechanisation depends in part on the production technology available, and the volume of the product to be produced.   Figure 9.4 shows the relationship between the volume produced by a process and the type of process.   In general, the higher the volume the more the mechanisation.

**Figure 9.4**  Volume and process relationship.

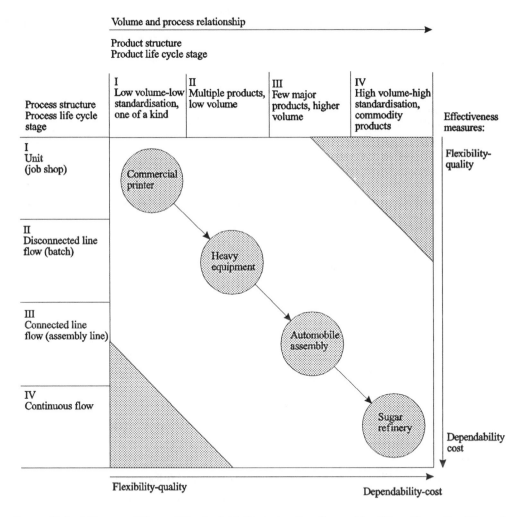

Source: Robert Hayes and Steven Wheelwright, *Restoring Our Competitive Edge: Competing Through Manufacturing.*  John Wiley & Sons, New York, 1984, p. 209.

New technology, especially computer technology does not always favour the larger plant. (See box 9.3.) Many of the traditional arguments are based on assumptions which were accurate enough before the advent of computers. Unfortunately, these outdated assumptions are often so well hidden in existing technology, by conventional wisdom, or by experience that they are rarely recognised.

---

In 1984, every expert thought you needed to have a giant blast furnace to produce sheet steel. Small mills could make bar steel, but only a large integrated producer could produce sheet steel. But the experts were wrong. In 1989, Nucor built a mini-mill to make sheet steel. The key to the process is a sophisticated computer technology to control the flow of molten metal in the process.

Nucor's mill takes takes less than one third of the time to make a ton of steel than the larger mills. This reduces the cost of a ton of steel by between $50 and $75; roughly 20 percent of the selling price.

**Box 9.3** Making steel in a smaller plant.
Source: Myron Magnet, Meeting the new revolutionaries, *Fortune*, 24th February, 1992, pp. 50-55.

---

However, each time a task is divided, the network which makes up the system becomes more intricate and therefore more difficult to coordinate. Unfortunately, this major cost of division of labour - the need for coordination - is often ignored (or poorly performed) by manufacturing management.

Two mechanisms are commonly used to coordinate activities within the manufacturing system. One is standardisation. If components are interchangeable, control of individual parts becomes less important. Standardisation reduces the uncertainty to which the process needs to be able to adapt.

The other mechanism is information. Internal information about people, plans, processes, and equipment is needed to coordinate and control the system. External information about customers, suppliers, competitors and technology is needed to define strategy and focus efforts. Enhancing the effectiveness of information is at the heart of several of the continuing attempts to improve the performance of production systems.

Integrating the elements of a divided task is never easy. Changes, which may make one element easier to do, may impact either on the performance of another element or on the final product. Integration becomes nearly impossible when the task changes significantly. Thus, manufacturing has traditionally been slow to change.

## 9.3 Manufacturing strategy

As a major component of the business system, the activities of production must be integrated into the overall strategy of the organisation.[1] Manufacturing resources must be configured to meet the competitive demands of the business strategy. It will do the firm little good to attempt a strategy differentiating their products based on quality, if the production function cannot deliver a product with a significant quality advantage.

Of course, manufacturing has the job of implementing the strategy. However, waiting until implementation to consider the manufacturing dimensions is too late.[2] Decisions which are apparently routine manufacturing decisions, can come to limit the organisation's strategic options. For example, the routine selection of a replacement for an old piece of equipment by a production function out of contact with research and development might result in the purchase of an identical technology, rather than purchase of an available new technology which will be needed to produce the next generation of the product. Because of the size of investment needed, this company may not be able to re-invest in the needed technology for several years; putting them well behind the competition.

If strategic decisions cannot be carried out, they have little effect. The manufacturing function is the portion of the company which performs the major function of the firm. It makes the products the company sells. If the manufacturing plant cannot make the product of the right quality, for the right cost, at the right time, no strategic plan will work. Box 9.4 illustrates the case of an organisation adopting a strategy incorporating flexibility.

A manufacturing system exists to produce products for customers. On the market products compete in five ways: quality, speed, dependability, cost, and flexibility.[3] Traditionally, the manufacturing role has been seen as balancing the costs of the resources against various objectives related to customer service: availability of the product, quality of the product, and dependability of delivery. The belief that no one production plant could be good at all of the objectives leads to a dilemma. For example, if you wanted higher quality you expected to pay a higher price. One way to address this dilemma is to focus on one particular objective, leading to the concept of a *focused factory*.[4] However, many of these 'trade-offs' are now recognised as false. An investment to improve production quality may lead to a reduction in scrap and rework, clearly a saving in cost.[5] Several of the following trends in manufacturing management attempt to address these false dilemmas.

In September 1982, Ind Coope Burton Brewery, a subsidiary of Allied Lyons and a traditional British brewery, had major facilities which had been developed to produce large volumes of a relatively narrow product range. The main product was Double Diamond in kegs for pubs.

The modern customer demanded something different. Beer drinkers were ordering a variety of different lagers, beers and ales. In addition they wanted them in a variety of different packages: kegs, casks, bottles, and cans. Overall demand was falling in Britain so the company had to deliver to more countries. This meant competing against new rivals who could deliver at lower cost. To stay in the market, to be considered by the customer, the company had to respond more rapidly to their demands.

The brewery's response to this challenge required a five year change programme, which included major organizational and cultural changes, as well as physical changes in layout and equipment: forty-six different projects including 37 physical changes, over £35 million in new capital investment and a reduction in staff of roughly 500 people. During the process of change it was necessary to continue to meet production schedules.

**Box 9.4**  The key to survival was to be found in one word - 'flexibility'.
Source: David Cox, *Exploiting Change By GABB and By GIBB*, David L. Cox, Lichfield, 1991.

## 9.4  Computer integrated manufacturing

Discussions of manufacturing usually conjure up visions of the *factory of the future*, populated by robots, running without lights, with no employees burdened with mundane manual tasks. For most industries that future is not yet feasible, but several steps have been taken in that direction. Various computer systems have been developed to perform or control elements of the production process. For example, *computer numerical control* (CNC) machines were developed to automatically perform the sequence for machining parts. *Computer aided design* (CAD) systems were developed to assist the designer in developing the product design. *Computer aided manufacturing* (CAM) systems help to plan and control the flow of materials through the production process. *Material requirements planning* (MRP) systems were developed to schedule and track the production of dependent demand items (see box 9.6). *Robots* and *automatic guided vehicles* (AGVs) are among the several types of handling equipment that have been computerised. *Flexible Manufacturing Systems* (FMS) are designed to handle several types of machining or assembly.

Computer integrated manufacturing (CIM) is directed towards gaining the synergies available by integrating all of the computer systems of the company. The database shared by parts of the system becomes the means of integration. In a CIM system a part is designed on the CAD system, which provides numerical data to the CAM system. The CAM system would provide the numerical cutting sequence for the CNC machines and the loading sequence for the FMS. When the MRP system calls for the production of that particular part, raw material stock is loaded and the entire process completed automatically. The machine tool industry is the most advanced in CIM, although various elements are used in many other industries. (See figure 9.5.)

**Figure 9.5** The development of computer integrated manufacturing.

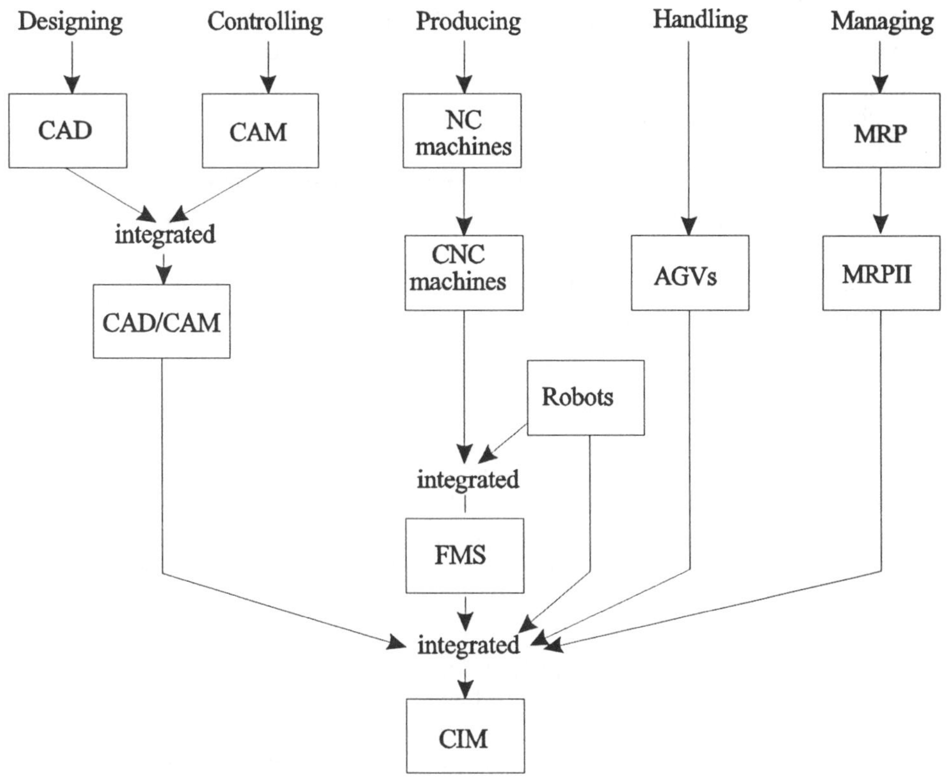

In factories with some elements of CIM, one of the major difficulties is tying the elements together.  Each "island of automation" would have been developed by different designers from different organisations, with few shared standards for either software or hardware.  It is not surprising that the pieces do not fit together easily.  In some cases they will not fit at all.

In addition to being developed by different sources, equipment has also been developed at different times.  As a piece of production equipment goes through the stages of its life-cycle - start, middle and end - different problems seem to arise.  At the start of life integrating the new equipment into the existing production system is the predominant problem. A new piece of equipment thus has a special advantage, it forces people to question everything that has been done previously.  Toward the middle of life the limits of machine capacity is usually a problem, which can be compounded by the integration with new equipment.  At the end of life, just as the equipment needs more extensive maintenance, the original equipment manufacturers are often phasing out their support for the old style of equipment.[6]

---

Even a small company can use computer integrated manufacturing.  Consider production of customized bicycles by National Bicycle Industrial Company, a subsidiary of Matsushita.  With a small plant, and only 20 employees and a computer, the company can produce 11,231,862 variations on its 18 models of mountain, racing and road bicycles.

When the customer visits the local bicycle shop, the shopkeeper measures the customer on a special frame and faxes the measurements to the factory.  At the factory, the computer takes about three minutes to automatically create a blueprint and produce a bar code, which is attached to basic materials which will become the bicycle.  At each stage in the production process the bar code instructs the worker (or a robot) where to cut, weld, paint and assemble the new bicycle. Production takes about 3 hours.

**Box 9.5**  Computerized custom manufacturing.
Source:  Susan Moffat, Japan's new personalized production, *Fortune*, 22nd October, 1990, pp. 90-92.

---

Several of the attempts to use information technology have met with limited success. For example, initial computerised MRP systems were designed based on assumptions about the speed at which information could be processed.  In the early 1960s a mainframe computer could take several days to complete the calculations for a medium sized company.  Therefore, a reasonable reporting period was once a week.  Since this was a significant improvement over monthly and annual reports, at the time MRP was an advance. Unfortunately, the inability to capture accurate information - specifically inventory status - led to weekly reports being both out of date and inaccurate. When used, they often led to costly decisions. One proposed solution, based on increased computing power, was to develop "real-time" MRP systems. However this solution does not address the basic problem - inaccuracy in the data collected; it only compounds it. Application of other technology, such as bar coding components and tracking the bar coded material as it moves through the system, addresses the problem, but can be very expensive.

---

The logic of MRP is fairly simple.

- If a wagon has four wheels, then the wheels must be made before the wagon can be built. (Dependent demand for a level of build.)

- If it takes a week to build the wheels, work must be started on the wheels a week before the wagon can be built. (The lead time necessary to produce components must be taken into account.)

- If wheels are a component part of several different models of wagon, the demand for each of the models must be added to find the number of wheels that need to be produced. (Aggregation of identical parts.)

- If 400 wagons are to be made in week 2, then 1600 wheels must be in stock at the end of week 1. (Similar time periods - called time buckets - are used at different levels of build.)

- If the facilities used to produce the wheels are used to produce other items, deciding what to produce when will require some planning. (Determining production batch size and timing.)

- If there are many other components which are needed to make both the wagon and the wheels, the process of deciding what to make when will become complex.

Material Requirements Planning is designed to reduce the complexity of this problem through a step by step hierarchical process. Manufacturing Resource Planning (MRP II) extends the planning logic to all of the resources used in the manufacturing process.

**Box 9.6** Material requirements planning.

---

Another problem is illustrated by the Optimised Production Technology (OPT) approach. *The OPT software system is based on a closely guarded algorithm which concentrates on identifying and scheduling bottlenecks in the manufacturing system.*[7] At the heart of this system is a proprietary algorithm, a black box.   The algorithm calculates the details of the optimised schedule for the production system.  This means that the manufacturing operation is coordinated by an algorithm the details of which it cannot understand.  This means that any proposed improvements in the production system cannot be checked against the assumptions built into the design of the black box.  If the change violates the basic assumptions of the algorithm, the results of the calculation may be far from the optimum solution.[8]

---

For years General Motors has been a giant of American industry.  In spite of significant investment in automation and quality, it is now foundering.  The synergies expected from wiring the entire company to one computer haven't been realized.  GM invested $77 billion to reduce labour costs; to automate.  Robots purchased in the mid-1980's are not being used, because the robots could not assemble the new models.  Productivity has fallen.  It seems that new machines were used to improve existing processes; to make the assembly line more efficient. Instead, the process became less flexible and less able to accomplish rapid change.

**Box 9.7**  The dangers of automating before you simplify.
Sources: Peter Drucker, The emerging theory of manufacturing, *Harvard Business Review*, May-June 1990, pp. 94-102; and Alex Taylor III, Can GM Remodel itself, *Fortune*, 13th January, 1992, pp. 22-28.

---

In 1989 MRP was being used by a small English plant building specialised pumps for the world market.  The original company, over 40 years old, was one of several in a highly profitable division of a diversified high-tech multinational.  The plant built a complete range of pumps, over 450 models in seven different product lines.

The plant also fabricated many of the mechanical components which were assembled into their products.  Purchased materials were brought into stores, issued to each department for processing, and returned to stores.  These inventory transactions were recorded on a sophisticated MRP system.  The MRP system tracked 600 different operations and 40,000 different component parts. Production was usually carried out in batches of 25, although orders ranged from 1 to 100.

When the components were ready, they were issued to assembly.  Assembly of a pump was (and is) a highly skilled and complex operation, so each pump was assigned to an individual assembly craftsman.  Since the assembly took some time, and much of the work was not readily visible to inspection, it was difficult to tell the stage of assembly of partially completed pumps.  Since assembly was the highest value added step in the production process, control was extremely important. The MRP system directly provided information to the management accounting system

Originally the structure of the MRP system incorporated seven or eight levels of build of a given pump. Since the MRP system worked with weekly time buckets, materials moved one stage in the build each week. This practice resulted in a lead time of as much as six months. In the spring of 1989, the plant managers changed the structure. By reducing the product structure, only major stages are recorded, the lead time was reduced to three months However, detailed information on each stage in the process was no longer available to the accounting system. This led to aggregation of accounting variances which were more difficult to explain.

**Box 9.8** MRP at the pump plant.

## 9.5 Design for manufacture

One possible measure of manufacturing flexibility is the speed at which a company can get a product to the market place. This is becoming one of the major means of competing in several industries, most notably motorcycles and radios. Traditional manufacturers develop products in a series of steps: concept development, product design, process development, pilot production, full production and marketing. Often these steps are done independently by specialised parts of the company. Overly complicated designs lead to unnecessary delays. Engineering changes, needed to correct design faults identified during production, cause major disruption to the production process and increase production costs significantly.

The strategy of offering the market a large variety of products has been very successfully used by Sony. In 1990 Sony had over 200 models of its popular personal audio-system, the Walkman, on the market. In many companies the idea of producing this many different products would appear impossible. Sony can do it because all 200 of the products are developed from three basic production platforms. All of the products with the same production platform share common design features and production processes. New hybrids, derivatives, and enhancements were developed to be easy to manufacture.

**Box 9.9** The Walkman - 200 models with only 3 platforms.
Source: Steven C. Wheelwright and Kim B. Clark, Creating project plans to focus product development, *Harvard Business Review*, March-April, 1992, pp. 70-82.

A different approach, sometimes termed *concurrent engineering,* suggests that these steps be done in parallel, with manufacturing providing a significant input at design and with designers involved until the production process is running smoothly.[9]   This practice has four beneficial effects.  Problems are identified and corrected early in the process before major investments in production equipment are made.  Since changes do not have to be referred across bureaucratic boundaries, the time and cost necessary to complete product introduction is significantly reduced.  Although each development phase may last longer, the total project is completed more quickly.  Finally, because the design incorporates production expertise the product is easy to make.  Information systems necessary to support such a system must provide consistent information at several locations.

**Figure 9.6** Sequential verses concurrent product development.

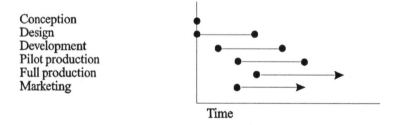

Based on Hirotaka Takeuchi and Ikujiro Nonaka, The new product development game.  In *Managing Projects and Programs*, Harvard Business Review, Boston, 1987, pp. 58-103.

# 9.6 Total quality management

Total quality management emphasises the interdependence in any production system.[10] The quality and cost of the final product is determined not simply by the reliable performance of the various stages of the production process, but by every function performed by the organisation. The performance of design, engineering, purchasing, maintenance, training, personnel, and accounting all impact either directly or indirectly on both the cost and the quality of the final product. Everyone is involved in quality and everyone is responsible for some element of quality.

Total quality improvement can be supported by several other movements, which are occasionally identified as independent trends in manufacturing: ISO 9000, and statistical process control.

## ISO 9000

In 1987 the International Standards Organisation published the ISO 9000 series of standards. The intent of ISO 9000, the international quality systems standard, is to ensure that the production process is fully documented and that this documented process is adhered to. The firm is responsible for developing detailed descriptions of the procedures necessary to complete each element of the production process. The company also conducts internal audits to ensure that the procedures are being followed. An external state agency oversees an external audit to confirm that the procedures are being followed. Of course, the impact of the system on product quality is directly related to the quality of the procedures documented. Information systems should be used to make the procedures easy to update, and easy to verify. The process of developing designs and certifying suppliers is also covered in the series.

## Statistical Process Control (SPC)

Variation is a characteristic of the output of any process. As long as the variation does not disrupt later stages of production, the product is 'within tolerance,' and the process is 'in control.' Disruption is expensive; out of tolerance performance must be eliminated. However, this is not the only cost of variation. In general, the wider the range of inputs a process must cope with, the more the process costs. Therefore reduction in the range of variation is also important. Statistical process control is aimed at recording variation in an effort to identify its causes. Once causes are identified, efforts can be made to eliminate them by improving the process. Although the statistics theory involved is moderately complex, the techniques of SPC have been successfully taught and used at the shop floor level. It is based on small samples taken regularly at the production location.

Sample results processed by the production operative provide rapid and regular feedback on the status of the process. The operative controls the process and does not have to wait for end of month results to know whether or not the process is performing. As variation in the process is reduced the need for quality inspectors, 'fire-fighters,' and supervisors is reduced, thus saving significant overhead costs. Visible information, available at the work station, in the form of charts and graphs, is an essential part of this process.

Recently the Whirlpool company invested $150 million to produce newly designed washing machines at its Clyde, Ohio plant. The new machines were designed to require fewer parts and a simplified assembly process. This helped improve the quality of the machines significantly. Whirlpool can now offer a one year replacement guarantee.

Workers are trained in statistical process control. They monitor critical dimensions and adjust machinery before it loses tolerance. The workers are involved developing assembly procedures and in the purchase of new equipment. In addition, new engineers spend a week on the production line to become familiar with the production process. This attention to quality in engineering and in production has resulted in a 68 percent reduction in service calls in the last five years.

**Box 9.10** Statistical process control at Whirlpool.
Source: Jack R. Meredith, *The Management of Operations: A Conceptual Emphasis*, 4th Edition. John Wiley, New York, 1992.

### The cost of quality

The cost of quality includes the cost of failure, the cost of appraisal and the cost of prevention. Failure costs are costs incurred when a bad product is made by the system. These include the external failure cost paid in warranties or lost sales and the internal failure cost paid in disruption, scrap and rework. Appraisal costs are the costs of inspecting out the bad products produced by the system. Prevention costs are those incurred to improve the design of the production system so bad products will not be produced. The Quality is Free movement claims, with some impressive examples, that application of this analysis usually indicates that significant savings (like 15% of sales cost) in failure costs and appraisal costs can be made by moderate investment in prevention.

**Figure 9.7** Cost of quality.

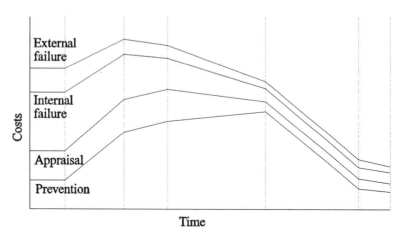

Increasing prevention of errors reduces the need for appraisal
and reduces the number of failures.

Source: Nigel Slack, *The Manufacturing Advantage: Achieving Competitive Manufacturing Operations*. Mercury, London, 1991.

Most computerised information systems have been designed to track cost and record performance. Unfortunately this has rarely led to interesting and new ways of presenting and analysing the information collected. Too often the computer system is just an automated version of the accounting system. An accounting system, based on the information processing capabilities of the 1920s has lost relevance for the control of modern production facilities.[11]

## 9.7 Just-in-time production

Just-in-time (JIT) is a philosophy that stresses the elimination of waste. Waste is defined as anything that adds cost, but not value, to the product. In essence this entails not being satisfied with current performance and constantly striving for improvement. Excess inventories is a usual, but not the only, example used to illustrate this philosophy. Inventories cost money, and add no value - if anything they reduce value due to deterioration, damage or obsolescence. Therefore they are waste. However, inventories are often justified on a number of grounds. For example, "we keep a safety stock of this part, because the machine that produces it breaks down every so often." Traditionally, elaborate models for deciding the 'proper' safety stock level have been developed. The JIT perspective would not directly challenge the current need for safety level.  Rather it would emphasise the urgent need to improve the reliability of the machine, and thus eliminate the long term need for the inventory.  The focus should be on doing something about the causes rather than modelling an unsatisfactory situation.  A key lesson here for information systems design is that the system must be robust enough to incorporate changes in information requirements which cannot be totally specified before the design of the system.  Designing the information system based on the assumption that the production system is static is a recipe for disaster.

---

- The logic of JIT runs throughout the production process.
- Any activity that does not contribute to the product is waste
- Materials that are not being worked on are losing value.
- Reduced setup and changeover times allow for reduced inventories.
- Removal of inventories reduces space and transportation costs.  Reduction of inventories expose:
    - unreliable equipment
    - unreliable production processes
    - sources of quality defects
    - unreliable materials and suppliers
    - slow management responses.
- More reliable equipment reduces stoppages due to breakdowns.
- Foolproofing operations removes the need for inspections.
- Removing quality defects reduces inspections, scrap and rework.
- Reliable suppliers reduce the need for inspections and safety stock.
- Placing management closer to the shopfloor speeds up reactions.

**Box 9.11**  The many elements of JIT.

---

In some manufacturing systems, however, the specific reasons for inventory are not known.  The system runs smoothly with high inventories.  From a JIT perspective, inventory has built up in systems because management has not addressed the actual problems in the system, but covered them with a blanket of inventory.  Often inventory, especially work in progress inventory, hides problems.  Incrementally reducing inventory will identify problems, which can then be addressed.  If no problems arise, then the inventory can be eliminated.

Of course inventory is only one of the buffers used to decouple elements of the production process.  Extra equipment capacity and extra personnel are also subject to the same process of improvement.  Improvement is not limited to direct activities. Overhead activities must also be subject to scrutiny.  In JIT the emphasis is on incremental and continual improvement rather than radical discontinuous improvement.

The materials manager at the pump plant discussed in Box 9.8 is interested in JIT as a means for reducing inventory and lead times. He feels that he can reduce the current 19 week inventory to 6 weeks and the current 3 month lead time to 4 weeks. He also hopes to negotiate JIT arrangements with suppliers. Small deliveries and short lead times would reduce the need to hold stock from a supplier.

The introduction of JIT at the plant has started, with a pilot study, which involves taking component parts inventory out of stores, and placing them in racks next to the work station where they are used. Eventually stores can be completely eliminated. Materials would be moved off delivery trucks directly into racks on the shop floor. Once this is accomplished the operations manager simply has to look at the shop floor to know that the plant is working and the materials manager only has to look at the shop floor to know materials are arriving as they should. Inventory status could be checked simply by looking in the appropriate bins.

**Box 9.12** JIT at the pump plant.

Rather unfortunately, the term "just-in-time", in several industries, now refers almost exclusively to the delivery of goods in small batches from the supplier. This external JIT is only a minor contributor of the potential of the concepts if they are internalised. This does however illustrate a danger potential in each of the trends discussed: oversimplification and misunderstanding are easy. An information system based on a naive view of the production system will be of significantly less value.

## 9.8 Involvement of employees

Employees are the most valuable resource of the company. In many companies much of this resource is being wasted. Direct employees - those employees that work directly on the product or operate the machines that make the product - often understand more about their jobs than their managers, maintenance specialists, quality inspectors or process engineers. They after all actually perform the job. All too often they are not consulted about changes and improvements and their ideas are lost or ignored.

Employee involvement is directed towards developing and strengthening this resource. All employees are trained in improvement techniques, for example statistical process control. Such techniques are used in one of two ways. When the system is running smoothly one of the functions of the worker is to record performance including minor problems and delays. (SPC is an unusually effective way of capturing this information.) This performance record becomes the subject of regular meetings of the production team, or some sub-set of the team. These productivity improvement meetings attempt to identify patterns in performance or problems. With investigation by the group, pattern identification may lead to actions to improve the production process.

A second opportunity to use problem solving skills of the employee occurs when the process breaks down. The production worker at the point of breakdown is the first person to address the problem causing the breakdown. The efforts of the entire organisation should be focused on supporting the worker in efforts to permanently eliminate the cause of the breakdown.

## 9.9 The learning organisation

The manufacturing organisation needs to be able to learn about itself in order to improve.[12]   Continuous improvement[13] is the goal of the modern manufacturing organisation, not simply getting the next shipment out the door. Improvement must be based on a clear understanding of the causes of current performance. This calls for clear and detailed understanding of the production system; a level of understanding which may take several years of experience to develop in an individual. Organisations, especially organisations with high personnel turnover, must develop mechanisms for capturing and recording experience. One way of doing this is to encourage people to explain the reasons for any given production practice and to share these reasons in improvement groups.

---

At the Ind Coope Burton Brewery discussed in Box 9.4, the changes discussed included new information systems. "The systems give previously undreamt of information and control to first-line team members. The operative running a filter now knows, via graphic display, about detailed conditions upstream and downstream of him. ... His workstation gives him complete control of all operations necessary for him to complete his tasks,without the need for hour-to-hour supervision. ... He can evaluate directly the results of his actions, analysed numerically or graphically in a form which he has designed to meet his own needs."

**Box 9.13** New information systems for the shopfloor.
Source: David Cox, *Exploiting Change By GABB and By GIBB*. David L Cox, Lichfield, 1991.

---

In 1984, on the brink of filing for bankruptcy, Harley-Davidson (America's last domestic motorcycle manufacturer) was in the process of adopting many of the practices used by its Japanese competitors, including JIT, SPC and employee involvement (EI). The story of their return to profitability is full of interesting accounts. For example, a quality circle at the York plant polishing department worked on the problem of reducing scratches and nicks that created rework costs on lamp brackets, saddlebag supports, fork brackets, and horn covers. This group came up with ideas that achieved net savings of more than $89,000 - and more importantly, cured a chronic quality problem.

**Box 9.14** Employee Involvement (EI) at Harley-Davidson.
Source: Peter C. Ried, *Well Made in America: Lessons from Harley-Davidson on Being the Best.* McGraw-Hill, 1990.

One method of focusing the attention of such groups is the concept of *benchmarking* which was discussed in chapter 2. It entails comparing your performance to the best in the world. Who is the best? How do you compare? What can we learn from them? Answers to these questions are the essence of benchmarking. For example, if your process produces 1% defective products, that is 10,000 bad products for every million produced, and the competition has a defect rate of 500 parts per million, two things are quite clear:

- they don't have to pay as much for rework, so you are at a cost disadvantage; and

- your work practices can be improved.

World class benchmarks, comparing the operation to the best in the world, and the progress being made by the organisation to achieve these benchmarks should be part of the formal information system.

At Boeing Aircraft, brainstormers still sit around a table and try to develop new ways of thinking about things. Instead of shouting ideas to a facilitator with a flip chart, they type their thoughts on networked personal computers. A new kind of software called *groupware*[a] keeps track of what everyone has to say, and shows the new ideas through monitors on the other PC's. Participants can screen more material faster than at any ordinary meeting.

The time needed to complete many team projects has been cut to one tenth of what similar work used to take. In the summer of 1991, a project team was formed to design a standardized control system for complex machine tools in several Boeing plants. The team included designers, engineers, manufacturing managers and machinists. Similar projects had taken about a year. With 15 electronic meetings, using TeamFocus software from IBM, it was done in 35 days.

**Box 9.15** A new way of brainstorming at Boeing.
Source: David Kirkpatick, Here comes the payoff from PCs, *Fortune*, March 23rd, 1992, pp. 50-55.
[a]Groupware is discussed in chapter 11.

## 9.10  Lessons about information systems for manufacturing

This chapter has introduced some of the concepts which are shaping modern manufacturing. These ideas impact on the type of information system needed by manufacturing. The lessons appear to include the following.

- *The information system includes all means of transmitting, storing and recovering information.* Electronic and computer hardware and applications are only a sub-set of this overall system.

- *Simplify before automating.* Incorporation of information systems technology should provide a way of reducing the complexity or enhancing the capabilities of the system.

- *Current performance measures may be based on pre-computer technology assumptions.* What used to take a week on paper may take less than an hour on the computer.

- *Go for understanding, not for complexity.* It is dangerous to use any bit of technology without a clear understanding of how it works; otherwise you are likely to be limited by its design assumptions.

- *Ask the question, how will the change improve the operation of the manufacturing systems performance on one of the competitive elements?* If it won't why do it?

- *Designing information systems to match the current situation without considering the need for changes is a recipe for disaster.*

- *Maintenance of an information system is like maintenance of any equipment, more complex than it appears.*

Another important lesson can be drawn from the examples in this chapter. Each of the examples illustrates the interdependent nature of the production system. None of the "trends" discussed above are independent from the others. Little can be accomplished in isolation.

Although the tone of much of this chapter is evangelical, none of the discussed techniques are without dangers. The primary danger is the tendency of top management to treat these concepts as easy to apply panaceas; to believe all the 'hype,' without accepting that the underlying goal in each case is developing a deeper understanding of the particular manufacturing system. To be useful, all of the concepts must be adapted to the organisation. Most of the benefit available from any of the concepts comes from struggling with the particulars of a given application: they can ignite innovative solutions to old problems. Uncritically applied they are subject to becoming unsuccessful fads; 'flavours of the month,' interesting for a while, but discarded when effort or commitment is needed.

---

*What's in a name? What we call a rose,*
*by any other name would smell as sweet.*

"We called it the materials-as-needed program, or MAN for short. ...Why? Mainly because JIT got a lot of bad press during the early eighties. Some large companies had said that they were introducing JIT, when they were really just pushing inventory back on their suppliers and it didn't work. So we thought we needed a different name and we came up with MAN."

Tom Gelb
Senior Vice President of Operations
Harley-Davidson.

**Box 9.16** JIT, MAN, or ZIP's - what's the difference?
Source: Peter C. Ried, *Well Made in America: Lessons from Harley-Davidson on Being the Best.* McGraw-Hill New York, 1990.

---

# Notes

1   Wickham Skinner, Manufacturing - missing link in corporate strategy. *Harvard Business Review*, May-June, 1969, pp. 136-145. Steeven Wheelwright, Manufacturing strategy: defining the missing link. *Strategic Management Journal*, 5, 1, 1984, pp. 77-91.
2   Terry Hill, *Manufacturing Strategy*. Macmillan, Basingstoke, 1985.
3   George Stalk, Time: the next source of competitive advantage. *Harvard Business Review*, July-August 1988, pp. 41-51; Nigel Slack, *The Manufacturing Advantage:*

*Achieving Competitive Manufacturing Operations*. Mercury, London, 1991.

4      Skinner, op. cit.
5      Richard J. Schonberger, *Building a Chain of Customers: Linking Business Functions to Create The World Class Company*. The Free Press, New York, 1990.
6      Based on Jack Meredith, Implementing new manufacturing technologies: managerial lessons over the FMS cycle. *Interfaces*, **17**, 6, 1987, pp. 51-62.
7      Jimmie Browne, John Harhen and James Shivnan, *Production Management Systems: A CIM Perspective*. Addison-Wesley, Wokingham, 1988.
8      Some insight into the OPT system is available in Eiliyahu Goldratt and Jef Cox, *The Goal*. North River, New York, 1986.
9      Otis Port, A smarter way to manufacture. *Business Week*, April 30th, 1990, pp. 64-69.
10     A.V Feigenbaum, *Total Quality Control: Engineering and Management*. McGraw-Hill, New York, 1961; and W. Edwards Deming, *Out Of Crisis*. Cambridge University Press, 1986.
11     H. Thomas Johnson and Robert Kaplan, *Relevance Lost: The Rise and Fall of Management Accounting*. Harvard Business School Press, Boston, 1987.
12     Robert Hayes, Steven Wheelwright and Kim Clarke, *Dynamic Manufacturing: Creating The Learning Organization*. Free Press, New York, 1988.
13     Richard Schonberger, *World Class Manufacturing: Lessons of Simplicity Applied*. The Free Press, New York, 1986.

## Additional reading

Deming, W. Edwards, *Out of Crisis*. Cambridge University Press, Cambridge, 1986.
Drucker, P., The emerging theory of manufacturing. *Harvard Business Review*, May-June, 1990, pp. 94-102.
Hill, T., *Manufacturing Strategy*. Macmillan, Basingstoke, 1985.
Meredith, J.R., *The Management of Operations: A Conceptual Emphasis*. 4th edition. John Wiley, New York.
Mofat, S., Japan's new personalised production. *Fortune*, 22 October, 1990, pp. 90-92.
Port, O., A smarter way to manufacture. *Business Week*, 30 April, 1990, pp. 64-69.
Wheelwright, S.C. and Clarke, K.B., Creating project plans to focus product development. *Harvard Business Review*, March-April, 1992, pp. 70-82.

# 10

# Expert Systems

As we progress through the 1990s one is continually astounded at the rate of decrease in cost of computing power available to the non-professional computer user. The computing power that is now available to today's "personal" computer user places no hardware restrictions on what can be achieved in terms of increases in efficiency, improvements in quality and personal productivity. In simple terms, spreadsheets have come a long way since Visicalc (the first spreadsheet), and wordprocessing capabilities available today outstrip anything that was available in the early 80s.

The only restriction that the professional user of microcomputers now faces is that of one's own imagination and time-resource. It is important to note that computing is no longer an insular discipline and as the increase of integration of the professions develops, the effect of advances in computer science and technology will become more widespread. Hardware is increasingly becoming a non-issue. Software tools are available today to achieve most anything that we would aspire to achieve in computing terms. The challenge that we now face is how to create systems that are evolutionary in terms of their being integrated into how we work. Expert system technology has an inportant role to play in meeting this challenge. Throughout the rest of this chapter we will outline some of the history of expert systems and express some views on how the technology can best be utilised to deliver business benefit.

## 10.1  Expert systems

After many years of research and seemingly endless endeavour, in the early '80s we began to see the emergence from the ivory tower of academia of a new multi-faceted commercially viable technology - expert systems.  Expert systems, as delivered at that time, were the latest form of productivity tool available to the professional PC user. Expert systems have unfortunately been shrouded with the same cloud of misinformation that surrounded the other data-processing functions at the beginning of the microcomputer era.  Expert system development tools are not any more mysterious than databases or 4GLs (4th generation languages) and are a lot easier to achieve productivity with than conventional programming languages such as C, Pascal, Fortran or Cobol. However, because of the lack of information forthcoming relating to expert systems and also because of the direct lineal relationship with artificial intelligence (and the consequent misconceptions from the most unfortunate nomenclature in the history of software development) the professional user of microcomputers has had a perception of expert systems that has predictably been erroneous.

Expert system technology is a software technique that is particularly appropriate when implementing computer solutions that require systems that are heavily dependent on high quality expertise to achieve maximum performance. The emphasis in the previous sentence should be placed on "high quality expertise". It is this emphasis which primarily differentiates expert system applications from spreadsheet or database systems. Expert systems are sophisticated computer programs that manipulate knowledge and expertise to solve problems efficiently and effectively in a specific problem domain. In recent times there has been an increasing awareness, however, that an expert system application, in a stand-alone environment, provides only a fraction of the benefit that it would do were it integrated effectively into an organisation's structure, both technological and cultural.  More about this later

Expert systems allow the user to encapsulate a body of knowledge, applied knowledge or expertise into a computer program in order that the knowledge or expertise can be made available to the non-expert or novice.  It is important to view expert systems alongside wordprocessors, databases and spreadsheets as another tool in your armoury, but not as a panacea for all ills. We will discuss suitable areas for expert system development later.

## 10.2 In the beginning ...

To create a machine that could think, perform intelligently or emulate "intelligent human behaviour" has, for decades, been the goal of computer scientists in general, and artificial intelligence scientists in particular. Can a machine think?  Is it possible to make a machine reason? While these questions are discussed and studied in the halls of academia and differing learned opinions postulate theories on scientific, social, economic or political significance of the latest knowledge representation techniques or inference methods, it is left to the PC user in the commercial environment to grasp some of the concepts of artificial intelligence and expert systems and to apply these concepts to the business at hand.

Research in AI from the mid-60s onwards was concerned with the study of human cognition and information processing. Natural language processing, machine learning, knowledge representation and understanding the components of search systems have all become distinct areas in AI development. From an expert system point of view we can loosely break the history of the AI story into three phases.

As mentioned earlier, man-the-scientist's greatest dream has been to create a machine or computer that could think for itself. Fiction writers have given us a glimpse of the potential of the computer with a brain of its own with HAL in *2001 - A Space Odyssey* in the '60s to Marvin - the paranoid android in Adams' *Hitchhikers Guide to the Galaxy* in the '80s - and *Time* choosing in 1982 as "Man Of The Year" a computer rather than a leading world political, religious or economic figure. In the early stages, the artificial intelligence scientists endeavoured to create a computer with general problem solving capabilities - like man. They tried to develop general methods for solving broad classes of problems and used these methods in general purpose programs. However as the scope of problems that was addressed by any one program increased, the effectiveness of that program for any specific problem decreased.

After a less than successful first phase, which spanned most of the '60s, the AI researchers decided that at least some of the general techniques must be useful through all classes of problems and set forth to develop general methods or techniques that could then be modified and used in more specialised programs. This was preferable to trying to develop complete problem solving programs. Consequently, there were significant advances in the seventies in the methods and principles used in "representation" - how to express in systematic terms the problem to make it clearer or the knowledge to make it easier to incorporate in the program, and "search methods" - how to find the correct path for the most efficient and effective solution to the problem.

The digital computer doesn't have any inherent knowledge. Any knowledge that you wish the computer to possess has to be fed into it. It was this realisation, combined with the realisation that any problem solving entity has to have a body of high quality expertise, that provided the biggest breakthrough in expert system development. This happened towards the end of the seventies and led to the development of programs which we now call expert systems. If a program is to assume intelligence, then it must be provided with a base of knowledge, rules and expertise to enable it to possess a significant degree of expertness.

The artificial intelligence and expert systems phenomenon has been much debated by scholars, system designers, computer industry commentators and traditional software developers. Passionate discourses on the unreliability, simplistic and limited nature of today's expert systems have been countered with arguments extolling the virtues of the technology, some making claims that even the most ardent artificial intelligence fan will concede to be overselling the science.

There have been many ill-conceived and heavily funded artificial intelligence and expert systems projects that have turned sour and the consequent backlash has adversely effected other more worthwhile ventures. In the UK and particularly in the US, the area of expert systems now has a bad name. Throughout the '80s many of the expert system product vendors promoted and sold the technology for its own sake, not for what the technology could achieve. Expert systems were designed as standalone applications, often developed as test or pilot systems and not applied to mission critical application where real benefits could be shown. The vendors of the technology, not for the first time, did not understand fully the commercial effects of their product offerings and the human issues that are so important in this area of technology. This has created difficulties for those people who do recognise the issues and who do want to introduce the technology into their organisations.

There have been a number of successes. In recent years, expert system applications built by or with the experts in both the public and private sectors have started proving their worth in a true commercial sense. It is in the fields of finance, industry and the professions that worthwhile implementations of the technology are beginning to emerge because of the results oriented aspect of commerce and the specific nature of tasks that the commercial entities are pursuing rather than the general nature of academic or scientific research. Box 10.1 describes a number of successful "early" expert systems.

Expert systems are different in a number of aspects. To implement them successfully, it is worth identifying the differences to assess the specific issues that arise.

## 10.3  Features of expert systems

One of the main differences between conventional programs and expert systems is that the conventional program solution is "algorithmic" while the expert system solution is "heuristic". A heuristic solution is a method or set of rules for solving a problem without the exhaustive application of an algorithm. Heuristics enable the human expert to make informed guesses when necessary. Typically expert systems require best-guess solutions rather than rigorous mathematical analysis or algorithmic solutions. Heuristics enable the system builder to use rules-of-thumb or tricks that have been learnt by experience. An important aspect of an expert system is that it works more

---

MYCIN

Developed at Stanford University in the early 1970s to diagnose infectious diseases and therapy selection. The system diagnoses the cause of the infection (e.g. the identity of the infecting organism) using knowledge relating infecting organisms with patient history, symptoms, and laboratory test results. The system recommends drug treatment (type and dosage) according to procedures followed by doctors experienced in infectious disease therapy.

PROSPECTOR

Prospector acts as a consultant to aid exploration geologists in their search for ore deposits. Given field data about a geological region, it estimates the likelihood of finding particular types of mineral deposits there. The system can assess the potential for finding a variety of deposits, including sulphide, lead/zinc, copper, nickel sulphide and sandstone uranium. Its expertise is based on geological rules which form models of ore deposits and a taxonomy of rocks and minerals.

XCON

The breadth and depth of Digital Equipment Corporation's products causes complexity when configuring computer system orders since each customer order is unique. The manual process for technically editing orders did not bring to bear all the available expertise needed to configure an order optimally and was showing signs of stress relative to increased order volume and complexity. XCON handles the configuration task by applying knowledge of the constraints on component relationships to standard procedures for configuring computers.

**Box 10.1** Expert system examples.

---

with information, which we can define as "knowledge acquired through experience or study" rather than with data which is "a series of facts yet to be interpreted". Box 10.2 summarises the distinction between conventional programs and expert systems.

| Conventional Programs | Expert Systems |
|---|---|
| Algorithmic | Heuristic |
| Right/Wrong | Probabilistic |
| Static | Evolving |
| Works with data | Works with information |

**Box 10.2** Conventional programs versus expert systems.

Expert systems have been defined by many erudite scholars who reference uncertainty, stochastic reasoning and Bayesian probability and other such learned terms.   The approach here is less sophisticated and addresses the question **what do expert systems mean to me in my business?**

*An expert system provides commercial benefit, through a well designed user interface, by making expertise more available to the non-expert by offering intelligent advice derived from a high quality base of knowledge.  Using rules the system can explain its reasoning process while being processed and provide an audit trail of how the knowledge was applied when the system arrives at its conclusion.*

To be effective, an expert system must have a knowledge base consisting of high quality knowledge about a specific problem domain organised in rules or some other representation. The knowledge base consists of facts and rules, facts being the short-term information that changes with each consultation with the system and rules the longer-term more permanent information. The knowledge in an  expert system is organised in such a way that separates the domain knowledge from other system knowledge such as knowledge about how to solve problems or how to interface with the user.

**Inference engine**

An expert system will have an *inference engine* which is that part of an expert system that contains the general problem solving knowledge and governs how the facts are dealt with by the rules and what inferences should be drawn based on changing facts. Connecting actions with fulfilled conditions is called inference and a series of inferences is an inference chain. Rules provide a clear way of describing knowledge and linking inferences. The processing of the rules can be stepped through with the opportunity to examine the state of things at each step. Rule based systems also provide an easy method for explaining the decisions taken at each stage of the rule processing.

There are two traditional methods of inference chaining: *forward chaining* and *backward chaining*.  Backward chaining is more rigid in structure than forward chaining and can only be used where all the possible goals or hypotheses can be determined in advance. This is normally the case in expert systems in the commercial world.  Forward chaining systems are sometimes called "event-driven" or "data-driven" systems and have been criticised for being unwieldy unless an effective strategy is provided as a guide from stored premise to conclusion.  Ideal inference systems will have the ability to deal with both these inference mechanisms and some of the countless others that have cropped up in recent years.

## The user interface

Presentation to the user of questions, prompts, explanations and conclusions must be totally free of ambiguity and open to interrogation. It is imperative to remember at all times the fact that the user is not necessarily expert in the given domain and consequently needs all the help and advice possible throughout the interaction with the system. How does the system handle uncertainty from the users point of view? What emphasis is placed on the wording of questions? When in consultation with an expert, the user will, through body signals, tonal inflections or other signs, be transmitting more information to the expert than will be passed on to the expert system. These factors must be considered in the system interface design and can only be perfected through constant modification and refinement. An ill-prepared user-interface can upset the implementation of the system in the workplace and consequently condemn a system which otherwise may have proved beneficial. The psychological effect of expertise in-a-box should not be underestimated and the reaction to, and level of acceptance of, this technology will be as varied as the personalities using it.

Figure 10.1 illustrates a conceptual model of an expert system with its component parts.

## 10.4  Why we should use expert systems?

There are certain aspects of expert systems that make them desirable in particular application areas. We will look later at suitable application areas for expert systems development, but firstly we take a glance at the advantages and disadvantages of expert systems.

Expert systems are being developed now because of the value being placed on human expertise and because of the increased competitiveness that can be gained from "working smarter". We are in the midst of a knowledge revolution with increasing emphasis being placed on information flow and knowledge accessibility. Particularly in transaction based business where customer knowledge and process knowledge at 'transaction time' is all important, that knowledge is the difference between your expert and your non-expert and provides decisive advantage to whoever possesses it. So what happens if the process knowledge is incorporated into a software program? There are commercial and social implications which are outside the scope of this chapter but we focus on a direct comparison between the human expert and the expert system.

**Figure 10.1** Conceptual model of expert system.

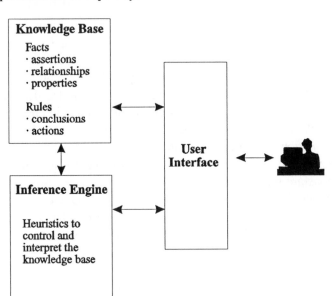

Before comparing expert systems with "real" or human experts let us first look to the *Collins Dictionary* for a definition of "expert":

*an expert is someone who has extensive skill or knowledge in a particular field.*

From the expert system point of view, the emphasis should be placed on "particular field". We are told also that the word expert derives from the Latin "expertus" meaning known by experience. An expert learns from years of experience. An expert system has to be told.

## 10.5 The advantages of expert systems

One advantage of expert systems is its consistency. Once the system has been designed to take a decision based on a given set of rules, then it will consistently carry out those rules. This will ensure identical implementation of those rules throughout an organisation because there is no limit to the number of locations that the expert system can be simultaneously. One of the largest difficulties professional firms face these days is maintaining the expertise level within the organisation when an experienced staff member leaves. Once knowledge is acquired by an expert system, it is around for all time. Human experts are very scarce and very expensive particularly in knowledge-based industries. Expert systems by comparison are relatively inexpensive. Box 10.3 outlines the advantages of expert systems over human experts.

| Expert System | Human Expert |
|---|---|
| Consistent | Inconsistent |
| Can be used in many locations | One location |
| Inexpensive | Expensive |
| Easily monitored | Difficult to monitor |
| Permanent | Temporary |
| Easily modified | Not easily modified |

**Box 10.3** Advantages of expert systems.

## 10.6 The disadvantages of expert systems

The rules change. An expert system cannot adapt to change unless it is told. A human expert sometimes applies more global or commonsense knowledge to a problem due to perhaps a sudden change in the world economy. An expert system without up-to-date knowledge is totally ineffective and potentially a liability. A human expert learns constantly and can be creative and inspired, weighing up new information or formulating totally new, more efficient algorithms to apply to existing problems. For an expert system to remain useful it needs to be constantly maintained by an expert. Box 10.4 outlines the disadvantages of expert systems over human experts.

| Human Expert | Expert System |
|---|---|
| Adaptive | Inflexible |
| Intuitive | Totally unimaginative |
| Global knowledge | Problem specific knowledge |
| Commonsense reasoning | No inherent reasoning ability |
| Self-learning | Needs maintenance |

**Box 10.4** Disadvantages of expert systems.

## 10.7 An expert system example

A large proportion of expert systems that have been developed have been built as assistants to the professional expert. The following example, which we will call the Investment Advisor, is an extract from one such system. This is intended as an example of an expert system's structure rather than professional investment advice or theory. Try and figure out, as you work your way through the example, whether this is a backward or forward chaining inference implementation.

**The problem**

When advising a client on investment strategy, the expert has to consider the client's requirements from the investment, the risk level that the client is prepared to take, his tax situation and whether he has a single lump sum to invest or intends to make monthly or annual payments to the investment fund. The expert has information on up to 100 different investment plans and seeks to match his clients requirement profile to the most suitable plan or selection of plans. The expert knows the features and benefits of each of the plans, but the sheer volume and permutations that arise with the changing fortunes of Government Securities and Index Linked funds means that he can only really feel confident recommending a minority of plans unless he is prepared to spend a considerable amount of his (expensive) time analysing each client's portfolio.

**The knowledge**

For the purpose of this example we will reduce the number of different investment plans to four so that we can look at the profile of each of the plans. The following plans are fictional and function to represent different types of investment plans only.

*Plan 1*
The Expert Edge Managed Growth Fund requires payment monthly and is suitable for the higher taxpayer who is prepared to take a medium risk for both growth and income return.

*Plan 2*
The Expert Gilt Edged Unit Trust provides high growth for the low taxpayer who is a high risktaker with a lump sum payment.

*Plan 3*
The Guaranteed Income Bond is for the investor with a lump sum payment, and provides income at zero risk for the low taxpayer.

*Plan 4*
The Expert Edge Fixed Interest Plan is for both high and low taxpayers who want growth in their investment with medium risk and either a lump sum or regular payment plan. Table 10.1 summarises these plans.

| Plan | Requirements | Risk | Tax rate | Payment |
|------|-------------|------|----------|---------|
| Managed Growth | Growth | Medium | High | Regular |
| Unit Trust Growth | High | Low | Low | Lump sum |
| Guaranteed Bond | Income | Zero | High | Lump sum |
| Fixed Interest | Growth | Medium | High/Low | Lump sum/ Regular |

**Table 10.1** Summary of investment plans.


**The rules**

Once the knowledge has been determined we must determine the rules to enable this knowledge to be used. The following is an extract of what these rules might look like:

| | |
|---|---|
| IF the investor's requirement is for growth | Condition 1 |
| AND the preferred level of risk is medium | Condition 2 |
| AND he is a high taxpayer | Condition 3 |
| AND the payment method is regular | Condition 4 |
| THEN advise the Managed Growth fund | Action 1 |

A managed growth fund (Action 1) is advised if conditions 1 to 4 are met. Other rules might be presented as follows:

| | |
|---|---|
| IF the investor's requirement is for growth | Condition 1 |
| AND the preferred level of risk is high | Condition 5 |
| AND he is a low taxpayer | Condition 6 |
| AND the payment method is lump sum | Condition 7 |
| THEN advise the Unit Trust fund | Action 2 |

OR

| | |
|---|---|
| IF the investor's requirement is for income | Condition 8 |
| AND the preferred level of risk is zero | Condition 9 |
| AND he is a high taxpayer | Condition 3 |
| AND the payment method is lump sum | Condition 7 |
| THEN advise the Guaranteed Bond | Action 3 |

OR

| | |
|---|---|
| IF the investor's requirement is for growth | Condition 1 |
| AND the preferred level of risk is medium | Condition 2 |
| AND he is a high taxpayer | Condition 3 |

|                                              |             |
|----------------------------------------------|-------------|
| OR a low taxpayer                            | Condition 6 |
| AND the payment method is lump sum           | Condition 7 |
| OR regular                                   | Condition 4 |
| THEN advise the Fixed Interest fund          | Action 4    |

## The conclusion

This is an obvious simplification of the rules and in this representation, conditions 1, 2, 3 and 4 would give actions 1 and 2. In the actual implementation of the system, each attribute of the client's profile is given a weighting and each plan is examined to see how it matches the weighted profile of the client. The plans are then scored and sorted to provide the top five most suitable plans for the client. It is obviously very easy to add new plans or change the weighting, without the expert having to calculate and analyse the effects of the changes.

## The result

The complete analysis procedure, which starts by keying in the client's profile and ends with the details of the five most suitable investment plans being presented to the user, takes just under 3 minutes. The same level of analysis used to take up to 2 hours. This system was developed in less than 6 man-weeks.

## 10.8 Expert systems in practice

The following few pages deal with some successful modern-day expert system implementations. It is not the intention to cover the more traditional systems such as Mycin and Prospector as these are sufficiently well covered in numerous other books. Most of the following systems have been developed and represent usage of expert system tools in commercial environments. Hopefully this will enliven by example your understanding of the practical application of the principles that were outlined briefly earlier. We have endeavoured to touch on a selection of systems that cover different types of problem areas. Hopefully at least one of these might prove instructive to each reader.

It is not practical to describe in detail the workings of the individual systems, but we will give an overview of the function and objectives of each system from the users point of view. In some instances we will then concentrate on a specific area within the program to delineate the method in which the knowledge is represented, the decisions taken, and the advice given to the user.

## Application Type - Advice

IMAGE (Intelligent Marketing Assistant and Guide to Exporting) is a system which was developed for a client that is involved in advising exporters when entering foreign markets. It is intended to give the new exporter assistance in preparation for the export market. The system contains general business theory and more specific marketing theory with particular reference to exporting procedures.

IMAGE can be broken down into four modules :

> Promoter Profile
> Market Analysis
> Product Analysis
> Advice Module

The first three modules are used to gather data about the promoter, the market and the product, all of which is assimilated and used in the final module to generate general advice, a research brief and a marketing plan specifically tailored to the characteristics of the promoter and his proposed product and market.

The **Promoter Profile Module** examines the trading position of the company, trading history, relevant export experience and number of employees. It looks at the proposed method of project financing and examines the levels of expertise the company has in relation to Financial, Technical/Production, Marketing and Management areas. The system analyses proposed levels of expenditure against in-house expertise and highlights such areas as working capital requirements and shortage of relevant business experience.

The **Market Analysis Module** assists the user in defining the profile of the market, looking at the position of the market on the market cycle, giving up-to-date financial information on all major world markets, establishes the promoter's reputation in the market, proposed distribution strategies and main market sector.

Products, like markets, go through cyclical stages of development. The **Product Analysis Module** looks at product sales, product profitability, cashflow and competitive products to determine the position of the promoter's product on the development cycle. Product quality and pricing (relative to competitors) is established.

At each stage throughout the usage of the system, the user is provided with theory and background information on the questions being asked and the advice being given. Before looking at the advice module, we will first examine the rule structure and the knowledge represented in the program.

## Rule structure

The position of the market on the market cycle is extremely relevant in establishing the basis for general advice to the user. Let's now look at the rules involved in this section. The knowledge relating to the Market Cycle section has eight subsections:

> Market growth
> Growth potential
> Product proliferation
> Number of competitors
> Market share distribution
> Customer stability
> Ease of market entry
> Technology

Each of these factors indicate whether the market is embryonic, growing, mature or declining. We will describe some of them.

*Market growth*
For the purpose of this exercise, we can state that a market is either growing, growing strongly, stable or declining. If this was the only factor governing the position of the market on the market cycle, we could define the following rules:

> IF the market is growing
> AND the growth is not strong
> THEN the market is at an Embryonic stage
>
> IF the market is growing
> AND the growth is strong
> THEN the market is at a Growing stage
>
> IF the market is stable
> THEN the market is at a Mature stage
>
> IF the market is declining
> THEN the market is at a Declining stage

However, if things were that simple, we wouldn't need an expert system. Marketing is a lot more complex and also a lot less defined. Let's look at the competitors in the marketplace.

Are there any competitors?
Are there lots of competitors?
Perhaps the marginal competitors are beginning to decline?
Are all the competitors nearly out of business?

The answer to each of these questions can indicate market position. At this point in the knowledge engineering process, what is becoming evident is that each of the factors must be weighted and an overall conclusion should be drawn based on the accumulated knowledge. Each of the following factors can be assigned weightings or confidence factors as follows:

Market growth: 0.8
Growth potential: 0.6
Product proliferation: 0.2
Number of competitors: 0.4
Market share distribution: 0.4
Customer stability: 0.2
Ease of market entry: 0.4
Technology: 0.2

Let's look at what happens if we process the rules in relation to a mature market:

> IF the market growth is stable: 0.8
> AND the competition is specialising to grow: 0.6
> AND product proliferation is slow: 0.2
> AND marginal competitors are beginning to decline: 0.4
> AND few companies control the industry: 0.4
> AND customer buying patterns are well developed: 0.2
> AND there are established marker leaders: 0.4
> AND technology process and material focus is important: 0.2
>
> THEN the market is mature: 3.2

The above is a simplification of what is happening in IMAGE. Each of the market cycle factors are being weighted to establish priorities and relative importance of each. When any condition for an Embryonic, Growing, Mature or Declining factor is met, then the confidence level of that factor is increased. Depending on the levels of confidence in each sector, IMAGE decides where on the market cycle the promoter's market is and tailors the advice to that sector.

**The advice module**

This module collects data from all of the previous modules and assimilates the inferred information. The advice that is given out depends on that information. For example, the information required in a Research Brief depends on the state of the market and the position of the product on the product cycle. We have outlined in brief how we determine what stage the market is at. There is a similar process for the product cycle. If we reduce the possible number of Research Briefs to four, it would be acceptable to use the information gathered on market and product to define the following rules:

> IF the market is new
> AND the product is new
> THEN use Research Brief 4
>
> IF the market is not new
> AND the product is new
> THEN use Research Brief 3
>
> IF the market is new
> AND the product is not new
> THEN use Research Brief 2
>
> IF the market is not new
> AND the product is not new
> THEN use Research Brief 1

where Research Briefs 1-4 are tailored to each of the specific circumstances above.
This is obviously a simplification of a minute portion of the total system. Its function is not to delineate expert marketing rules but rather to be elucidative from a system structure viewpoint.

IMAGE is a combination of both backward and forward chaining and is a typical example of where expert systems can be applied to assist professionals give high quality consistent advice.

**Application Type - Interpretation**

The Companies (Amendment) Act 1986 implements the Fourth EC Council Directive on company law. Much of the Directive leaves little choice to the national legislator, but there are however variances between countries on implementation. The CAAA (Companies (Amendment) Act Advisor) addresses the implementation of the Companies (Amendment) Act in Ireland. This system was developed in association with a professional accountancy firm.

**The problem**

The Act requires all companies limited by shares or guarantee (including dormant companies) to publish their accounts by filing them with the Registrar of Companies. Fixed formats for profit and loss accounts and balance sheets are laid down and these, together with extra note requirements, give rise to considerable new disclosure. The act introduces two new classes of company, medium and small, which modify the format of the accounts and the disclosure requirements.

Who knows what needs to be disclosed?
What are the new formats for balance sheet and profit and loss?
What are the exemptions for small and medium companies?
What is a small company?
What is a medium company?

One of the provisions of the Act states that all companies affected by the Act, with an accounting year-end after the 31st of December 1986, must publish accounts and make the required disclosure to the Companies Office within 11 months of the year-end. The difficulty however is that because of the complexity of the legislation and because it is new, the vast majority of professional auditors have yet to gain significant experience in this area. Typically the auditor will be asked by the client how they are going to be affected by the Act. There are however as many answers to that as there are auditor's clients. The CAAA addresses these issues.

The system can be divided into four modules:

Scope of the Act
Balance Sheet
Profit & Loss
Disclosure

The Balance Sheet, Profit & Loss and Disclosure sections all inter-relate and the CAAA determines the format of Balance Sheet and Profit & Loss required for each company and the items that must be disclosed when filing the return with the Companies Office. We will concentrate on the first section, looking at the rules used to establish the effect of the Act for specific instances.

The difficulty with legislation, from the layman's point of view, is the nature of the wording. (It sometimes appears that this is also the case with expert systems and artificial intelligence.) The Companies (Amendment) Act is a fifty-page A4 document, each paragraph of which is a challenge to read. The accountancy firm, when holding a series of one-day seminars on the Act, used a manual which came to about two-hundred pages. It occurs to me that it is much easier to embody this type of knowledge in an expert system than in any other vehicle.

One of the items to consider in relation to the Companies (Amendment) Act is the incorporation date of the company. Let's see what the Act says about that.

*A private company which was incorporated before such commencement shall qualify to be treated under subsection(1) of this section as a small company or, as the case may be, as a medium-sized company, in respect of the first financial year of the company in which accounts of the company are required to be prepared in accordance with section 3 of this Act if it satisfies at least two of the relevant qualifying conditions specified in subsection (2) or (3), as may be appropriate, of this section in respect of either that first financial year or the financial year immediately preceding that year.*

That's all one sentence!

It would be necessary for any person reading the above paragraph to examine the sections referenced in order to establish the size of the company. If we take the reference to "at least two" from this subsection of the Act, and look at subsections (2) and (3), we can work out that the rules for small companies are such that if any two of the following conditions apply, then the company can be classified as a small company:

balance sheet is not greater than 1,250,000
turnover is not greater than 2,500,000
average number of employees is not greater than 50

Looking at the paragraph of legislation above we can work out (with some difficulty) that these rules can be applied to either the first financial year of the company affected by the Act, or indeed the financial year preceding that. So for each of the two years in question we can say that:

> IF the balance sheet is not greater than 1,250,000
> AND turnover is not greater than 2,500,000
>
> OR turnover is not greater than 2,500,000
> AND average number of employees is not greater than 50
>
> OR balance sheet is not greater than 1,250,000
> AND average number of employees is not greater than 50
> THEN the company can be classified as small

As with all expert systems, the primary concern of the knowledge engineer is to provide a system that is not only easy to use, but also emulates, in so far as is possible, the working procedure of the expert, taking cognisance of the processes which are normally applied in the working environment.

One of the most useful features of the CAAA is that it monitors its own usage. In other words it remembers every question that has been asked and notes all questions that have either been answered in the negative, or have not been addressed at all. This is to facilitate the review process which is common practice in the professional accountancy firm. Frequently one of the junior members of staff would undertake a task which would later be checked and reviewed by a senior. The CAAA eliminates the requirement for review at this level, printing out an audit trail of all questions answered and decisions taken.

**Application Type - Planning**

CATALYST (Capital Acquisitions Tax Advisor) is an expert system developed in conjunction with a local tax expert. The system concerns itself with the effect of Capital Acquisitions Tax (CAT). CAT, which used to be known in the UK as Capital Transfer Tax, more latterly restricted to Inheritance Tax, is a tax which deals with the benefit gained by a donee or successor when in receipt of gifts or inheritances. The tax liability which accrues as a result of CAT is assessed on an ongoing basis on the aggregate amount of the gifts or inheritances received throughout the lifetime of the beneficiary.

The Capital Acquisitions Tax Act, 1976, makes provision for

a *gift tax* on the taxable value of every taxable gift taken by a donee on or after the 28th February, 1974, and

an *inheritance tax* on the taxable value of every taxable inheritance taken by a successor on or after the 1st April, 1975.

The scheme of the Act is to tax property to which a person becomes beneficially entitled in possession otherwise than for full consideration in money or money's worth. A gift or an inheritance is taken from a "disponer" who is the financial source of the benefit and may be, for example, a testator, intestate, donor, settlor etc. The actual relationship of the donee or successor to the disponer is important in computing tax payable.

The core function of the Catalyst is to assist the professional Capital Acquisitions Tax practitioner process these complex computations correctly. There are however a number of operational aspects stemming from this which make a more practical contribution to the actual process that takes place.

**Estate planning** - The primary reason CAT occurs is because a gift or inheritance is donated to a beneficiary by a donor. The consequential tax liability is dependent on the profile of the beneficiary in terms of his/her previous aggregated benefits and his/her relationship to the donor.

Some simple rules ..

> IF The relationship between donor and donee is spouse
> THEN the threshold amount is £150,000
>
> IF The relationship between donor and donee is nephew/niece
> AND the nephew/niece is not a favoured nephew/niece
> THEN the threshold amount is £20,000
>
> IF The relationship between donor and donee is none
> THEN the threshold amount is £10,000

If we look at the second of these rules, we must examine what is meant by a favoured nephew/niece. By going through the legislation we can tell that a favoured nephew/niece is one who has worked with the uncle/aunt in the latter's business for a significant period of time and should then be treated as a son/daughter. As we examine each possibility it becomes clear that it can all be defined in rules.

The Catalyst is being used by individuals now to plan their estates and to bequeath their assets in the most tax effective manner possible. This is particularly true in the case of agricultural property where the cash-flow effect of CAT can be so immense that the property may need to be sold to meet the tax liability.

**Revenue returns** - As with most other areas in this tax, the required documentation that needs to be returned to the Revenue Commissioners can be quite time-consuming and complicated to complete. The Revenue Commissioners have welcomed Catalyst and have suggested ways that it can be used to help practitioners make their returns more effectively.

The complexity of this tax is immense and it causes great concern among solicitors, accountants and investment houses, who all have to deal with the possible consequences of a client's death.

This system has no uncertainty, it does however have an extremely large base of expert knowledge. That knowledge is scarce and expensive. Expert Edge were fortunate with the expert in this case, who was a CAT expert and a computer fan also. As an example of a suitable application for expert system development, the Catalyst is ideal with a heavily rule based nature. The problem can be well defined and the pay-back is significant. This system will now process a complex CAT computation in five minutes which before may have taken up to five hours.

**Application Type - Monitoring**

The Analyst is being used by a Government Department to assist the user monitor the performance of a segment of the business community, by analysing the accounts and financial returns of each organisation within that segment.

The Analyst assists in the interpretation of the accounts in respect of financial status, profitability, asset utility, productivity and overall health. The system calculates key ratios and then draws conclusions upon them about particular aspects of the organisation. The main source of information is the organisation's financial returns, which are compared against the ratios and standards that are considered a norm in that specific sector. The conclusions are derived from the ratios calculated using company data compared with other company data and figures for the previous year. In addition, it compares those figures with the relative and absolute measures for the sector.

Financial managers control and monitor performance of divisions, companies and business units. Once the core data has been compiled, the Analyst produces quick conclusions about key areas, with the supporting data, for further study or distribution to other management. In particular, this will help to identify those areas which require further investigation whether for positive or negative reasons.

## 10.9  Exploiting expert systems[1]

By now you should have an understanding of expert systems, how they differ from conventional systems, their advantages and limitations.  However, *how might an organisation exploit knowledge-based systems?*

There are three basic ways in which expert systems can be exploited:

- *Aggressively*, to create strategic and competitive advantage;

- *Defensively*, for knowledge capture and the retention of knowledge within the business;

- *In a neutral manner*, where there is no significant effect on the business.

The choice of strategy will depend on a number of factors, including the type of industry, its competitive situation, the position of the corporation in the industry and, of course, the goals and objectives of the corporation. Each strategy will produce different results.

## 10.10  Expert systems for competitive advantage

We can analyse the contribution and impact of expert systems by following the Porter and Miller framework which was introduced in chapter 1. They identify three ways in which information technology (of which expert systems are an element) can affect corporate strategy:

- by improving competitive position;
- by enhancing productivity and improving performance;
- by assisting the development of new businesses.

There is obviously some overlap between these three approaches. For example, by increasing productivity a business could dramatically improve its competitive position with the production of a product at a lower cost.

### Improving competitive position

We have seen in the first three chapters that because of increasing competition the organisation must constantly consider new ways to maintain or improve its competitive position. All the leading banks are active in building expert system applications. However, detailed information on these products is scarce since their developers seek an advantage in a most competitive business. Foreign exchange advisory systems are used by number of Wall Street and City financial institutions. Such systems can qualitatively evaluate currency-option trading strategies over varying market conditions. These systems incorporate complex arbitrage transactions and can assist hypothetical trading strategies under many possible market conditions.

Many banks have developed systems for processing home-loan applications. In France, where interest rates are controlled by the government, the quality of service offered to clients is often the deciding factor in gaining business. To meet this challenge, most banks have systems designed to speed up the mortgage offer process.

For competitive reasons the American Express Card has no fixed spending limit. Limits are personalised, but determining the spending limit for each customer poses a tough administrative challenge. To overcome this problem, they developed the

*Authorisor's Assistant* to sanction credit requests. This system approves certain purchases by American Express cardholders using rules and knowledge of such factors as spending habits and previous monthly billings. American Express is now building a "knowledge highway" to help employees manage every step of the job of managing credit from card applications to collecting overdue accounts. The business goal is to shield both credit card holders and employees from the bureaucracy needed to manage American Express's vast business - so leaving employees free to devote their efforts to building relationships with customers.

We have seen in chapter 10 that, for the manufacturing firm, product innovation is of critical concern. The key to its success lies in creating better products or processes than the competitors and to introduce these before competitors catch up. In the conceptual product design stage expert systems can usefully complement existing computer-aided design (CAD) systems since the actual design drawing phase is preceded by a longer phase for specification, preselection and decision making in which the possible solutions for the product to be manufactured have to be compared from various points of view.

Strategic advantage can also be created by diagnosis and monitoring systems. Krupp, for example, has developed a computer-aided diagnostic system for diesel engines in which data on the new engine, measured on the test bed, is stored and compared with the values of the engine installed, for instance, in a ship. Sensors, installed at roughly 30 locations, monitor the thermodynamic process. This early warning system recognises and assesses signs of impending damage. The expert system makes the diagnosis and recommends what corrective action should be taken. Preventive maintenance can be planned and spare parts procured in time. In this way, engine manufacturer and customer keep in contact throughout the life of the product, a major strategic advantage.

We have seen that competitive advantage can be achieved in two ways: lower cost, or differentiation relative to competitors. American Express's Authorisor's Assistant allows for customers to get individual credit limits. Digital Equipment Corporation's XCON (Expert CONfigurer) permits DEC to offer customers many configurations and architectural options when buying DEC equipment.

Both direct and indirect costs can also be reduced, paving the way for selling a product or providing a service at a cheaper price than competitors. Expert systems applications can point out ways to maximize the use of raw materials and optimise equipment and labour scheduling. Increasing productivity may also result in decreasing costs, especially labour costs.

**Enhancing productivity and performance**

By using expert systems many organisations have realised vast productivity gains. The performance of the organisation is contingent on the knowledge and skill of the employees. Expert systems can be used as an extension of an expert to take over routine tasks and free that person for more demanding problem solving, or they can be used by staff less experienced in the domain of the expert. Further, managers who are afraid to ask questions because they feel they should know the answers can consult an expert system in private.

Expert systems permit tasks that previously required an expert to be carried out by less qualified staff. They can also increase productivity where job performance is inconsistent. For example, the majority of numerically controlled (NC) systems used in computer-aided manufacture (CAM) are geometry-oriented, i.e. they contain only basic functions for geometry-dictated tool selection and cutter pattern. In most cases, such data as selection of tools according to material and cutting data, and selection of machine tool and workholding devices, have to be determined and input by the programmer. Expert systems can readily make up for a deficit of technological and product-specific knowledge. On the financial side, *ExperTax*, developed by accountants Coopers & Lybrand, allow them to have superior tax expertise on a disk for each of its 100 offices in the US. This ensures that quality information and analysis is uniform throughout the corporate system. Tax experts can now devote more time to more complex non-routine situations.

Diagnostic systems can significantly increase the productivity of those involved in fault detection. MENTOR was developed by Honeywell to give its field technicians a portable expert system for troubleshooting and performing preventative maintenance. Formerly constrained by a limited number of refrigeration experts, Honeywell can now support a large number of less-trained field technicians with a portable expert assistant. MENTOR has improved both the quality and efficiency of Honeywell's field technicians and resulted in a lower service fee charged to its customers.

The British National Health Service is using a system called *DHSS-PA* (Performance Analyst) to evaluate the quality of medical care provided by individual health authorities. An evaluation that previously took six experts two hours to achieve is now done in less than ten minutes. A striking feature of this system is that it does not make value judgements, leaving interpretation to users.

**Developing new businesses**

Knowledge is a valuable asset. By capturing an expert's knowledge in an expert system, the expert system provides the organisation with the opportunity to market the skill and expertise of employees without them leaving the office, even when they move to a different employer. The Irish practice of Coopers & Lybrand, together with Expert Edge, developed *The Data Protection Advisor* to help prepare and guide companies through registration and management of data, thus ensuring compliance with the Data Protection Act. This system is now available for other accounting firms and businesses to purchase and use.

Applied Expert Systems Inc. have developed a personal financial planning system called *PlanPower*. What is unusual about this system is that it is sold fully packaged, without the need for customisation. It automates the knowledge of general financial planners (for overall strategy) and specialists (tax, stock market).

Both Texas Instruments and Digital Equipment Corporation first developed expert system for internal use but have since spun off organisations based on this technology that offer new products such as "shells", consulting and training. The international management consulting firm Andersen Consulting have developed a new business building and selling a variety of small expert systems

## 10.11 Knowledge capture and preserving fragile expertise

While information is an organisational resource, equally important is the knowledge which is also contained in the organisation. The modern organisation is increasingly faced with the problem of greater turnover and mobility among employees, especially those with specialist skills and knowledge. Very often the success of corporate activities is due to the performance of a few individuals. Expert systems provide a means of preserving their expertise and skills, as well as making it available to other employees, thus creating a tangible and permanent "organisational memory" of corporate know-how. Expert systems can also readily make up for a deficiency of technological and product specific knowledge. This is important as products and services become more and more complex.

Arthur Andersen have developed the *Financial Statement Analyzer* (FSA) for the US Securities and Exchange Commission. This system is used to analyse and consolidate incoming financial statements. Due to the relatively unstructured nature of financial statements, FSA is required to interpret incoming source data by enabling accounting elements to "find" themselves in the data.

As one of the largest on-line services providing financial information, Dun and Bradstreet's strength is based on its ability to use up-to-the minute financial and commercial information in its analysis. The company is developing a financial analysis update system that will intelligently process on-line information and determine important events that will affect its updates of a company's financial strength, rating and financial position.

## 10.12  Conclusion

Artificial intelligence, in the guise of expert systems, is delivering its long awaited potential. With many successful systems developed over the past number of years, the time is now ripe for organisations to develop a coherent strategy to investigate this technology with a view to exploiting it. Perhaps it should be located in the high potential quadrant of your organisations application's portfolio.

- *Develop a coherent strategy to investigate and explore expert systems.*

- *Be aware of the nature of corporate competition and how it competes.*

- *Select an appropriate area of expertise.*

As Tom Peters (co-author of *In Search of Excellence*) has written:

*Any senior manager in any business of almost any size who isn't at least learning about AI, and sticking a tentative toe or two into AI's waters, is simply out of step, dangerously so.*

## Notes

1     Adapted from J.W. Peppard, Corporate knowledge-based systems: implications and impacts. *Management Decision*, **27**, 5, pp. 48-52.

## Additional reading

Feigenbaum, E., McCorduck, P. and Nii, H.P., *The Rise of the Expert Company.* Macmillan, London, 1988.
Harmon, P. and King, D., *Expert Systems: Artificial Intelligence in Business.* John Wiley & Sons, Inc., New York, 1985.
Leinweber, D., Knowledge-based systems for financial applications. *IEEE Expert*, **3**, 3, 1988, pp. 18-31.
Leonard-Barton, D. and Sviokla, J.J., (1988) Putting expert systems to work. *Harvard Business Review*, March-April, 1988, pp. 91-98.
McDonald, M..H. and Wilson, H., State-of-the-art developments in expert systems and strategic marketing planning. *British Journal of Marketing*, **1**, 2, pp. 159-170.

Peppard, J.W. and Henry, P.L., Corporate knowledge-based systems: a framework for management. *Management Decisions*, **26**, 6, pp. 42-46.

Shiel, B., Thinking about artificial intelligence. *Harvard Business Review*, July-August, 1987.

# 11

# Future Technologies and their Business Impact

The LP *Days of Future Past* by the Moody Blues was a seminal piece when issued in the late 1960s. With its very evocative title, it reminds us that we must look upon the future as a natural progression from the past and see therein that many of the things that will come to pass, have in one guise or another gone before us and the lessons of history, even industrial history, are learned the hard way and often so easily forgotten. In this chapter we want to set the scene for some challenging issues and questions that the reader must address in the future. These issues and questions will affect every fabric of our working lives and, indeed, many of the same issues will affect our personal lives just as much.

We live in challenging times, of that there is no doubt, but we observe in the world of business that the extent of these challenges is underestimated and the nature of them disguised by the prejudices and mores that govern our business lives as we struggle from day to day to address the ever present crises that affect us all. Nobody is immune from these crises. In fact, they are even proportionally the same in their effect on us, irrespective of our position in life. For the sublime *One Minute Manager*, the paragon of efficiency, a ten minute lunch break is a lost opportunity, for a starving child it could be a matter of life or death. It is a question of degree, but for both it represents an immediate problem.

Why is all this important? This chapter argues that many crises in modern business have a common thread and the traditional reactions are becoming less appropriate to solving these.    Major changes are afoot in all spheres of business and radical restructuring of business is inevitable.    Those of us that adapt will survive, the others will falter and wither away.


# 11.1  Future business


### Alvin Toffler - Future Shock

Some of you may remember the book *Future Shock* by Alvin Toffler.[1]  At the time of its publication in 1970, it caused much controversy due, partially at least, to the forthright prognostications of Toffler about the nature of the impending crises set to befall an unsuspecting world in the late 20th century.    While largely a work dealing with social issues, its underlying theme was one of accelerating change and a world overwhelmed through lack of adequate response to that change.

No conventional wisdom has prepared us adequately well for the forces that technology have unleashed upon society.    We are grappling with technology-induced problems in a world, both business and social, that has no capacity to shift quickly enough to react.    We see these problems daily, and indeed the very visibility of them has de-sensitised us to the problems.    Ecologically, we have nuclear power stations less than forty years old that have presented us with dangerous waste that will take 500 years to get rid of.    We have medical techniques that keep us alive and eat up our expensive medical resources doing so.    We can watch from a nose camera, as it happens, a "smart" bomb wing its way down a ventilator shaft in Baghdad, yet cannot find jobs for "smart" bomb makers when there are no wars to fight.

We have a problem with technology today, we use it, we abuse it, but we have not mastered it.    Technology is an obedient servant, but the mastering of it is for future generations.    Our role is to transform our business and social worlds to allow the future generations to master and exploit technology.[2]  Never has it been more obvious that we are the guardians of our children's future.


### Is all this technology relevant to me?

None of this is probably relevant to you, of course.    You are, by your training and education, well fitted for your role in business.    You have many years practical experience behind you, or else, perhaps, you have attended all the right management schools  where you have learned how to take your place in business as befits your station.    You are widely versed in management theory and thus you **know** how to tackle the impending crises, because that is what management is about. Technology is for the technologists, and if required, you can manage them as well as you can manage the marketing department. You are a generic manager with skills that are above technology or marketing or whatever. You also will be extinct in 15 years time.

The fundamental fabric of business and business practice is changing. If you do not think that technology is the key to your effectiveness in business then you are not adequately prepared for the Information Age. Be not afraid, for you join 90% or more of your colleagues in this unhappy state. The fact that you are reading this gives you a clear edge, however.

### I'm a manager - these are tactical not strategic issues

From hereon this section will take a somewhat contrarian view, although the issues raised *are* strategic. You will rarely see these views expressed in conventional business course or seminar materials. Think of these views as extreme perhaps, but they reflect one way of thinking on the organisational structures necessary to exploit future technologies.

### Workplace

The early years of this century saw the introduction of office equipment. In displacing the traditional clerical role, the new processes sought to introduce efficiency by way of automating routine clerical tasks. The introduction of today's office equipment has sought to replicate the former gains in productivity when the typewriter was first introduced in the 1880s, and has been applied against a background of organisational structures that have altered little since the mid 19th century. By continuing to pursue this mechanism of automating clerical tasks, many companies, large and small, are relinquishing the many competitive advantages that the information technology tools can bestow.

We have heard a great deal in the last ten years about competitive advantage and how the application of information technology, among other things, can improve the prospects of firms who adopt it. There is a great difference between adopting new technology and adapting to take in new technology. It is widely considered that the adoption of new technology has not led to the productivity gains that were forecast. This is true. No company will see a great net gain in productivity solely by the adoption of new technology. Only those companies that adapt their business to exploit the real benefits of new technology will find that the investment is worth it. Many companies throw good money after bad trying to automate procedures that fail to enhance the competitiveness of these companies in any material way. There are many reasons why this should be so and one can find an excellent study of it in Zuboff.[3]

## Rebirth of Scientific Management

It is all too easy to consider that increasing automation will allow the concentration of decision making in the hands of the organisation's management. By flattening the organisational hierarchy, improved use of automation and technology will allow managers to be more productive and creative.

So, what do you as executives need to do to grasp these ideas and exploit them for your corporations' benefit? Well, let us disabuse ourselves first of the idea that management has a God given right to ideas. This attitude was prevalent for many years. The philosopher and economist John Locke was very influential in expounding the ideas of social Darwinism in business. People like himself, and Frederick Taylor later on, fostered the ideas of scientific management. This attitude fostered the idea that success was built on expropriation of knowledge into the ranks of management. Thus was born the idea that knowing how it was done was more important than doing it. As Taylor put it when talking about managing a pig-iron foundry, *I can say without the slightest hesitation that the science of handling pig-iron is so great that the man who is fit to handle pig-iron and is sufficiently phlegmatic and stupid to choose this for his occupation is rarely able to comprehend the science of handling pig-iron.*[4]

## Management in crisis

The information age is going to deal these concepts a deadly blow. How many times have you heard it said, seen it written, perhaps even said it yourselves -

> *"I don't understand computers"*
> *"All this high technology is beyond me"*
> *"I don't have to understand wave propagation to play my stereo"*
> *"These new fangled phones are too complex"*

These are the comments of executives in stress. We are losing control of our businesses but precious few realise it. To manipulate information one has to understand the data that forms the basis of that information. Those divesting themselves of the task of manipulating information for strategic purposes are in serious danger of letting these strategic decisions slip from their grasp. Senior executives must be in a position to take strategic decisions and whether or not they generate the information on which such decisions are made, they must be comfortable with the data or else they are reduced to rubber stamping strategic decisions made by others.

**Information Age is upon us**

This problem would go away if only information flow would slow down. This will not happen. How many organisations in the last five years have we seen struck down by the early signs of this organisational dysfunction? We need to look very carefully at the pre and post Big Bang situation in the financial services market. Financial services, and arbitrage and index trading in particular, require nigh on instant decision-making. The senior management just had to leave it to the market traders to keep positions and maintain liquidity. Many of them failed to do so, not because their telecommunications were inadequate, nor their information systems under-powered, but rather that a serious mismatch developed between the speed of decision-making required and the organisational structure in place to take those decisions. A few companies have even begun to address these problems seriously. For those involved in planning, now is the time to start addressing the issue as it will take 5-10 years to complete restructuring and small efforts now could avert a disaster for your business. We must not underestimate how difficult this is, both politically and conceptually for many people, and there is indeed a tendency to want to leave it for another day, but time waits for no man and it only requires micro-seconds for a machine to screw everything up.

We may quip about some of these issues but they are, of course, very serious ones, and we want to stress how important it is to examine them. Each and every one of you may find no cause or justification for action within your organisations, but you owe it to yourselves to address the issue *before* you dismiss it.

**Why business needs transformation**

Several of the contributers have mentioned the need for business transformation. By this they generally mean business *process* transformation. This chapter takes a much more radical role on this question and will explain why.

**Outdated Corporate structures**

As has already been mentioned, the post industrial information age is going to cause a massive shift in thinking about business and workplace practice and little attention is paid to the transformations necessary to effect those changes. Many studies have been done on the impact of automation in the workplace but not many authors have proposed alternative management and organisational structures to effectively translate new processes and structures into forms that better suit the informated organisation. Toffler calls it the *Organisational Ad-Hocracy* and Zuboff refers to the *Informated*

*Organisation* as models of the organisational structures that will emerge in this decade and the next.

To envisage how an organisation should be structured to cope with the new realities, it is recommended that you dismiss any organisational structures that you consider as constants, the pillars of the organisation today. The structures of today will not fit tomorrow and little is to be gained by trying to squeeze old structures into new realities. This is not to say that any particular structure will fit any particular organisation but in figure 11.2, a prototypical structure for a truly informated organisation can be viewed alongside the current equivalent (figure 11.1).

**Figure 11.1** Typical organisational structure in a pre-Information Age company.

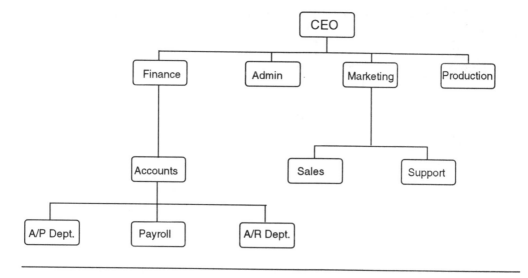

## Information Age companies

Information Age companies will exhibit a radically different structure from that which prevails today. One might see a structure not unlike that in figure 11.2. The impression one gets immediately is the strong shift from a hierarchical structure to a more relational one, reflecting perhaps, as has happened in the information systems area itself, that strictly hierarchical mechanisms are unwieldy in fast moving situations. While it is unlikely that the relational model structure will be entirely appropriate for business, it will form the basis for business structures that are responsive to rapidly changing business environments of the next century.[5]

**Figure 11.2**  Structure of Information Age organisation.

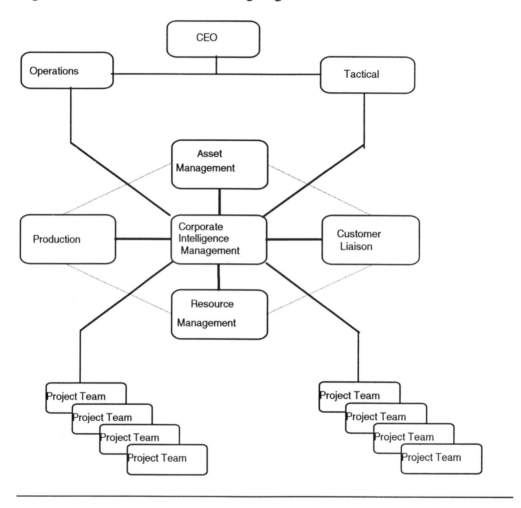

## What will these companies produce?

How representative of the industrial and service workplace will these new companies be? Another way of addressing that question is to ask what is it that these companies will produce in this new Information Age? The answer is stark but likely to be very true. These companies will produce information. Information will be the lifeblood of all companies in the coming decades. Those that produce information and use it effectively will be the companies that survive. In a short period of time, we will see developing a society where structural unemployment will become the norm. Since 1945, we have seen the so-called smoke stack industries vanish as the huge industrial concerns have automated or closed. In the period 1990-2010 the same fate will befall lighter manufacturing. As processes are automated the requirement for human labour will diminish. The currency of labour will be the currency of intellective skills.[6] The ability with which a company can innovate and adapt based on maximising its information skills and resources will be the critical factor in the future.

### Evolution or revolution?

The history of computing in particular and technology in general is one of gradual evolution interspersed with revolutions of major importance that lead to frenzied activity followed by further evolution. Thus, the cycle of evolution and revolution is symptomatic of development. This will continue to be the case. We stand at the brink of revolution. The last computing revolution was the advent of the IBM personal computer 10 years ago. For purists, of course, personal computers did not start with the IBM PC, but it can be argued that the impact of the IBM PC was of greater importance than the introduction of the Apple II in 1977. In computer terms, there is a mini revolution every time a new hardware or software product is introduced that achieves market share and alters the way we do business. The personal computer has radically changed business procedures in the last 10 years. In the next 10 years, we will see similar changes of even greater magnitude by products as yet not developed. We have reached a critical mass in the understanding of the impact of technology on business. We now have to harness that knowledge effectively and efficiently.

## 11.2  Future technologies

Any section of this book can only give the reader the briefest of introductions to the topics discussed. You are at a technological wine tasting, where you can sample and try everything but you will have to savour the full product at some other time. We can provide the insight and, hopefully, direct you to more comprehensive cellars where you can concentrate on areas of importance and savour the contents at your leisure. The technologies chosen here are those of most relevance to business at the operational level. There are technologies that are more important as fundamental drivers of technological evolution but they are largely invisible to the average user and as such are not of primary interest. The technologies chosen are a sample of telecommunications, computer and software developments that are important, but the list is by no means exhaustive. A subsection of any one of these could easily fill a book in itself.

## Telecommunications

In chapter 7 and elsewhere we looked at the great changes in telecommunications over the last twenty years. Yet, in the future we are likely to see even greater change. Nothing has impacted our lives as much as the invasive power of communications and how they have literally shrunk the world. Today, telecommunications gives us a window on the world; tomorrow will see that world inside our offices and homes in a way that we can little imagine. Let us examine some of the technologies that will impact us in this way.

## Digital high speed communications

Today, most people in Western Europe and North America access the telephone network via digital communications. The ubiquitous telephone communicates, for the most part, in the zeroes and ones of binary digital logic. We have reached a critical mass in the availability of digital communications such that an explosion in the availability of services is coming. In a relatively short period of time you will be able to shield yourself from the angry creditor by routing his calls away from you automatically via *Call Identification*. Access to vast amounts of knowledge, indeed perhaps even the sum total of human knowledge, will be available easily and cost effectively. Even today, the availability of vast databases of information is a business resource under-utilised and largely unknown. This will have a profound effect on the businesses of knowledge brokers, generally management consultants and other professional consultants, who can be eliminated by the judicious use of these information resources.

Today's high speed is tomorrow's crawl. We consider 64k (64,000 bits per second) as high speed data lines. Tomorrow's lines will be 1 terabit (1,000,000,000,000 bits per second) and beyond. What difference will that make to the average user? It is analogous to the difference in the information content and speed of a Morse code message and TV.

## Less travel needs

The profound effect on business will perhaps be on travel. As full motion, large screen video conferencing comes on stream there will be less need to hop on a plane to New York. The video screen will be wall sized with very high definition and you will dial the participants as easily as you can create a telephone conference call today. Even now the equipment to do this on a point-to-point basis has dropped to $10,000 for each end. This point will be touched on further in a subsequent piece on virtual reality.

**Still greater speed of business and the profound implications**

As outlined earlier, the pace of business is increasing at breakneck speed. High speed communications will increase that further. Imagine as a product supplier to the supermarkets of the continent, that your products are being ordered within seconds of consumers picking them from the shelves. Your flexibility to schedule production is being eroded because competitors who can meet the consumer need faster will be poised to take your shelf space if you leave it vacant for long. In retailing, these trends are already manifesting themselves within store chains. In time, the processes of electronic trading will reach a critical mass and those geared to respond will survive. We are not talking about the current levels of EDI, but trading an order of magnitude more integrated, timely and efficient than anything available today.

**Artificial intelligence**

*Artificial intelligence - a definition*
Artificial Intelligence is a very complex field. Like all new buzzwords, Artificial Intelligence ( AI ) is used and abused, to hype products in the market. The formal definition of AI was expounded by the British scientist Alan Turing in the 1940s. He defined a system thus: *a machine has artificial intelligence when there is no discernible difference between the conversation generated by the machine and that of an intelligent person*[7]. It was not until late 1991 that the first system ever passed that test, and only just. However, we should not be too pedantic about this, as many AI systems, while less than perfect, do exhibit intelligent behaviour and provide real benefits to users.

Taking a simplistic view, AI can be broken down into two areas - symbolic (rule based) systems and non-symbolic systems (neural networks). These technologies are in use all around you but you may not realise it.

**Rule-based expert systems**

In chapter 10 we explored expert systems. So for example, when you fill out a life insurance policy, most insurance companies will use a rule based-expert system to evaluate your proposal. In "conversation" with the client, the system will ask a series of questions. Based on the responses of the client, the system will weigh up the answers and give a response. This is different from an ordinary computer program, in that the AI system will take a probability-based line in response to any particular answer. Thus, the response of the system is conditioned upon weighing up all factors in the client's answers and comparing these to the base of knowledge that the system already has.

As a practical example, if the client is a smoker, the system could evaluate on the basis of his/her response that they are a higher insurance risk than non-smokers. So far so good, any computer program can do that. But how easy is it to determine the relative risk between two potential clients, one of whom smokes 60 cigarettes a day and drinks 5 beers a week, and another who is a non-smoker but drinks 5 beers a day. Suddenly the problem has got murkier. The system will have a base of knowledge on which to work and will start to evaluate these proposals from a probability standpoint. But it is hoped that you can see that all the possible combinations would make a non-rule-based system very unwieldy. The difference between a non-AI program and an AI program is that the AI program will have an inference mechanism, i.e. it will infer an answer based on inconclusive or conflicting inputs. The techniques of inference was briefly looked at in chapter 10.

While these systems have been around for the last decade at least, they will really assume a very important part of all our lives in the decade ahead. The implications for you are myriad. Many of the routine, albeit highly skilled jobs will be capable of being replaced. In the office environment, skilled personnel who have to make value judgements based on their knowledge of the subject area will find their roles changing. On the factory floor, the rapid automation of processes will see an acceleration of employee displacement. The machines will be able to manufacture, process, evaluate and deliver faster and more efficiently than ever the human could do it. In the services sector, the increasing automation of all things, from cash dispensers to credit card verifiers, from automatic traffic lights to intelligent alarm systems, will continue until some time in the period 2005-2015 when all services capable of being delivered by machine *will be* delivered by machine. All these issues will affect you profoundly as a business executive and you seriously need to ask yourself if you are prepared for them.

## Neural nets and genetic algorithms

Neural nets are very different from the type of computer systems you may be used to. The original work on neural networks was conducted in the 1940s by McCullough and Pitts. They sought to model how a neuron in the brain held and passed information. Thus, their research sought to construct a device that would emulate biological systems, albeit very simplistically. Neural networks are very foreign to most conventional computer people. This stems from the fact that neural networks are not programmed by a series of computer instructions, but rather, they are "trained" on a series of inputs and they "acquire" knowledge as a result of that training. Following a lapse of many years of inactivity in this field, the mid 1980s saw an explosive growth in neural networks and their applications. Neural networks are known by many names - neural nets, adaptive networks, abductive information modelling, adaptive logic models. While each of these are different in their approach to a problem set, they all share the common trait of addressing a problem by training rather than programming.

Neural nets have seen their greatest penetration to date in the military and financial services arena. In military applications it is generally the pattern recognition abilities of neural nets that have been dominant. Neural nets, if properly trained, are very good at picking identifiable patterns out from background noise. The human brain is also very good at this activity. Where they differ is that research has shown the human is unable to juggle more than seven external inputs at once, whereas the net is able to handle hundreds of simultaneous signals. Neural networks are at an early stage, however. It takes very skilled computer scientists or cognitive psychologists to train a network properly. A network, like a child, takes much careful tuition, makes many mistakes in early life and can burn out if over-trained. Approach teaching with skill and a network will deliver great benefits to its creator.

**Fuzzy logic**

Fuzzy logic is the darling of the production world today, and it is in production and manufacturing that it has found its greatest expression. Fuzzy logic is about real world decision making, where nothing is ever black or white. Decisions that depend not on whether the input is right or wrong, but more akin to "nearly" right or "marginally" wrong. These inexact value judgements are at the heart of fuzzy logic. This is a very precise mathematical concept, developed in the 1960s at Berkeley by computer science professor Lofti Zadeh. It attempts to model human judgement by quantifying such "fuzzy" ideas as long, very short, nearly right, etc. In its short history fuzzy logic has had a major impact on consumer goods. Before the end of this decade, it is not inconceivable that all consumer electronic goods, from vacuum cleaners to telephones to automobiles, will be crammed solid with fuzzy logic controllers.

# 11.3 Object oriented systems

**What are they?**

Norway is famous for many things, Vikings, fjords, merchant ships and cross country skiing. It is not quite so famous as the birthplace of object oriented systems, but in time this may be seen as Norway's greatest contribution to mankind. The computer language Simula was created in Norway in 1967 and it contained many of the structures and concepts that we now label as object oriented.

From humble beginnings, object oriented systems have had a long gestation period and only in the last five years have they made any headway in the commercial programming world. The techniques of object oriented programming will continue to supplant and supersede procedural programming techniques to an extent that it is unlikely that by the year 2000 any systems will not be created in an object oriented way.

Object oriented systems have several properties ( as foreign to most IT professionals as they may be to you ), including *objects, classes, encapsulation, inheritance* and *polymorphism. Objects* are representations of data and the processes that act on that data, *encapsulated* or hidden within the object itself. (See figure 11.3.)

---

**Figure 11.3** Object oriented metaphor.

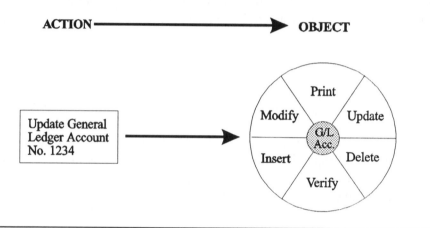

---

Think of these objects in real world terms. A particular man, Albert Einstein, is a member of *class* human. A human *process* or action is to walk. Thus, Albert Einstein *inherits* the ability to walk from his membership of the class of humans. Walking is not something a class of objects with no feet can do. Thus, the class of flowers cannot walk, leading to the inevitable conclusion that the particular flower, Tulip, as a member of the flower class, cannot walk either. Returning to old Albert, if we issue him with the instruction "Walk Albert!", he will do so. We have instructed a specific *instance* of *class* human (Albert) to execute a process (walk) that is a characteristic of this class. Perhaps you can see that we only have to program once the process "walk" for the class of all humans. Any instance of this class (Albert) will inherit this process without us having to code it specifically for him. This saves an incredible amount of time over the traditional approach to the problem. Finally, let us examine the final property - *polymorphism*. To do this let us introduce Stephen Hawking, the great English scientist whom many regard as Einstein's successor. Dr. Hawking has been struck in latter years with Motor Neurone disease, gradually reducing his abilities to move. Still, of course, a member of class human, Dr. Hawking can no longer respond to the instruction "Walk Stephen!" as most other instances of class human can.

However, we need not be concerned because we can reprogram the "walk" process for a new subclass of humans (Motor Neurone sufferers) to have them respond to the "walk" instruction by moving their motorised wheelchair. Again, we have redefined the process once for a whole class of people who *inherit* human characteristics but are, unfortunately, unable to perform this particular process. This process of *polymorphism* has allowed us to issue the same instruction to any *instance* of a *class* and that class "knows" how to respond effectively to the instruction. These very powerful programming techniques allow great flexibility and speed of development of systems that more reflect real world situations than the abstract ideas of representing data and procedures as distinct and unrelated.

Let us take a quick tour of the difference in a procedural programming approach to a problem and an object oriented one. Let us examine a real business issue and see how an object oriented approach may help. In the Albert Einstein example, it was argued that the development process, once mastered, is much faster than traditional approaches. To illustrate how that might happen in a business environment, examine the common situation of changing the General (Nominal) Ledger. For those who have gone through the process, changing GL account code structures in a functioning business can be a nightmare. Notwithstanding the business disruption and heartache, it can be a major challenge to the programmers to come to grips with the cascading effects of changes in perhaps hundreds of programs. If the GL code is 5 digits long with a range from 00001-99999, then traditionally the programmer would check the ranges and perform actions based on that. Alter this to 6 characters, 1 alpha and 5 digits (A00001-Z99999), and a whole suite of programs will have to be changed. Everywhere within the suite of programs the programmer will have to check that every use of the GL code is not dependent on it being only 5 digits.

In an object oriented approach, any process being performed will be sent to a GL object and it will deal with its internal structure and procedures privately. It is analogous to posting a letter. You put a letter in the post tray, and next morning it arrives at its destination. You don't need to know if it got there by air or truck, if it went through one sorting office or many. You issued one instruction ("Deliver Letter") and the Postal System "object" privately carried out its processes. If the Postal System was to change its processes every week, you would be unaware as long as your letter arrived as expected. Traditionally, in computer terms you defined all the processes and then submitted a letter to them. In the object oriented world you address your letter object and it "knows" what has to be done.

It must be emphasised that this whole object oriented approach is no panacea for programming problems. There is nothing magic about the way things are handled, it is just that it more reflects the real world than traditional mechanisms. The people having most difficulty with this change in programming practice are computer people. End users are more at home with the approach than most programmers or analysts have been to date. It has much more of a common sense appeal about it, and programmers are used to abstracting reality so that they can code it as they have been trained to do. This whole object oriented approach is too "unreal" to them to allow them to abstract reality from the real world.

## Another fad or fundamental change

Is object oriented programming a fad? Probably not. It is the first fundamental change in mainstream programming that we have seen in the short history of commercial computing. We have barely scratched the possibilities of the technique, and all the work to date will look childish when examined in ten years time, but there is a distinct shift in thinking about addressing problems and that will mature. The pain of adolescence will of course cause much grief and anguish to older generations as has been the case in all walks of life.

## Benefits

It is possible to summarise the benefits of an object oriented approach as follows:

- Increased modularity allowing more rapid and cost effective development.
- Decrease in maintenance cost due to effective development and localisation of problems.
- Difficult business problems can be addressed that were heretofore intractable to a programming solution.

# 11.4 Imaging

## Humans deal with images not data

Looking at today's typical office, there is a very evident gap in the way we deal with information. While our systems deal with keyboard-entered data they have little stomach for non-textual data, i.e. images. We would ideally like to be able to photocopy a page of information into our computers and manipulate that in the same way as we manipulate text. It is possible to do this, but with nothing like the ease with which we would wish. The facsimile, which in a decade has achieved almost 100% penetration in business, has almost totally displaced the telex. Humans deal with many objects of information, only one of which is text. Our current systems prevent us from dealing with information in non-textual form with ease but that will change.

By the end of the decade, images will be the norm and text the exception. The profound effect of this will manifest itself in yet another way within the office. More and more external information will be delivered electronically, stored electronically and read electronically. The paperless office will only arrive when it is easier to deal with information electronically than it is to deal with it on paper. But filing assistants will be able to file ten times as much information in one tenth of the time in electronic storage cabinets that will hold a million times the paper equivalent and allow us to retrieve it for reading in one millionth the time it takes to do manually.

## Multimedia and user interfaces

The deficiency our computer systems have in working with non-textual data was alluded to earlier. Allied to this is the whole area of multimedia. We receive our information from many sources, many of which are visual. Multimedia is a term used to designate a class of computers that have a capability of dealing with input and output that is non-textual in character. A multimedia machine can record and playback sound, display images, photographs, video and facsimile. Most of these additional features are used in very specialised niche applications today but they will become an integral part of general applications in the near future. A standards council, known as the MPC Council, has specified a standard configuration for personal computers that will allow manufacturers to design computers and software for interchangeable use on MPC certified configurations.

## Ease of use

The reason multimedia is important is that there is a requirement to make computers easy to use and human interaction with multimedia computers is more instinctive and productive. The cognitive psychologists who study human response find that multimedia computers allow interaction with the computer to be more intuitive and responsive.[8] The term GUI (graphical user interface) has been spawned and taken on the mantle of all that is good about modern software. If a software product does not have a GUI it is unlikely to remain mainstream for very long. With the headlong rush to Microsoft Windows as the GUI of choice (over 11.4 million copies sold in 15 months), the scramble to bring applications to market with GUI interfaces is well under way.

## Why interfaces are important - car facias etc.

User interfaces, whether graphical or not, are key to the productive use of computers. They alleviate the huge hidden cost of constant retraining that has been necessary prior to their widespread introduction. To illustrate this point, look at any DOS based software package that people are familiar with. Lotus 123 is a prime example of a well designed DOS application that does not use a graphical interface (in the DOS version). Wordperfect 5.1 is an extremely popular DOS based word processor, again well designed and relatively easy to use. The problem with these, however, is that they each have their own set of commands, ways of doing things and very little commonality in operation. For the user, this means learning a new way of doing things each time a new application comes along. Users have to concentrate too much scarce time on learning how to use the software, as opposed to learning how to maximise the functionality contained therein.

Contrast this with the same products in a Microsoft Windows or OS/2 or Macintosh environment. Because these environments are richer and graphical, each application, more or less, operates in the same way with regard to the interaction with the user - learn one and you have learned them all. The user can now concentrate on the functionality of the program rather than the quirkiness of its operation. Think of it as being analogous to car instrument panels and operator controls. The pedals are always in the same order and the facia has a standard set of outputs including a speedometer, odometer, fuel gauge, temperature gauge and oil pressure. This allows the driver to transfer with ease between vehicles and concentrate on the items of greater functionality because he brings with him knowledge of how the basics work.

## 11.5  Geographic information systems

In the vast majority of information systems today, we find that information is presented in the form of textual data. As stated earlier, however, the real need for non-textual data is becoming more apparent and a genuine business requirement. All data has a context and place. Most people view data in context but visually out of place. This is where Geographic Information Systems (GIS) come into play. A GIS allows for the interpretation of data by relating it to its physical location and presenting it in a visual format. Typically, this involves displaying a map with relevant data. GIS has a relevance to every business although the use of it has been patchy to date. To enable GIS systems to be effective there has been a requirement to have digitised maps available and these have been very expensive or hard to find. That has all changed and digitised maps have been developed, largely from satellite sources in the last five years. They are now very reasonably priced and can be cost justified very easily.

**Who benefits from a GIS?**

Every company with customers can benefit from a GIS. If you have ever tried to analyse your customer base by region then elements of that analysis can be overlooked because of the lack of a geographical perspective. An example of this might involve an analysis to determine the siting of a new customer service centre. Instantaneously, a visual presentation of customers on a map can give a visual clue to customer clustering. This type of information content is only available from poring laboriously over textual customer account records.

The most dramatic implementation of GIS systems in the 1990s will be in the transport arena. Coupled with Global Positioning Systems (GPS) they will allow transport managers and planners to more effectively manage transport systems. This will entail having transponders fitted to all vehicles but this will be commonplace in ten years time. A GPS transponder acts like a car radio but it signals back to a central source the vehicle position which the transponder picks up from a satellite.

## 11.6 Virtual reality

A term you are going to hear a lot of in the next five years is VR or virtual reality. Virtual reality is an extension of robotics into the world of computers and it has major implications for all. VR is already well out of the laboratories but its current use is niche oriented and expensive. Virtual reality is defined as the simulation of real world events and responses in a computer generated environment. If you have ever seen the Holo-deck in *Startrek - The Next Generation* you will see where the simulation is heading. VR grew out of NASA's programme to develop remote robotic devices that could allow a human to interact with an environment that would simulate a real world situation in the future.

While they are not VR devices, aircraft simulators are along the same lines as VR devices. The training a pilot gets in a simulator is intended to provide him with a realistic approximation of the real experience he will have in flight. The crucial difference is that a VR equivalent of a training simulator would have no real parts, they would all be computer simulations. You may have seen examples of current VR interfaces in the popular press. They consist of VR gloves and wraparound headsets, in the main, and while practical for use in specialised environments they are not practical, yet, for use in normal office environments.

VR devices work in a manner akin to the 1950s 3-D glasses you received on entry to see a 3-D film, they seem to take you into a three dimensional environment. An application of today's technology is where the participant dons a headset and gloves for a walkround of a virtual building. As you progress through this 3-D building you can open doors, just as you would real doors, but your hand actions are transferred into the computer simulated landscape and as you reach for the door your hand "appears" in the computer scene and opens the door. You can look around the scene by turning your head and look up and down also. It is easy to envisage the major impact such devices will have on architects and engineers. They will be able to take clients on full walkthroughs of buildings not yet built, change designs as they "stand" in the building and generally get client approval without the expensive errors and reworks that are necessary during the physical construction stage of the building.

### Reality is hard enough

The impact of VR will be very strong on design environments of all descriptions. That is not to say that it will not strongly affect other business activities. Reality is harsh and virtual reality will be virtually harsh. As this technology permeates the office environment, it is conceivable that simulations of all descriptions will become as everyday events as we today simulate business decisions and effects by using spreadsheets. The concept of planning merchandise presentation on supermarket shelves by a virtual reality simulation is not far off. Jaron Lanier coined the term "Virtual Reality" in the early 1980s. As chief scientist of VPL Research he is a pragmatist about the impact of VR on business and social environments. Concerns about the use and abuse are real, but he dismisses many of the concerns in the 10-20 year time frame because he firmly believes that *there is absolutely no chance whatsoever of virtual reality becoming so good or so cheap that it will be confused with reality.*

VR will give us a new 3-D spreadsheet type tool. If we forget that spreadsheets are only simulations and have no validity in the real world (they are, at best, only approximations), then VR will have serious impact and not all of it will be for the best. If we remember that simulations allow us to speculate about possible future events, and use them to determine the optimum actions we should take, then we will find that they further revolutionise how we do business and we will in twenty years time look back and ask how did we ever manage without it.

## 11.7  Group decision support systems

We referred earlier in the section on Future Business to the increasing imbalance between the speed of everyday business operations and the decision making processes inherent in managing that business. To conclude we will bring into focus all those elements that have been touched on in this chapter and see how the application of these technologies will form an information infrastructure around which businesses will grow and flourish. Again, this structure is quite foreign to most computer people and is probably unlike any structures you may be used to. Notwithstanding this fact, this is a structure that you will see developed, deployed and utilised in companies that will remain competitive in the coming decades. These companies will have achieved a balance that will allow them to manage information effectively and expeditiously.

Today's Decision Support Systems (DSS) are clumsy, centred on financial data and totally dependent on manual feeding for any meaningful results. Systems that depend on explicitly feeding day to day information to them will never achieve the responsiveness necessary to assist the decision making processes in a company. At best, the DSS gives results that approximate the real world of the business at some time in the past. The system has no memory of past decisions that brought the company to this point and is unable to evaluate changed circumstances that might assist it in giving more meaningful assistance to the humans who need to take new decisions. This inability to respond effectively has led to the euphemistic cliché to *align the technology with business goals*. This is not an alignment problem. Managers make decisions based largely on information provided from inadequate information systems. When the strategies unfold, inevitably there is a mismatch between the new state of the business and the systems in place to support that business.

Why does this occur every time? It is a problem of construction. Even the most far sighted of companies who design systems to support their business find that after the 2-3 year construction process the wonderful new system is ready for a company that existed 2-3 years ago but does not exist today. The dynamism of a changing business environment is not compatible with the relatively slow process of system construction and can never be compatible using current techniques. It is akin to building a frontline supply depot in time of war. If, by the time the depot is finished, the front has moved on by 300 km then it is no longer a frontline depot. Construction of frontline depots requires different techniques to peacetime supply depots. In information system terms, we have not yet deployed the techniques for staying with the frontline. This is a business issue as it is usually the core business people who have final say in how systems should be developed.

In figure 11.4, you can see the radically different structure that is needed. The intelligent corporate database becomes the hub of the decision making process. After construction it becomes a dynamic core to the business. Unlike current systems that need constant programming and reprogramming, this system will learn from experience. It will be a passive observer of all the elements influencing the decisions that drive the company. More importantly, it will remember decisions taken and allow for modification of past behaviour in the light of changed conditions. This type of system is trained rather than programmed. Its training never ceases and it continues to learn by absorbing all the external stimuli it has been trained to heed. It will contain the sum total of corporate experience of its specific company and it will then be a true decision support system supporting all facets of the business with which it interacts.

**Figure 11.4** Relationships in an Information Age organisation.

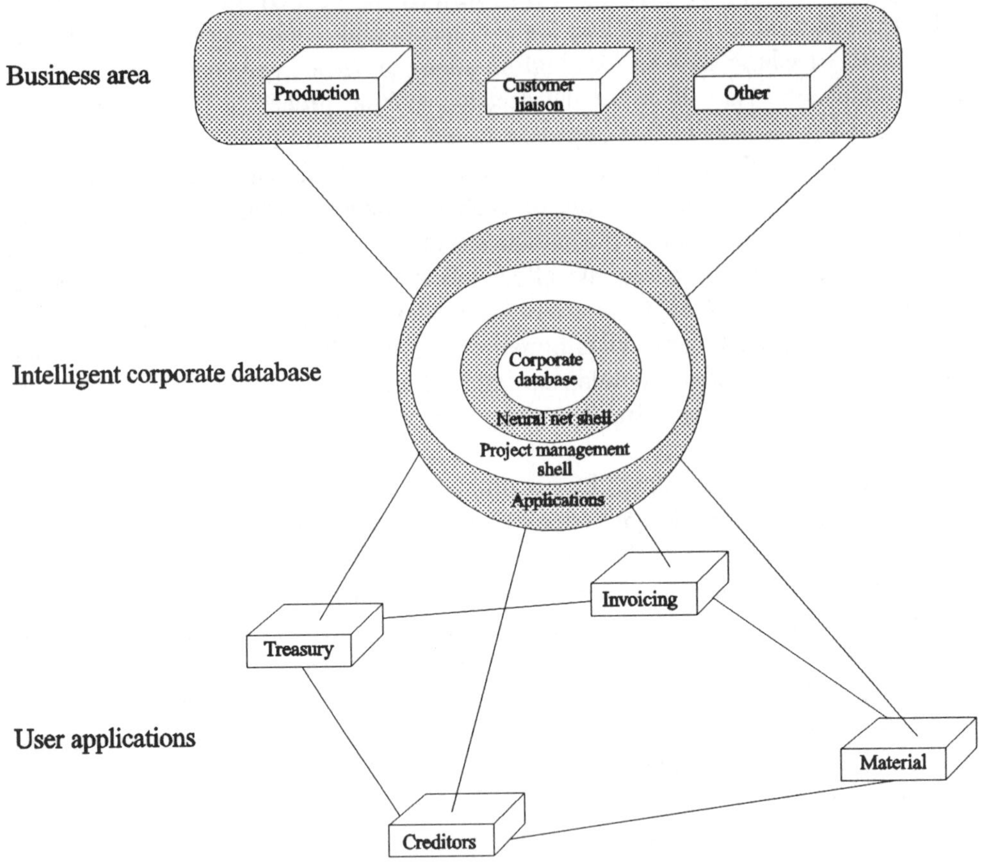

Business area

Intelligent corporate database

User applications

## 11.8 Conclusion

It is hard to remember a time without pocket calculators, fax machines and photocopiers. Progress is unstoppable and accelerating. We are on the fast track whether we like it or not. Unpalatable as it may be, the invasive nature of technology is going to cause you to reassess your knowledge of, and attitude to, technology. You will no longer have the luxury of leaving technology to others, unless you have decided to leave your business to others as well. If your position reflects your ability to get the job done then you will no longer be able to adjudicate on the decisions of others, if you are not in command of the technology that was the basis of those decisions. Technology has the capacity to be used to deceive and if you can't spot the flaw, you have problems. In 20 years time the essence of management will be the management of information, this will be the heart of every business and if you wish to be at the heart of your business you owe it to yourself to get to grips with technology sooner rather than later.

# Notes

1    A. Toffler, *Future Shock*. The Bodley Head, 1970.
2    J. Ramchandran, Post industrial manufacturing. *Harvard Business Review*, November-December, 1986.
3    S. Zuboff, *In the Age of The Smart Machine*. Basic Books, New York, 1988.
4    M. Dubofsky, *Industrialism and the American Worker 1965-1920*. Cromwell, New York, 1975.
5    Zuboff, *op. cit.*
6    *Ibid.*
7    *Electronic Computer Glossary*. The Computer Language Company, 1991.
8    S.L. Smith and J.N. Mosier, *Guidelines for Designing User Interface Software*. NTIS No. AD A177198.

# Additional reading

Hartson, H.R. and Hix, Human-computer interface development. *Communications of The ACM*, 21, 1, 1989.
Howard, R., *Brave New Workplace*. Viking, New York.
New Science Association, *Object Oriented Technology: Commercial Scope and Limits*. New Science, CT., 1989.
Redmond, C., *Strategic Importance of Advanced Telecommunications*. Eolas, Dublin.
Winblad, A., Edwards, S. and King, D., (1990) *Object Oriented Software*. Addison Wesley, Mass.
Zdonik, S. and Maier, D., eds., *Readings in Object Oriented Databases*. Morgan Kaufmann, California.

# 12

# Implementing IS/IT Strategies

This part of the book is concerned with defining an approach which will lead to *successful* implementation of IS/IT strategies. These are rocky shores upon which many IS/IT strategies have come to grief. Consultants reports and internal strategy documents have sunk here without trace, leaving those on shore looking out in vain and wondering if their investments in time and money will pay off.

One major cause of these disasters is that many IS/IT strategic plans were incomplete when they were launched. Often these reports identified excellent opportunities for using IS/IT to gain competitive advantage; they may even have recommended significant changes to the technology platform being used by the organisation. This in fact may have admirably honoured the terms of reference, but it *primarily* reflects the *infancy of our understanding* in relation to IS/IT planning and has failed to give a complete map for successful implementation.

There is a growing realisation that *successful* implementation depends on an IS/IT planning process that is comprehensive and multi-faceted.[1] This chapter advocates that successful implementation of an IS/IT strategy depends on the IS/IT planning process integrating *demand, supply and application development* and providing an on-going framework for organisational decision-making. Before proceeding too far we would like to relate the terms demand, supply and application development to the context of IS/IT planning and, during the remainder of the chapter, describe an approach to ensure their inter-relatedness.

## 12.1 The terms and the linkages

The need to link IS/IT planning to the business planning process has been well researched. However, in many organisations IS/IT planning may be synonymous with IT planning, that is, technology issues dominate from an early stage. This usually results in disaffecting senior management of the organisation who may not feel able or willing to contribute effectively. Additionally, organisational or managerial issues are usually squeezed out by this predominance of technological issues.

In chapter 4 we highlighted the need to separate IS and IT during the planning process to provide focus and clarity, but to retain their overall inter-relatedness in the total planning process. This is illustrated in figure 12.1.

**Figure 12.1** The relationship between IS strategy and IT strategy

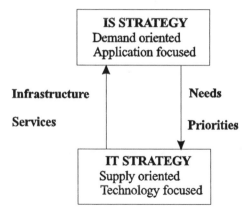

**IS strategy is concerned with demand,** i.e. the nature of the business applications required by the organisation. This process must be owned by the senior management of the organisation and must focus on the total information needs of the organisation, not only applications concerned with potential competitive advantage.

**IT strategy is concerned with supply,** i.e. the way technology will be applied to deliver the different types of applications required by the organisation. This process should be the responsibility of the IT management.

**Application development is concerned with benefits,** i.e. the way in which information systems are progressed to ensure the desired benefits are realised. This process should determine the actions of both business management and IT professionals.

The most critical aspect of implementing IS/IT strategies is to ensure that the above areas are coordinated and that a framework for consistent and integrated organisational decision making is given. Too often demand, supply and development decisions are uncoordinated; perhaps undertaken at different times, by different people with different perspectives. Each decision, when taken in isolation appears rational. This frustrating and mysterious lack of coordination within organisations, of which IS/IT is only one of many examples, is the rocky shoreline which sinks many IS/IT strategies.

The approach advocated here is to use and develop the applications portfolio, described earlier in chapter 3, to provide a shared understanding within the organisation in relation to IS/IT. The applications portfolio provides the strategic inheritance for an organisation's applications which will give consistency and coordination between demand, supply and development.

**Figure 12.2** The applications portfolio.

| Strategic | High potential |
|---|---|
| | |
| Key operational | Support |
| | |

## 12.2 Demand: understanding the importance of the applications portfolio

Chapter 3 highlighted the usefulness of the applications portfolio in classifying applications. It is a powerful tool for senior management to make decisions in relation to IS/IT and its contribution to the business. These decisions need to be made thoroughly, with full understanding of the organisational consequences. They also need to be explicit and communicated throughout the organisation as the basis of subsequent IS/IT decisions.

## An applications contribution to business strategy

The starting point for understanding how applications support business strategy and the achievement of its objectives is to position each current and potential application onto the portfolio. This activity must be undertaken by the senior management of the organisation together, which in itself can be the single most important contributor to successful implementation of IS/IT strategy.

Differences in understanding as to the real objectives of applications may be highlighted. For example, in one building society during such a meeting the chief executive realised that a major system he had been told was 'strategic', i.e. going to give competitive advantage was in fact 'key operational', i.e. they were catching up and avoiding disadvantage. This in itself was important but as the chief executive angrily put it 'it changes the emphasis'.

We have seen many such changes in emphasis as applications are evaluated critically against organisational objectives when using the applications portfolio. Correct positioning and a clear understanding of the required benefits are vital otherwise the emphasis at implementation may be wrong or the expected benefits may not be realised. For example, many companies have recently decided to invest in significant amounts of office automation technology believing if each department or member of staff used the same technological environment they would gain competitive advantage by getting their product to market sooner, or by being able to make better and faster decisions, etc. However, to achieve these strategic benefits, organisational changes will be required, for example changes in working practices. Leading edge technology will not in itself deliver these benefits let alone the introduction of inappropriate technology.

Hence it is necessary for management to undertake an impact analysis to determine what changes are necessary in order to realise the desired benefits. Often these changes affect organisational issues, such as structure, working practices as well as technology. It is important to gain understanding and commitment at this stage to these changes and their consequences, particularly the resources likely to be needed to facilitate implementation. In figure 12.3 a number of applications are placed on the applications portfolio. Note that an application's position will vary from organisation to organisation.

**Figure 12.3**  Positioning applications in the portfolio.

| Strategic | High potential |
|---|---|
| Distribution system<br>EDI<br>Geographic<br>Information system | Expert systems<br>Imaging |
| Key operational | Support |
| MRP system<br>Billing system<br>Production planning<br>system<br>Stock control<br>system | Accounting system<br>Word processing<br>Electronic mail |

## Apportioning the total spend

Having positioned each application in the applications portfolio senior management can see where the emphasis in their use of IS/IT lies. This often shows for the first time the emphasis from an organisational perspective rather than a departmental perspective. The impact for senior management can be increased if the total spend on each system (development, technology, maintenance, operation, and user time) is shown. Figure 12.4 illustrates this idea for the applications portfolio in figure 12.3.

Management can decide if this is the optimum way of utilising the spending on IS/IT in relation to the organisations objectives. Often there is a desire by senior management to increase the strategic applications by releasing resources from the support sector. Any shift in emphasis or spend if agreed by senior management at this time has a greater chance of successful implementation.

## Generic critical success factors for applications in the applications portfolio

In chapter 4 the concept of critical success factors (CSFs) was introduced to help identify IS/IT opportunities. It was suggested above that different IS/IT applications may require different emphases and therefore an understanding of these differences is vital for successful implementation. CSFs can also be assigned to applications in the portfolio.

**Figure 12.4** Current IS/IT spend.

| Strategic | High potential |
|---|---|
| Distribution system £20K<br>EDI £20k<br>Geographic<br>Information system £10k | Expert systems £5k<br>Imaging £10k |
| **Key operational** | **Support** |
| MRP system £100k<br>Billing system £40k<br>Production planning<br>system £75k<br>Stock control<br>system £50k | Accounting system £70k<br>Word processing £30k<br>Electronic mail £30k |

*High potential applications*
The objective here is to develop a system in order to evaluate a new business idea or technological opportunity.

The CSFs are:

- a rapid evaluation capability, probably using prototyping

- an evaluation which reviews business, technological and economic issues, particularly the potential contribution to organisation objectives

- identification of the best way to proceed, including a migration policy as few systems start from a green field site

- the ability to kill inappropriate ideas before they take on a life of their own.

*Strategic applications*
The objective is to gain competitive advantage from innovation in support of business strategies.

The CSFs are:

- rapid development and implementation to gain the business benefits as far in front of the competition as possible

- a flexible solution which can be enhanced as the markets detailed needs become better understood

- parallel and complementary business and technological initiatives

- continuous review to monitor market reaction and competitor activity.

*Key operational applications*
The objective here is to provide effective systems to support existing customer critical activities and avoid disadvantage in performance relative to competitors.

The CSFs are:

- robust, reliable, high quality systems which are technically efficient

- provide an appropriate solution to business risks resulting from any system failures which lead to poor customer performance

- integrated systems, avoiding duplication, inconsistency and providing for rapid processing.

*Support applications*
The objective of support applications is to improve productivity and efficiency in relation to the internal activities of the organisation.

The CSFs are:

- lowest cost long term solution when considering total costs including maintenance and user costs

- standardisation where ever possible yet still offering flexibility in use.

**Gap Analysis**

Senior management should now review current applications to ascertain if these applications are complying with the above generic CSFs. Any shortfalls need to be highlighted and organisational consequences determined. Clearly the significance of the shortfalls can act as a basis for priority setting.


## 12.3 Supply side: understanding the importance of the applications portfolio

Critical to successful implementation of the IS/IT plan is having an adequate and appropriate capability to supply the technology and technological skills needed in relation to the organisational demand for applications. Essentially supply issues and decisions are the responsibility of IT management, but the framework of the portfolio provides criteria and CSFs to deliver against.


### Supply capability around the applications portfolio

The demand decision making processes have determined different CSFs for different types of application, hence supply management should not treat systems in a homogeneous manner but incorporate different supply approaches around the applications portfolio.

The key to supply management is to identify the most appropriate approach and hence resources needed to cater for these differences in approach. Each quadrant requires a separate approach and dedicated resources with different management styles, skills, technology, etc.


*High potential applications*
Here the emphasis of supply is on rapid evaluation; an entrepreneurial style focused on key business issues should be the culture. Prototyping, piloting, and business feasibility skills should dominate so that a full evaluation of all the issues will lead to a comprehensive set of recommendations about the way to proceed.

The technology and methods should support this experimental approach. Outsourcing could be used as a way of buying specialist skills the organisation does not have. However, as this is the seed-bed or research and development of future business innovation the organisation must retain close control over these applications.

*Strategic applications*
With strategic applications the emphasis of supply is on the understanding of market needs and rapid development of systems and organisational change to gain competitive advantage.   As these applications are intended to differentiate the organisation a package solution is unlikely to suffice, hence a bespoke system of some description is likely to be needed.

A project management style and will to succeed should be the culture.  Analysis, development and change management skills should predominate.   Rapid development tools and techniques should support this time constrained approach. However, the methods adopted should facilitate subsequent enhancements as greater knowledge becomes available or market needs develop and changes are needed to remain ahead of the competition.

Outsourcing can be used to reinforce organisational strength, for example buying programming skills to cope with once off peaks or obtaining new database skills to provide for future flexibility.  However these applications require the secrecy of a new product launch and so must be kept very close to the heart of the organisation.


*Key operational applications*
Here the emphasis of supply is to provide high quality technical solutions to known business needs to deliver effective customer service and avoid competitive disadvantage.  Hence, since being as good as the rest is the issue here, industry packages should be considered along with bespoke systems, particularly if the organisation needs to catch up.

The culture should reflect technical excellence.  Systems engineering, integration, database management and methodology should dominate.  Outsourcing can be used to provide specific skills and expertise but under the control of organisation personnel.  These are business critical systems and responsibility should remain with the organisation.  Additionally, as integration is critical these applications should all be run on the same platform.


*Support applications*
Here the emphasis of supply is to provide applications to increase productivity and efficiency at the lowest total cost.  This often leads to the adoption of package solutions, which conform to organisational standards thus facilitating interfacing.

The culture should reflect a scarce resource approach with a strong emphasis on tangible savings through a rigid cost benefit analysis.  Package evaluation and support skills are essential here, as are implementation skills, even at times requiring the company to bend if the economics say so. Clearly packages are a form of outsourcing, the cheapest long term solution is required here, so facility management offerings should be considered for particular applications. Specialist maintenance organisations could be considered for older or more off-beat packages.

### Infrastructure

For supply management the applications portfolio can provide a framework to ensure optimum use of IS/IT expenditure both in the short and long term in line with business objectives. This will ensure the appropriate resources and policies to implement IS/IT strategies. A key supply issue has been to determine the nature of future infrastructure. Justifying this investment has been difficult when applications have been developed piecemeal. As the portfolio can take a longer term and organisational perspective, it could show future application requirements, hence indicating the nature of infrastructure investments to support these future applications.

## 12.4  Application management and the portfolio

The essence of application management is the ability to ensure the desired benefits are realised. The key to this is understanding the strategic inheritance of the application. Hence, the applications position in the portfolio and the issues made explicit by senior management at the 'demand' discussions need to form the heart of the approach to the development and introduction of the application within the organisation.

### Approach to application management

To ensure an application meets the business objectives set for it the 'demand' discussions need to be explored in depth. In particular, the specific benefits to be realised need to be understood, the critical success factors of the application, the nature of the organisational change issues, the senior management responsible for the application and the criteria which will be used as the basis of the post implementation review. No misunderstandings can be allowed at this stage.

### Applications into projects

The term application has been deliberately used to refer to the business task which is under consideration in order to retain a top down and organisational perspective. Too often applications have been seen as synonymous with computer projects.  This loses sight of the inter-relatedness and complexity of modern information systems.

The figure below showing a very simple model begins to hint at the interrelated nature of systems development; in particular it shows the critical role of the user. Not only are they key to the activities of the technologists, they also have their own work to do in preparation for the introduction of the new system.  These include organisation changes, data cleaning, with perhaps additional coding and classification, revising procedures, training, etc.

**Figure 12.5**  Application development effort contribution diagram.

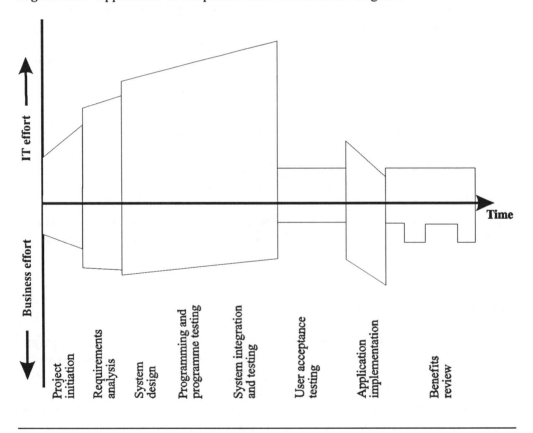

It is important at this stage for an Application Manager to be appointed who will take responsibility for the delivery of the benefits.  This application manager should be selected in relation to the CSFs of the application, i.e. it will be business led when appropriate.

Also the application manager will break the application into smaller and more manageable projects as appropriate. Some of the projects may be technical, for example system development or telecommunications, others may be business oriented like revising working practices or a structural reorganisation. The application manager must ensure a consistent strategic inheritance to these projects from the application. Additionally, there is a need to ensure the projects are well coordinated and do not drift.

**Figure 12.6** Application to projects.

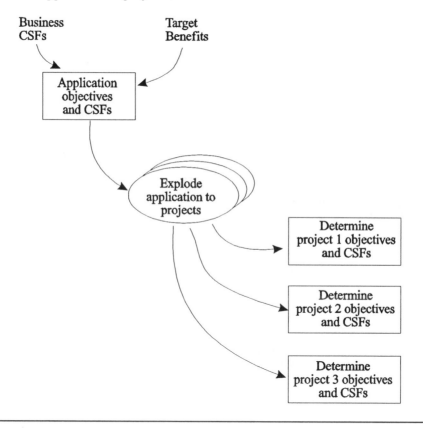

**Project planning**

The project manager for each project will be expected to plan the detail of their project. This project planning should identify:

- the activities to be undertaken
- resources needed

- timescales
- interdependencies (both within and between projects)
- budgets
- CSFs for the project
- risks.

Clearly there is likely to be a wide variety of projects which need to be undertaken and so the specific activities will vary. However for those projects concerned with system development, a useful model for initiating planning is the V-model shown below.

**Figure 12.7** The V-model of IS development.

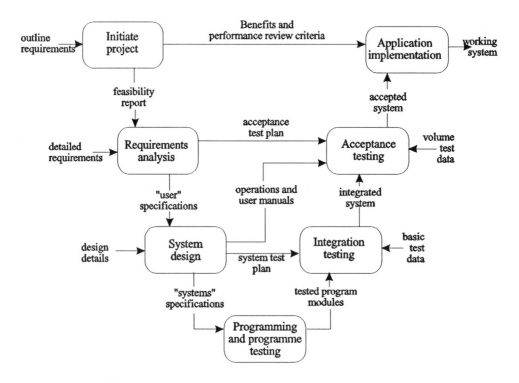

Adapted from the NCC Starts Program.

The V-model shows the general case for systems development. From each major stage a deliverable is produced which provide the basis of input to the following stage. However the real power of the V-model is the horizontal links it shows between the specifying activities, i.e. those shown on the left hand side, and the testing activities, i.e. those shown on the right hand side. This means that at the time of specifying or producing something, then the way in which it will be checked and the criteria to which it must conform are defined.

In essence the main stages of the V-model are

- project initiation
- requirements analysis
- system design
- programming and programme testing
- system integration and testing
- user acceptance testing
- application implementation

*Project initation*
The outcome of project initiation is the feasibility report. This should specify the objectives and scope of the project, the desired benefits and potential risks. The classification of the project in terms of the strategic grid will provide a basis against which to evaluate the expected resource, cost, dependency, technical and organisational issues. It will also specify responsibility and the criteria for success.

*Requirements analysis*
This is concerned with clarifying the precise impact of the change, who will be affected and the business tasks involved. Considerable detail may be required here describing processes, volumes, data structures, etc. The main output is a statement of functional requirements and the key features of an acceptance test plan.

*System design*
System design reviews the business requirements and examines alternative technical solutions. The major deliverable at this stage is a system specification describing the nature of the system in terms of processes, datafiles, hardware and security. This document can act as a basis for programming, package selection, or invitation to tender. Importantly, the system specification should provide evaluation criteria for both the systems integration testing stage and user acceptance.

*Programming and programme testing*
At this stage individual programme modules are written and tested.

*System integration and testing*
The individual components of the system may work in themselves, but they may not perform as expected when combined with other system components. Software integration checks the operation of the system as a whole to ensure its technical correctness in relation to the system specification.

*User acceptance testing*
This is a key stage in the development of an application, one where the users of the system along with the developers will need to invest a considerable amount of time and effort ensuring the system meets its requirements.  In particular the system needs to be evaluated to ensure that when the system is implemented it will allow the realisation of the desired benefits.  The accompanying documentation, including operation and user manuals, should be checked for adequacy.

The impact of the system on the organisation's operations should also be evaluated in detail to help prepare for implementation.

*Application implementation*
This can be a fraught time as the new IT-based application is introduced into the working practices of the organisation.  Many of the shortcomings or omissions during the development phases may begin to reveal themselves.  Even without these problems the additional workload can be immense, under resourced and often underestimated.  The change issues involved in implementation are explored in more depth in the following chapter.

## 12.5  Development and the applications portfolio

Earlier the importance of the applications portfolio was emphasised as a key tool for integrating demand, supply and application management.  We have already discussed its usefulness in highlighting the key issues of demand and supply.  The portfolio can also focus attention on the particular key issues of an application and suggest an emphasis of approach depending on the type of system.

High potential systems require rapid evaluation, using prototyping tools, and is best undertaken by an individual or small team.  The development stages may blur and organisation documentation should focus on the quality of the analysis and not inhibit it.

Strategic systems require fast, effective development and implementation.  Matrix and project management techniques should be used to pull the required resources together. The emphasis of development should be on understanding market/customer needs of the system as well as the required organisational changes.  Good organisational understanding and a strong analytical approach are needed, hence the requirements analysis stage is vital here as with innovative systems precise needs are not known.  Prototyping can be critical to ascertain these needs and evaluate their impact.  Documentation and techniques should detail needs and rapid development.

Key operational systems are about technical excellence with essentially known requirements. Prototyping may be useful to evaluate technical alternatives. High quality control and technical documentation are essential to give reliable and efficient integrated systems.

Support systems, when using packages, obviate much of the programming but emphasise package evaluation, acceptance testing and implementation.

Estimating the resources, timescales and costs of an application can be a hazardous activity. Using the portfolio and reviewing the detail of the projects which comprise the application facilitate good estimating by making more explicit and more manageable **all** the activities which need to be undertaken. Reference to previous projects and organisational metrics can be helpful here.

Quality in its fundamental sense is concerned with fitness for purpose. Clearly fitness for purpose varies around the portfolio as described above. A *Quality Plan* will describe in detail the standards, timescales, targets, risks methods and responsibilities of the project and reflect the different needs around the portfolio.

### Managing resources and project control

All projects require good project management and control; the use of the portfolio and CSFs helps to focus attention on key areas and highlight critical areas for control.

### Realising benefits

Realising benefits must be undertaken as a specific activity, indeed responsibility and resources should be allocated to ensure this happens. Too often in the past benefit realisation has not been managed effectively and has been left almost to chance. Reference should be made to the original benefits. Lessons can also be drawn from the experiences of each project to improve organisational processes in relation to the development of applications.

## 12.6  Conclusions

Successful implementation of an IS/IT plan depends on successfully linking demand, supply and application management. We have advocated the use of the applications portfolio as a technique for linking these together, however for this to happen successfully requires changes in perception and approach within the organisation.

Senior management must take responsibility and ownership for managing *demand* in a way they have not done in the past. IT management need to review their structure and emphasis to ensure they have within their department the appropriate resources to meet the demands placed on them and are prepared to continually review *supply* issues critically to ensure they are making the most effective use of organisational resources.

Applications should not be managed homogeneously but reflect differences in requirement. The business change issues must be made explicit and real commitment given to these projects.

For the above to happen a major commitment to education is needed to facilitate the change management process. Approaches to change management in IS/IT implementation are the subject of the next chapter.

## Notes

1    See the work of C. Edwards, J. Ward and A. Bytheway, *The Essence of Information Systems*. Prentice-Hall Inc., 1991; J. Ward, P. Griffiths, and P. Whitmore, *Strategic Information Systems Planning*. Wiley, 1990; and M. Earl, Approaches to strategic information systems planning in twenty-one United Kingdom Companies. In J.I. DeGross, M. Alavi and H. Oppelland, eds., *Proceedings of the Eleventh International Conference on Information Systems*, December 16-19, 1990, Copenhagen, Denmark, pp. 271-277.

# 13

# Managing Change in IS/IT Implementation

In the previous chapter on implementing IS/IT strategies we used the applications portfolio as a framework to ensure the integration of information systems demand with information technology supply and applications development. We also adopted a rigorous approach to ensure that the applications which result from the planning process are developed as efficiently as possible. The concentration was clearly on constructing the IT solution and managing the process. This approach is valid for all information systems development projects whether or not they result from a formal IS/IT planning process.

However, organisations are social systems composed of people and this critical human dimension must not be neglected. Information systems used for strategic purposes are likely to cause significant changes in an organisation. These changes can manifest themselves in many ways from how the employees perform their jobs to a complete redefinition of the way in which a company conducts business. Further, information is a resource which is closely linked with status, power and authority. By redefining or redistributing information in an organisation both positive and negative consequences can be expected for all parties involved.

Ultimately, the success of the IS/IT planning process is governed by how well the accompanying change is managed. It is fruitless developing a superior strategy which fails to be realised or building an IT based solution which is resisted. In this chapter we address change and issues in managing change. We consider these issues from the perspective of organisation theory and attempt to provide some insights into the organisational context behind the change process.


## 13.1  Understanding change

Before exploring the concept of change, let us first look at three scenarios. We will then identify the changes that are likely to occur in these situations with the introduction of IS/IT and the implications of these changes for the wider organisation.


*An expert system*

An engineering company which designs and manufacturers engines identifies customer service, particularly in regard to responding to service calls, as being a critical success factor. It sees its ability to respond effectively and in a timely manner to service calls as permitting it to differentiate itself from competitors. As a result of the IS/IT planning process, it was decided to investigate the potential of artificial intelligence techniques to aid in diagnosing faults in its engines (high potential quadrant as per the applications portfolio). Initially, a prototype was developed and evaluated and it was clear that an expert system could significantly improve the diagnostic process. Presently, over 70% of faulty engines have to be taken by the technicians to the organisation's repair centre where the cause of the problem is identified and remedied by company engineers. This often results in turnaround times of up to ten days. Field service technicians equipped with laptop computers would now be able to diagnose the cause of faults and repair the damage at the customer site. The company estimated that now less than 10% of faulty engines would need to be taken back to the company's repair centre, significantly reducing turnaround times.


*Computer integrated manufacturing*

A successful manufacturing firm has been losing competitiveness over the last few years despite considerable investment in technology. A study by a team of management consultants identifies a number of causes:

> ineffective planning of IT investment resulting in 'islands of automation', i.e. unintegrated machines and systems;

> inadequate inventory control; and

> inefficiencies in production planning and control.

The consultants recommend that a more integrated approach to manufacturing be adopted. A plan is developed to achieve an integrated manufacturing environment within the next three years.


*Electronic data interchange*
A supermarket chain initiates an electronic data interchange project with the objective of moving towards paperless trading. Initially key suppliers, who account for up to 70% of all orders placed, will be approached with a view to developing EDI links. Eventually it is hoped that invoices, debit and credit notes and payments will be sent via EDI.

Each of the above scenarios could conceivably result from the IS/IT planning process. Each will involve change, although the extent of this change will depend on a number of factors including the IT base of the organisation, the skills and abilities of organisational members and the attitude of both management and employees. Implementing similiar IT solutions in two organisations will not necessarily result in the same level of change. Although we don't have the full background to the organisations in these scenarios we can suggest where potential changes are likely to occur and the implication of these changes.


**The expert system**

- Changes in the position and status of engineers at the organisation's repair centre.

   Implications for:

   *job security of the engineers;*
   *how power relations between field technicians and engineers are managed, when power is based on possession of 'expert' knowledge.*

- Changes the existing definition of tasks and responsibilities.

   Implications for:

   *the redefinition of responsibilities;*
   *the provision of measures for enforcing new responsibilities, such as rewriting job descriptions and reassessment of criteria used for performance appraisal and evaluation;*
   *the coordination of activities between field technicians and centre engineers;*

*how systems for remuneration and recognition of field technicians are planned to ensure that their rewards are commensurate with the division of labour with engineers.*

- Changes the existing systems of control.

Implications for:

*the forms of 'control' chosen in the switch from a centralised to a decentralised system with mobile field technicians;*
*consideration given to technical controls;*
*how systems for 'internal' control can be developed and maintained amongst distant field technicians.*

### Computer integrated manufacturing

- Changes to the organisation of tasks and responsibilities.

Implications for:

*job security;*
*potential for mass or union action.*

- Changes to existing work practices.

Implications for:

*how job redesign, including the introduction of more flexible work practices, is managed;*
*replacing individual responsibilities with team work;*
*the redefinition and codification of responsibilities.*

- Changes to existing reward systems.

Implications for

*how performance is evaluated;*
*how individuals are motivated.*

- Changes to existing skills.

Implications for:

*skills development and training;*
*the recruitment policy;*
*promotional structures.*

- Changes to the existing centralised operational structures.

  Implications for:

  *accountability of decentralised units;*
  *coordination between sub-units;*
  *control of manufacturing system.*

- Change to management philosophy.

  Implications for:

  *their attitudes and decisions about 'control' issues and following from*
  *this,*
  *their commitment to notions of delegation and empowerment;*
  *their conceptualisation of the business as an integrated system.*

### Electronic data interchange

- Changes in business practices.

  Implications for:

  *the ordering process;*
  *job design, job functions;*
  *service levels;*
  *security of data.*

- Changes in business structure, particularly with the move to partnerships.

  Implication for:

  *the degree of formal control buyers have over supply companies;*
  *the degree of influence suppliers might have over buyers through 'single*
  *user agreements' and exclusive contracts;*
  *the level of accountability to other companies on, for example issues*
  *relating to their viability;*
  *security of company information.*

- Changes in management philosophy.

  Implications for:

  *the conceptualisation of the organisational boundary;*
  *how the company  treats and deal with suppliers;*

*organisation of the division of responsibility with the suppliers.*

## Planned and unplanned change

In order to gain a deeper understanding of change, it is important that we understand what we mean by the term. Simply defined, change can be viewed as the alteration from one state to another, for example the change from an activity that is manually carried out to one that is now fully automated. Sometimes this change is planned for; at other times it occurs spontaneously in response to some event, the effect of which was not anticipated.

Unplanned change, on the other hand, occurs spontaneously and emerges unpredictably from a situation. It is not necessarily negative, and many new strategies and products are the outcome of unforeseen changes which force the company to seek new 'ways of doing things'.

Following this line of reasoning, we can differentiate between between *planned change* and *unplanned change*. Planned change is that change which is intentional and goal oriented and deemed necessary to sustain competitiveness. It involves *unfreezing* the current status quo, *movement* to a new state, and *refreezing* the new change to make it permanent[1] as illustrated in figure 13.1.

**Figure 13.1** Unfreezing, movement and refreezing.

Planned change is change which is *managed*. This includes calculated innovations, whether to structure, culture, technology, skills or the strategy of a company. Restructuring or downsizing is one example of planned change, implementation of a new MRP system or billing system is another.

In the above scenarios we looked at the planned changes arising from the applications resulting from the IS/IT strategy and tried to identify what the implications might be. They included changes to job design and responsibilities, changes in human resource management including new skills development and training and changes in the organisation's structure.

The introduction of new technology can have many consequences. Typically, as routine tasks become automated, people are being freed up. Some may take on more varied and challenging tasks, for example when a printer using new technology gets involved in design and layout rather than just printing. Many jobs are reshaped, for example when an architect using a CAD system performs stress analysis on designs, a task typically undertaken by an engineer; new skills are required but with these skills becoming obsolete more quickly as technology develops. Job design must change to reflect new roles and responsibilities. Individuals doing narrow, specialised, and routine jobs may be replaced by work teams whose members can perform multiple tasks and actively participate in team decisions.

These are tangible changes. Other, more subtle changes such as the impact on worker satisfaction, motivation, job committment are also likely to accompany the introduction of planned changes. In practice both planned and unplanned changes are likely to occur in implementing the IS/IT strategy. A well managed change program will aim to anticipate and minimise the negative consequences yet maximise the benefits of new information technologies by preparing the 'groundwork' for them.

The above scenarios highlight the interdependencies between organisational elements and the fine balance that exists between them. By introducing new technology the equilibrum which exists is disrupted. We shall build on this notion subsequently. First, however, we will explore some of the key factors which make up organisations and which should be considered when considering any sort of change.

## 13.2  An integrated approach to change

Organisations who wish to manage change effectively, do so through people. Figure 13.2 illustrates the pivital role of people in the linkage between strategy, organisation, business processes and technology.

- **Strategically** - by setting the direction of the organisation towards a vision of the future

- **Organisationally** - by providing the environment where ownership is accepted by people within the organisation

- **Business processes** - to ensure that operations positively support and improve day to day business and the quality of service to customers

- **Technically** - by making the most of current technology while building an architecture for future developments.

**Figure 13.2** Managing organisational change through people.

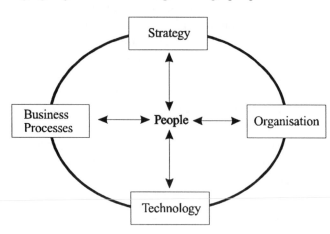

## 13.3  Resistance to change

Probably one of the greatest barriers to the management of change is the assumption that it simply happens or that people must simply change because it is necessary to do so. Even if planned changes are achieved this is no guarantee that they can be maintained. For instance a relatively simple change like getting workers to keep more accurate inventory records, usually requires a considerable amount of management time spent on ensuring that workers understand why greater accuracy is needed, and in listening to and learning from what workers perceive as the obstacles to achieving greater accuracy. Resistance is adverse reaction to a proposed change.

In his book *The Unbearable Lightness of Being*, Milan Kindura explores the notion that our existence in the world has a great deal of chance contained within it, for example the chance meeting which changes our life. The irony is that if we really believed that our lives were so 'light' (to use Kindura's phrase) life would be quite unbearable. That is, we need to believe that we are in control. Change in the organisation context is resisted for this very reason. People feel that a change from the status quo will affect their ability to have control in their lives.

As mentioned before, change may also have positive effects and is not always resisted. If an employee is given a top-of-the-range company car, fully expensed, is it likely to be met with much resistance? Is a salary increase likely to be rejected? The answer to these is probably no. However, to understand resistance we need to understand the *scope* of the change, that is, we need to understand any possible *knock on effect* of the single change suggested.

The degree of resistance to change depends on the kind of change involved and how well it is understood and the degree of actual or perceived disruption which is likely to accompany that change. The uncertainty which accompanies a major change initiative has a major bearing on the level of resistance to that change. Consider the decision to automate a previously manual task. Resistance may occur due to the following perceived threats:

- uncertainty in relation to the future (will they still have a job?)

- need to learn new skills (they may feel that they are unable to do so)

- loss of status, money, authority, etc.

- loss of power due to removal of discretion in performance of task

- requirement to relocate to a different geographical location

- breakup of a work group which has been together for a number of years.

A prime objective in managing change is to ensure that resistance is reduced and does not become a major barrier to achieving the planned goal.


**Role of perceptions**

One of the ways in which resistance is reduced is to attempt to change people's attitudes about the change process. In section 13.4 below we look at ways in which this can be managed through the use of education and communication. As we saw above, what people perceive to be a likely threat will determine their degree of resistance to change. As managers we should remember that in the change equation people's behaviour is based on their perceptions of what threat and reality are rather than on a single 'objective' reality.

The same is also true of how people perceive opportunity. Research in the business strategy area shows that managers from different firms operating in the same industry can perceive the same environment quite differently and will therefore implement different strategies to meet competitive challenges. How people *enact* or bring about change is also, therefore, determined by their perceptions. Because of this, a dominant perspective taken in examining the change process is the *science of interpretation*. This perspective assumes that people's actions are best understood from the perspective of the actor and must be understood in the context in which those actions are performed. This is the view shared in disciplines such as anthropology and ethnography. Human behaviour is guided by the constructs and meanings which individuals use to interpret their surroundings.[2]  This interpretative approach requires that we understand the change process by understanding the individual *frame of reference* which guide the actions and decisions of those involved in the process.

## 13.4  Issues in managing change

To overcome resistance to change a carefully planned implementation approach is needed which will ideally bring about a change in people's attitudes as well as behaviour.  Yet there are a number of issues and how these are addressed will have significant impacts on the direction of change, the degree of cooperation, and ultimately whether or not change is likely to be successful.

In relation to culture change, Marshall and McClean[3] ask whether change in culture can ever be fully identified from within by internal employees or whether the very process of change requires that a fresh perspective freed from the traditions and 'enculturation' must be bought to bear.  This might be especially true for family firms with strong traditions or ethics of 'how we do business'.  Culture change has become very popular over the last decade both in theory and in practice.  In this section we deal with culture and other processes which exist in organisations and consider how they might be effected by change.

### Power and politics

*Who makes the decision to change?*
Within organisations there are many different *interest groups*: collections of people with different goals and ambitions.  Interest groups may comprise individuals or whole departments who feel that their interests or needs differ from other groups in the organisation.  *Coalitions* are formed from the alignment of different interest groups with and against each other.  Interest groups will compete with each other to try to maximise the likelihood of securing outcomes and resources which are compatible with their particular goals.  Competition is likely to be more acute when resources are limited.  Competition might be overt, wrangling or conflict such as between departments, or covert where perhaps information necessary for the decision to be made is withheld or massaged.  The individuals or departments which control who gains access to valued resources will have particular *power*.  Consider the following example:

> Funding available for developing new applications for a manufacturing
> process is limited.  There is competition between the IT department and the

> Research and Development department over which applications should be developed. The interest groups, in this case representatives from the R&D and IT departments, might discuss the decision openly with the project manager around the conference table or be forced to lobby the project manager, resorting to catching him in corridors and putting their case. The project manager has the final decision over the selection.

In this example, the sources of the project manager's power are control over decision outcomes and over funding. The interest groups are engaging in political activity by competing for a scarce resource.

Such political competition in organisations will pervade the change process. Introducing a new resource or innovation has the effect of creating new alignments and unleashing competition. Change is necessarily destabilising. Two obvious interest groups are the users and those involved in developing the IS/IT strategy. Even within the top management team there may also be interest groups whose goals differ, or who propose different change strategies and compete, for example, for recognition by the process as the chief 'change agent'. What resources does each control which will give them power over the other? Management power is one important cornerstone of the change management process.

## Management: a dominant interest group

Managers have considerable power in an organisation to shape the direction and extent of change. But they are not the only power group and cannot be said to have absolute power. Any interest group in the organisation can, by withholding information, goods or services, exercise power. The threat of the use of power is often as influential and potent as the actual withholding of power. Unions are one interest group who by threatening to withhold their labour power can exercise influence over management's plans for change.

## Decision making

*Irrationality in the change process*
In chapter 4 we attempted to introduce rationality into the IS/IT planning process. We presented an approach to aid in formulating an IS/IT strategy which is closely aligned with business strategy. This approach matches closely with what is generally accepted as the basic steps involved in the rational decision making process. These are:

- recognise and define the problem or opportunity

- identify and analyse alternative courses of action
- choose a preferred course of action
- implement the preferred course of action
- evaluate results and follow up as necessary.

Researchers of organisation theory have long been aware that there are constraints on people and managers which prevent them from making purely rational decisions. These constraints may be political, economic or cognitive. March and Simon[4] recognised there was a tendency to 'satisfice' rather than to optimise in decision making when they coined the term *bounded rationality*. Some sources of sub-optimisation in the decision making process which occur at different stages of the strategy formulation process are:

- constraints on time and/or money which reduces the search for alternatives
- political competition between interest groups which may in extreme cases lead to the suppression of relevant information
- distortion of information due to the 'chinese whispers' effects, or vested interest.

It has also been said that as most bureaucratic organisations are modelled on Weberian notions of rationality in which decision making is the ultimate form of rationality, information gathering in such organisations has a special symbolic value. This explains why in many cases excessive quantities of information are gathered which is not used in decisions.[5]

**The two-culture problem**

Even though organisations will have a unified set of values at some level (usually about the need for survival of the organisation) there are also different *subcultures* within organisations. Subcultures are groups of people whose values may differ from others or the organisation as a whole and who appear to have a different culture. These values may be about seemingly superficial things such as the preferred style of dress in that subculture, or their preference for being allowed to take their own decisions rather than being given strict guidelines. However, in an organisational context, these cultural differences signify the potential for conflict and can pose obstacles to communication.

Users and IT professionals are from different 'subcultures'. They often dress differently, have different codes of behaviour, have different goals for their departments, think in different time scales or have different types of educational background. Even 'jargon shock' signifies a difference between the cultures. While simple stereotyping should not be encouraged, research scientists typically adopt a long term perspective in terms of problem solving, while operations and production people are generally seen as thinking short term. The former are used to solving problems over years, the latter must solve problems, for example maintaining and re-tooling equipment, 'by yesterday'.

There is too often an implicit assumption that the thinking and problem solving styles of the IT professionals and users of the system are similiar. Very often, IT professionals assume that all problems have a technical solution and in failing to see the political nature of organisations fail to take proper account of problems of vested interest in implementation. IT professionals are trained to be highly disciplined. They tend to have a low tolerance for ambiguity and often shy away from dealing with emotions.

While communication between users and IT professionals must be two way this must be reconciled with the project management dimension. IT projects do have milestones and targets which must be met if system implementation is to be kept on schedule.

## Communication

Resistance to change can be broken down by opening up lines of communication and understanding. To a large extent this can be accomplished by education programmes, one-to-one discussions, group presentations, memos and reports. Communication effectiveness, or the quality of communication, is enhanced through developing shared 'frames of reference', critically involving shared interpretation of the benefits of the new technology, and definition of the underlying problem(s) which the technology seeks to tackle. Communication can also help employees see the logic of change. However, this method is only likely to be successful if the source of the resistance is inadequate communication. And very often it is.

## Leadership issues

In chapter 4 we emphasised the importance of having top management involved in developing the IS/IT strategy. It is paramount that they are also involved in implementing this strategy by being directly involved in leading the change process.

The MIT study *Management in the 1990s*[6] present the following guidelines for the role of top management:

- set policies regarding where to introduce information technology and how to establish priorities for competing projects
- develop an understanding of the capabilities and limitations of IS/IT
- establish reasonable goals for IS/IT systems
- exhibit a strong commitment to the successful introduction of IT
- communicate the corporate IS/IT strategy to all employees.


*Education*

The thesis of this book is that management must be aware that being competitive in the 1990s will depend on the effective application and use of information technology. Senior executives need a clear vision of the competitive impact of IS/IT. Line managers must also be able to identify opportunities for applying IS/IT to business problems.

We saw in chapter 1 that an IS/IT strategy must be an integral part of the business strategy. Senior management and planners must be given frameworks to develop this IS/IT strategy. However, to be effective in the strategy formulation process they must have an appreciation of information technology.

The recent British Computer Society report[7] claimed that hybrid managers - that is *managers possessing business understanding, technical competence and organisational knowledge and skills* - are needed for the following reasons

- because information management is becoming the major value-added of all professionals

- because of the compression of corporate hierarchies and reduction of middle management with the aid of information systems

- because of the globalisation of production and markets regarding the development of sophisticated information systems

- because 'Open Systems promise to reduce the cost of computing hardware and software so dramatically that IT budgets can buy almost any product' (p. 8). The speed of conception and implementation for business applications will become the limiting factor.

Earl[8] presents a useful framework for management education, which he sees as being more as re-education programmes. The objective is to reorientate their focus and position IT in their domain of expertise. This framework is based around four key concepts: refocusing, retooling, reskilling and reinforcing. These are illustrated schematically in figure 13.3.

**Figure 13.3** Re-education for information management.

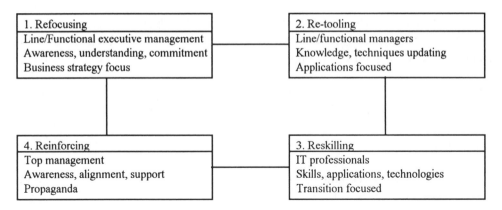

| 1. Refocusing | 2. Re-tooling |
|---|---|
| Line/Functional executive management | Line/functional managers |
| Awareness, understanding, commitment | Knowledge, techniques updating |
| Business strategy focus | Applications focused |

| 4. Reinforcing | 3. Reskilling |
|---|---|
| Top management | IT professionals |
| Awareness, alignment, support | Skills, applications, technologies |
| Propaganda | Transition focused |

Source: M. J. Earl, *Management Strategies for Information Technology*, Prentice Hall, p. 201.

- **Refocusing** - increasing senior managements awareness and understanding of the strategic importance of IS/IT.

- **Retooling** - developing management or application skills and knowledge to follow any new initiatives defined in refocusing.

- **Reskilling** - training and educating the IT professionals, for instance in object oriented programming, design methodologies, etc. Pay particular attention to their business skills.

- **Reinforcing** - increasing top managements' understanding and committment to support the effects of other re-education programmes.

*Training*
Training is of critical importance in introducing new technologies and thus reducing the associated resistance to change. Early automation projects resulted in de-skilling workers. More and more, new information technologies require workers to gain new skills. For example, CIM usually results in increased skills and levels of knowledge required by employees. Operators require new skills to operate new machines.

For many information technologies the learning process must entail a user actually using the technology, so called 'on-the-job' training. Zuboff[9] reports the case of the introduction of a heavily computerised paper machine where the users were initially allowed to experiment with the technology. Such an approach promotes critical understanding of the technology and of the new work practices which would be expected.

**Human resources**

In many of the chapters the importance of people in todays business organisation was highlighted. It is interesting to note that the recognition of human resources as being strategic has parallels with IS/IT: only recently have both been recognised as such.

Strategic human resource management is made up of all activities affecting the behaviour of individuals in their efforts to formulate and implement the strategic needs of the business. It is largely about integration and adoption.[10] The concern is to ensure that

- human resource management is fully integrated with the strategy and the strategic needs of the organisation

- human resource policies cohere both across policy areas and across hierarchies

- human resource practices are adjusted, accepted and used by line managers and employees as part of their everyday work.

Rhone-Poulenc is the seventh largest chemical company in the world with revenues of $14 billion and conducts business in 140 countries. The firm has grown through acquisition and is decentralised into 5 major sectors: health, agriculture, organic and inorganic intermediates, speciality chemicals and fibers and polymers.

Anthony H Sugden is the international IS/IT consultant for the company providing international IS/IT consultation and coordination throughout the company's five sectors. Having previously worked in Germany, UK, France, Sweden, Denmark and the US, his experience has convinced him that both company and country culture must be considered when assessing personnel and organisational issues.

Sugden sees a change in Europe away from a broad humanistic perspective and increasingly toward issues of change management, quality initiatives, decentralisation and downsizing. Meanwhile, he sees a change in the US towards humanism and establishing cultural values in order to achieve business objectives. He thinks that the ideal lies somewhere in between.

Sugden believes that partnership and team players are critical to success for the IS organisation of the 1990s. Partnerships are essential for successfully conducting business, both within the company as well as with external suppliers. In particular, IT professionals need to create partnerships with users. The key to understanding the nature of the partnership is aligning work efforts with the company mission statement and its stated cultural values, and its business objectives.

Sugden suggests that US companies practice many more human resource activities than European companies, which makes them more adaptable and better positioned for the challenges of the decade. He cites the fact that there are more appraisals, evaluations, and career planning, yet fewer complex administrative policies. However he sees European companies now beginning to use human resources to facilitate corporate-wide career planning and relocations. In the past, it was often necessary to leave a company to make a career advancement.

As the way to conduct business change, people must change with them. Those who cannot change must step out of the way for those who can can, and seek employment elsewhere. The world recession is making people more realistic about the way business must be conducted.

The challenge for the information systems organisation is to make more important contributions to business needs. Communication must improve between the information systems organisation and senior management - in both directions - as well as between IS and its users.

To achieve this, Rhone-Poulenc is working with a new concept, that of the *business advisor*. The business advisor is an individual from the information systems organisation who works for and supports business needs. He or she acts as an internal consultant to a user organisation's business manager. The role of the advisor is not project management or day-to-day problem solving, but rather a strategic management position. The business advisor is outward-looking and outward-thinking, considering such matters as the company's products, services, external relationships, its mission, and so forth.

**Box 13.1** Managing change at Rhone-Poulenc.
Adapted from Assessing the personnel and organizational issues of the 1990s, *I/S Analyzer*, Vol. 29, No. 11, 1991.

Investing in a human resource strategy must go hand in hand with information systems. An integrated approach to HRM makes sure that training systems complement job design; that promotion prospects and career planning is supported by appropriate training and individual opportunities for growth; and that each employee is evaluated and appraised on terms appropriate for the job and set of responsibilities. Such policies can create a climate conducive to adopting new technology and thus reducing the associated resistance to change. The *Management in the 1990s* Research Program clearly indicated that the full potential of advanced information technologies can only be realised if it is associated with appropriate changes in organisation and human resource practices.

## 13.5  The culture dimension

### What is organisational culture?

Organisational culture can be defined as *the shared values and beliefs which take the form of rules of behaviour in a work group or organisation.*  Culture will be influenced by many variables including gender, nationality and the 'cultural baggage' which people bring in from their educational and social background.  This very functionalist perspective has recently been questioned by Smircich[11] who sees culture more as something an organisation *is* than has.

Culture is described as particular to each organisation and evolves over time.  It develops out of the interactions between individuals, groups including managers, and the social structure.  Culture is the *cognitive map*[12] which enables participants in a given context to interpret others' actions.  It is also the *social glue* which binds members of that context together by allowing them to interpret others' actions in a similiar and consistent way.

This view of culture encourages questions about the extent to which people, particularly senior managers, can influence or 'mold' culture in the organisation.  In Peters and Waterman's book *In Search of Excellence*, the 'excellent' companies were those which had a strong culture with values directed towards the market-place (such as responsiveness, quality and determination to be the best).  In these companies the culture was managed:

- through education and training

- through changes to reward and remuneration systems, e.g. bonuses for extra effort or improved quality

- through intensive 'socialisation' into the organisation; the six month JP Morgan training programme is an example of this

- the perpetuation of company myths as at Hewlett Packard which reinforces the key guiding principles in the organisation for all its members

- cartoons and competitions at the work site which again reinforce key values.

# 13.6 Strategies for managing change

As seen above, there are many elements in the organisational setting which need consideration when thinking about change. The picture depicted so far is of the need for an integrated process of change which takes into account all the factors which will be affected.

There are three general types of change strategies for managing change in organisations: rational persuasion, forced-coercion, and shared power.[13] In different ways they seek to overcome resistance to change. A central obstacle to change is the problem of persuading people of long term gains in spite of short term losses (of jobs, for example). People's willingness to accept this argument may also be affected by the broader social and cultural environment in which they operate.

## Rational persuasion

The underlying theme of this strategy is to bring about change through rational argument. It is essentially a top down approach where rationality in the arguments are used to persuade of the necessity for change. This strategy basically assumes that the source of resistance lies in mis-information or poor communication. Education therefore plays a key role in presenting the full facts and the reason for the change. However, a distinct problem with this strategy is that people don't always recognise the need for change.

## Forced coercion

This strategy entails making direct threats if the change is not accepted. As a corollary, it includes the use of rewards as well as punishments. Examples include loss of promotion, threats of transfer, negative performance evaluations or a poor letter of recommendation. However, to what extent does this technique affect peoples' understanding of the need to change? Is such change likely to be lasting?

## Shared power

The shared power approach entails involving others in the taking of key decisions. The argument is that people are less likely to resist change when they have participated in the change decision. The emphasis here is on creating new norms and values so that support for change naturally emerges.

**Counterimplementation strategies**

Keen[14] suggests that the lack of success of implementation is due to the counterimplementation strategies adopted by users who oppose change. These are covert and overt attempts by users to sabotage or make ineffectual the various implementation strategies.

Keen recommends counter-counterimplementation approaches:

- make sure that a contract for change has been agreed by all parties
- seek out resistance and treat it as a signal to respond to
- rely on face-to-face contracts
- become an insider and work hard to build personal credibility
- co-opt users early.

## 13.7  Is change forced on organisations?

We started off this chapter by distinguishing between planned and unplanned change. The notion that the organisation can plan change presupposes that many of the factors which effect it can be predicted. But changes include things like the arrival in the market of new competitors, rapid changes to markets resulting from demographic or political shifts, or dramatic technological developments with far reaching implications and opportunities.

Because of the awareness that change can not always be predicted, there are divergent views of what 'drives' change: is it a rational, cognitive evaluation of the environment and anticipated developments, which results in rational action and planning, as illustrated in Porter's five forces strategic thinking or the IS/IT planning approach outlined in chapter 4? To what extent does the firm operate less 'rationally', for example by reacting to some changes and not to others or because of apparent 'irrationalities' in the decision making process of managers for reasons seen earlier? Or to what extent is supposedly 'rational' reaction limited by the competing or vested interests of the strategic managers?

Both of the approaches above imply that organisations do at least recognise the need for changes even if their reaction is not always rational. But some organisations do not always see that they are falling prey to inertia: failing to read the environment, make important changes or slowly losing their competitive edge. Consider the analogy of the boiled frog.[15] You can put a frog into boiling water and it will jump out. But if you put a frog into cold water and raise the temperature the frog will boil to death. The same is true of organisations.

In addition to issues about the rationality of change, there is another set of important questions in business strategy and organisation theory. To what extent are the structure, culture, size, etc. of an organisation determined by their environment or conversely do they 'shape' the environment in which they wish to act? *Contingency theorists* claim that the structure of the firm is determined by the strategy it pursued in the marketplace. The *strategic choice* argument proposes that an organisation's strategy is the outcome of *management choice* and determination by changes arising in the environment.[16] Thus the organisation does create opportunities in the shape of markets it selects, technologies, or regions of cheap labour where it chooses to operate. This is the management choice. However, it is also constrained by aspects of the 'objective' environment.

## 13.8  How do organisations learn?

The dramatically increased pace of change in the political, trading and informational environments means that organisations which can adapt and learn have a competitive advantage over those which are slow and cumbersome in their reactions to environmental change. For some theorists this means distinguishing between organisations which are *reactive* and those which are *proactive*. The latter anticipates the need for change and initiates changes which will limit their exposure to environmental jolts. Organisations which have both a structure and culture which is conducive to such ongoing change are thought to be better at *organisational learning*.

A term frequently used to characterise such organisations is flexibility. Over-structured bureaucracies might be delayered to devolve responsibility to smaller, autonomous units. One advantage is that critical communication processes such as decision-making and problem solving are speedier and more effective. Through attention to the internal processes of communication the company aims to build a culture which promotes problem solving, decision-making, idea generation and inter-disciplinary and group communication on a day-to-day basis. In this way the company develops its capacity for self-renewal by learning how to implement similar cycles of problem diagnosis and problem solving, and curiosity for change.

Change programmes often have the objective therefore of creating an environment where change is accepted as part of the continual adaption to the environment so that the organisation is constantly changing. By this definition then, change programmes are not a finite process with a well-defined beginning, middle and end.

## 13.9  Conclusions

Implementing an IS/IT strategy involves change, and this change needs to be managed if the IS/IT strategy is to be successfully implemented.  In this chapter we have portrayed organisations as collectives of people bound together by processes.

- *Change management requires that technology is closely integrated with the people, strategy, structure and culture of the organisation.*

- *Changing technology will have a 'knock-on' effect in all of these arenas.*

- *A coherent approach to human resource management should go hand-in-hand with new technology as at Rhone Poulenc.*

- *Change management begins with managers understanding the nature of change itself.*

- *Senior management should initiate the IS/IT implementation process.*

- *Introducing a programme of change means accepting that there may be resistance to change, and implementing schemes to minimise that resistance.*

- *Users should become involved once the IS/IT plan has been devised. They should become involved as early as possible in the application design.*

- *Motivate users and gain support of stakeholders.*

- *Human resource policies can create a climate conducive to adopting new technology and thus reducing the associated resistance to change.*

## Notes

1   This terminology was proposed by Lewin;  for more information on Lewin's model see Kurt Lewin,  *Field Theory in Social Sciences*, Harper & Row, New York, 1951.
2   For more information about how these constructs are built up, refer to C. Geertz, *The Interpretation of Cultures*. Basic Books, New York, 1973.
3   J. Marshall and A. Mclean, Exploring organisation culture as a route to organisational change.  In V. Hammonds, ed., *Current Research in Management*, Francis Pinner, 1988.
4   J.G. March and H.A. Simon, *Organisations*. John Wiley & Sons, New York, 1958.

5    M.S. Feldman and J.G. March, Information in organisations as sign and symbol. *Administrative Science Quarterly*, **26**, pp. 171-186.
6    Reported in M.S. Scott Morton, ed., *The Corporation of the 1990s: Information Technology and Organisational Change*. Oxford University Press, 1991.
7    *From Potential to Reality: A Report by the British Computer Society Task Group on Hybrids*. British Computer Society, Publications, London, 1990.
8    M.J. Earl, *Management Strategies for Information Technology*. Prentice Hall, pp. 200-208.
9    S. Zuboff, *In the Age of the Smart Machine*. Basic Books, New York, 1988.
10   R.S. Schuler, Strategic human resource management: linking the people with the strategic needs of the business. *Organisational Dynamics*, Summer, 1992, pp. 18-32.
11   L. Smircich, Concepts of culture and organisational analysis. *Administrative Science Quarterly*, **28**, 3, 1986, pp. 339-358.
12   See K.E. Weick, *The Social Psychology of Organisations*. Random House, New York, 1979.
13   J.R. Schermerhorn, J.G. Hunt and Osborn, R.N., *Managing Organisation Behaviour*, 4th Edition. John Wiley & Sons Inc., 1991.
14   P.G.W. Keen, Information systems and organisational change. *Communications of the ACM*, **24**, 1, 1981, pp. 24-33.
15   Example adapted from J.R. Schermerhorn, J.G. Hunt and Osborn, R.N., *Managing Organisation Behaviour*, 4th Edition. John Wiley & Sons Inc., 1991.
16   See J. Child, Organisational structure, environment and performance: the role of strategic choice. *Sociology*, **6**, 1972, pp. 1-22.

# Additional Reading

Beer, M., Eisenstat, R.A. and Spector, B., Why change programs don't produce change. *Harvard Business Review*, November-December, 1990, pp. 158-166.
Johnson, G., Managing strategic change - strategy, culture and action. *Long Range Planning*, **25**, 1, 1992, pp. 28-36.
McKersie, R.B. and Walton, R.E., Organisational change. In M.S. Scott-Morton, ed., *The Corporation of the 1990s: Information Technology and Organisational Transformation*, Oxford University Press, 1991, pp. 244-277.
Rochester, J.B. and Douglas, D.P. Change management in information systems. *I/S Analyzer*, **28**, 8, 1990.
Schaffer, R.H. and Thomson, H.A., Successful change programs begin with results. *Harvard Business Review*, January-February, 1992, pp. 80-89.
Swanson, E.B., Information systems in organisation theory: a review. In R.J. Boland and R.A. Hirschheim, eds., *Critical Issues in Information Systems Research*, John Wiley & Sons, Chichester, pp. 181-204.
Walton, R.E. and Susman, G.I., People policies for the new machines. *Harvard Business Review*, March-April, 1987, pp. 98-106.
Wijnhoven, A.B. and Waisenaar, Impact of IT on organisations: the state of the art. *International Journal of Information Management*, **10**, 1, 1990, pp. 35-53.

# Glossary

Note
Acronyms are given in their acronym form.

**ABI**
Application Binary Interface. A standard interface for an operating system and a specific processor (or processor series) which enables machine code to be ported from one computer to another without modification.

**Account control avoidance**
Avoiding a situation where a user is dependent on one supplier for key systems.

**ADA**
Programming language developed originally for the US Department of Defence. One of the most highly specified languages ever devised.

**API**
Application Program(ming) Interface. An add-on to a programming language which shields the programmer from the specifics of the operating system. A half-way house between an ABI and source code portability.

| | |
|---|---|
| **Application Transparency** | Used to describe an environment where the user is unaware of the underlying technology and does not have to learn different ways of doing things depending on which machine or package is being used. |
| **ASCII** | American Standard Code for Information Interchange. A standard for representation of numbers and characters in binary code. |
| **BASIC** | Beginners All Symbolic Instruction Code. Third generation language, originally designed (as the name suggests) for teaching purposes. Still quite widely used in some commercial applications, notably on VAXes. |
| **C** | A third generation language with low level functions and the native language of Unix. It is widely used for development of packaged products and is the basis for the POSIX standard. |
| **CASE** | Computer Aided Systems (or Software) Engineering. A series of (usually integrated) tools designed to assist software developers and engineers. They generally combine (amongst other things) drawing, data dictionary set up and maintenance, consistency checking and, in some cases, code generation facilities. |
| **CASE Generator** | Contrary to what the name might suggest, a CASE tool (or an add-on to a CASE tool) that generates computer application code from the CASE diagrams and the data dictionary. |
| **CIM** | Computer Integrated Manufacturing. The use of a shared database to electronically control machinery throughout the production process. |
| **COBOL** | COmmon Business Orientated Language, a very widely used third generation language. |
| **DEC** | Digital Equipment Corporation. |
| **DIBOL** | DIgital Business Oriented Language. Variant of COBOL used on DEC machines. |
| **EDI** | Electronic Data Interchange. The transfer of structured data, from computer to computer, using agreed communications standards. |

| | |
|---|---|
| **EDIFACT (UN/EDIFACT)** | United Nations/<u>ED</u>I <u>F</u>or <u>A</u>dministration, <u>C</u>ommerce and <u>T</u>ransport. Comprises a set of internationally agreed standards, directions and guidelines for the electronic interchange of structured data, and in particular that related to trade in goods and services, between independent computerised systems. |
| **Electronic Mail** | Computer-based system that allows people to communicate either character or graphics information by electronic means. It allows messages to be sent when desired, stored when necessary, routed to designated destinations and subsequently retrieved. |
| **Ethernet** | A common local area network standard based on the statistical theory that if messages on the network collide, they can be detected and retransmitted and that under certain traffic density, the chances of a collision are very small. |
| **Excel** | Spreadsheet software package from Microsoft Corporation. |
| **FMS** | <u>F</u>lexible <u>M</u>anufacturing <u>S</u>ystem. A configuration of computerised production machinery including at least two computer controlled production machines and one materials handling component. |
| **FOCUS** | Fourth generation language and database management system from Information Builders Inc. |
| **FTAM** | <u>F</u>ile <u>T</u>ransfer and <u>A</u>ccess <u>M</u>ethod - OSI standard for transferring files between two computers over a network. |
| **GUI** | <u>G</u>raphics <u>U</u>ser <u>I</u>nterface. Way of interacting with a computer based on graphics, icons, a mouse and pull down menus of the point and click type. |
| **HDLC** | <u>H</u>igh Level <u>D</u>ata <u>L</u>ink <u>C</u>ontrol. OSI standard in the Data Link layer of the OSI model. |
| **Interoperability** | Strictly speaking, the ability of two machines to communicate but more often generalised to mean the ability of different software, operating systems and machines to communicate and interwork or to share the same network. |

**ISDN**                                Integrated Services Digital Network. A single network for the transmission of voice, image and data in digital form.

**ISO**                                 International Standards Organisation. Key international body responsible for a wide range of standards including the OSI model.

**ISO 9000**                            International Standards Organisation quality system certification, published in 1987. The standard states the requirements necessary for certification of the procedures used by the firm to document and adhere to its production process.

**JIT**                                 Just In Time manufacturing. Producing sub-assemblies or products precisely when they are needed by the following process or the customer.

**Mailbox**                             A storage facility within a VAN service which is maintained for a specific user so that the user can store and retrieve messages contained there.

**MRP**                                 Material Requirements Planning. A method for determining the production schedule based on time-phased decomposition of the components necessary to produce sub-assemblies or final products.

**Message**                             A collection of data organised in segments and exchanged between organisations via EDI. Messages contain the data for any transaction that is agreed by the various partners concerned.

**Messaging**                           The technique of addressing and sending messages between applications and machines.

**MIPS**                                Millions of Instructions Per Second. The number of basic machine code level instructions executed by a processor each second. A common, if somewhat crude, measurement of processor power. (Also, the name of a US manufacturer of processors and Unix-based minicomputers.)

**Modem**                               Device for converting computer signals into a suitable form for transmission over ordinary voice telephone lines and decoding the result at the far end.

**MS-DOS**                     MicroSoft Disk Operating System.    Single user
                               operating system from Microsoft Inc.   Used on most
                               IBM compatible/Intel processor-based microcomputers.

**MVS**                        IBM's mainframe operating system.    Used on very
                               large and powerful computers.

**Novell (Netware)**           A leading network management system supplied by
                               Novell Inc.

**NT**                         New Technology.    New operating system being
                               developed by Microsoft as a replacement for DOS.

**Open System**                A system where the various components (hardware,
                               software, communications etc.) can be provided by
                               more than one vendor and which readily interrelate.

**Operating System**           The fundamental piece of software that makes a
                               computer run.    Provides functions such as file
                               management, security, access, printer control, etc.

**OPT**                        Optimised Production Technology.    A proprietary
                               computer algorithm and its associated practices
                               focusing on bottlenecks in the production process.

**OSI**                        Open Systems Interconnect (or interconnection).
                               Seven layer model developed and promoted by the
                               International Standards Organisation for computer
                               communication.

**Packet Switching**           The process of breaking data down into packets, each
                               with its own envelope and address.   Packets may be
                               sent out at different time intervals over a network and
                               may even travel by different routes.  On arrival at their
                               destination, packets are reassembled in order to extract
                               their contents.

**PDP/11**                     One of a range of DEC minicomputers (the PDP series)
                               which originated in the 1960s.   Only phased out of
                               production in the late 1980s.

**Pink**                       Code name used by Apple and IBM for a new joint
                               operating system they are developing jointly.

**PL/1**                                        Programming Language/1. third generation language originally designed to combine the best features of COBOL and FORTRAN while overcoming some of their drawbacks.

**Portability**                                 The ability to move a piece of software from one machine and operating system to another. There are various degrees of portability.

**POSIX**                                       Portable Operating System Interface for Computing Environments. A set of operating system standards based on Unix and the C language to which many operating systems can, in theory, be made to comply. A POSIX compliant system will permit a reasonable level of software portability.

**Powerhouse**                                  Fourth generation language from Cognos Corporation.

**Processor**                                   In general any device that processes information but more colloquially an integrated circuit or circuits which form the heart of a computer system and carry out all computations.

**Progress**                                    Fourth generation language and database management system sold by Progress Software Corporation.

**Proprietary**                                 Generally used to describe a computer system which can only be supplied or supported by one vendor.

**Relational Database**
**Management System (RDBMS)**                    Database management system based on tables of data and the relational algebra devised by Ted Codd. Unlike other database management systems, there are no physical links between tables. Linking data is done using the SQL language.

**RPGII/III**                                   Third generation language native to the IBM System 34/36/38 and AS/400 IBM proprietary and mid-range minicomputers.

**Scaleability**                                The ability to increase the size and power of a processor without altering its basic characteristics so that the software designed to run on it will run with modifications.

| | |
|---|---|
| **SNA** | System Network Architecture - IBM's network architecture developed from the mid 1970s onwards and now standard in all IBM proprietary environments. |
| **Source Code Portability** | When a language enables the source code written by a user to be recompiled on different machines irrespective of the underlying processor and operating system. The crudest form of software portability, only a few specialist languages have ever really attained it on any scale. |
| **SPARC** | Scaleable PRocessor ARChitecture, a scaleable processor RISC chip developed by Sun Microsystems and used in a number of machines. |
| **SPC** | Statistical Process Control. The use of various techniques to track, understand and reduce variation in production processes. |
| **SQL** | Structured Query Language. Database enquiry and update language key to the operation of relational database management systems. Enables the extraction, update, deletion and manipulation of data as well as creation and management of the databases. |
| **TCP/IP** | Transmission Control Protocol/Internet Protocol. Suite of communications protocols developed originally for the US Department of Defense and now widely used in Unix networks. Covers layers three and four (and some of layer two) in the OSI model. |
| **Telecom Gold** | British Telecom X.25 packet switching service. |
| **TELNET** | TELetype NETwork, terminal emulation system and a widely used *de facto* standard in Unix networks. |
| **Token Ring** | Network protocol developed by IBM which uses a token to carry traffic around a ring. Messages can "grab" the token until they reach their destination. |
| **TQM** | Total Quality Management. Management based on the awareness of the potential impact that every action of every employee has on the competitiveness of the product in the marketplace. |

| | |
|---|---|
| **Unix** | Operating system originally developed by AT&T (Bell Labs) and the first to become widely available on a wide range of machines. A key factor in the evolution of open systems. |
| **Unix SVR4** | See Unix System V Release 4. |
| **Unix System V Release 4** | Latest (1989) fully standardised version of Unix from the Unix International consortium. Embraces AT&T System V, Berkeley and Xenix. |
| **Upwards Compatibility** | Generally, the ability to move software and applications up a range or generation of machines. |
| **VAN** | Value Added Network. A service which allows many users to share its communications facility. *Value* is added by managing the sharing of costs among many users. |
| **VAX** | DEC's minicomputer (the replacement for the PDP series), a 32 bit minicomputer based on a proprietary processor. Uses the VMS operating system but will also run Ultrix, DEC's version of Unix. |
| **VisiCalc** | Invisible Calculator. The first commercial spreadsheet developed for the PC (circa. 1979). |
| **VS** | IBM proprietary operating system used on their main minicomputer range. |
| **Windows** | Microsoft graphical user interface product that sits on top of MS-DOS and provides windowing and pseudo multitasking. |
| **WordPerfect** | Advanced word-processing package from WordPerfect Corporation. |
| **X.25** | A standard package switching protocol (q.v.) |
| **X.400** | A standard governing message transfer between computer systems. It covers such matters as addressing conventions. |

**3rd Generation**    Common, if sometimes loosely used, term used to describe computer programming/development languages which lack certain facilities (such as screen generators and report writers). Examples are COBOL, BASIC and PL/1.

**4th Generation**    Term used to describe languages developed in the early to mid 1980s which automated many basic functions of programming (for example report writing, screen painting, standard libraries and so on). Many have their own file management system and English-like code. The term is much abused.

**286**    Short for 80286, 16 bit processor from Intel Corporation.

**386**    Short for 80386, 32 bit processor from Intel Corporation.

**486**    Short for 80486, 32 bit processor with enhanced features from Intel Corporation.

# Index